Design for Leisure Entertainment

Design for Leisure Entertainment

Anthony Wylson FRIBA

Newnes-Butterworths
London   Boston
Sydney   Wellington   Durban   Toronto

United Kingdom/London
Butterworth & Co (Publishers) Ltd
88 Kingsway, WC2B 6AB

Australia/Sydney
Butterworths Pty Ltd
586 Pacific Highway, Chatswood, NSW 2067
Also at Melbourne, Brisbane, Adelaide and Perth

Canada/Toronto
Butterworth & Co (Canada) Ltd
2265 Midland Avenue, Scarborough, Ontario M1P 4S1

New Zealand/Wellington
Butterworths of New Zealand Ltd
T & W Young Building, 77–85 Customhouse Quay, 1
CPO Box 472

South Africa/Durban
Butterworth & Co (South Africa) (Pty) Ltd
152–154 Gale Street

USA/Boston
Butterworth (Publishers) Inc
10 Tower Office Park, Woburn, Mass 01801

First published 1980
© Butterworth & Co (Publishers) Ltd, 1980

British Library Cataloguing in Publication Data

Wylson, Anthony
  Design for leisure entertainment.
  1. Recreation centers 2. Architecture and
  recreation
  I. Title
  725'.8   NA6800   78–41340
  ISBN 0–408–00343–X

Set, printed and bound in Great Britain by
Fakenham Press Limited, Fakenham, Norfolk

Foreword

by Edward D. Mills, CBE, FRIBA, FSIA

This new *Design* Series of books is a direct development from *Planning 9th Edition*, and will be complementary to the five volumes comprising this work. The subjects for the books in this new series have been carefully chosen, and will fill a number of obvious gaps in the current literature relating to specific architectural design problems.

Design for Leisure Entertainment follows this pattern, as there are few books dealing with the subject of buildings for leisure which cover the wide range of activities that are now generally popular. The leisure industry is expanding rapidly throughout the world and with ever increasing living standards the demand for leisure facilities will inevitably grow.

The world wide interest and expansion of new technology in both commerce and industry is already resulting in a drastic reduction in manpower requirements as the computer, the microprocessor and other developments take the place of the human agency particularly for dull and repetitive jobs. The result is greater leisure for many workers as their working hours are reduced. Whatever view individuals may hold regarding this new industrial and commercial revolution, it has now become inevitable, and irreversible. The results will be an ever-decreasing working life for many people and a corresponding increase in leisure time, which can be used profitably or wasted.

Fifty years ago people developed their own leisure pursuits, if they were fortunate enough to have time to enjoy them. Today the trend is for large numbers of people to rely on leisure activities organised for them; the leisure industry is therefore becoming very important in the economy of most countries. Already it employs large numbers of people and caters each year for millions of people of all ages, and nationalities.

Leisure entertainment is therefore a most important subject, and this book reviews a wide range of activities in broad terms, and in a way which will ensure that it is of value to promoter, designer and user. For readers requiring detailed planning data on many of the building types described, the appropriate volume of *Planning 9th edition* will provide essential information and indicate further reference where this is necessary. Together, the two series will form a valuable reference library for all concerned with the design and use of buidings.

Acknowledgements

The research for this book has provided an opportunity to visit many organisations concerned with leisure entertainment. In most cases, this has provided a very pleasant preoccupation. I am grateful to those that have given time to explain their enterprise and those that have provided background and illustrative material: Rank Leisure Services and Butlins; Club Mediterranée; Las Vegas Convention Authority; Walt Disney Organisation; The Blackpool Pleasure Beach Company; Dr Walter Stahl; The Hamburg Press Office; Freie und Hansestadt, Hamburg; The GLC Parks Dept; The GLC Architects Dept; Handicapped Adventure Playground Association; Directeur du Servic de Loisir Pro-Juventute; Architects Dept, Tivoli Gardens; Publicity Dept, Knott's Berry Farm, Showmen's Guild of Great Britain; Japanese Information Office; Biwaters; Marineland, Florida; Seaworld, Florida; Hanna-Barbera Marineland; Benneweis Cirkus, Copenhagen; Ringling Bros and Barnum & Bailey; Gerry Cottle's Circus; EMI Blackpool Tower Circus; Hall Stage Equipment; Société d' Etudes et de Réalisation d' Equipements Spéciaux (SORES); Sound Research Laboratories Ltd; Monsieru Boudre, Paris Lido; The BBC Television Centre; Thames Television; EMI Leisure Limited; Phyllis Haylor, Phyllis Haylor School of Dancing; Victor Lownes, The Playboy Organisation; Ladbrokes; Dr Leslie Knopp; The Home Office Fire Dept; Fire Research Dept; Inter-Action Arts Group, Camden; Longleat Stately Home and Safari Park, Wiltshire.

I am also grateful to the many consultants referred to in the text; the Press Officers and Information Officers, for providing illustrations and information on individual projects, the patient manuscript reading by my wife Patricia and the time spent by her and John Hoile preparing illustrations. I would also like to thank Jan Creamer, Philippa Gunn and Susan Chester, for typing the manuscript and dealing with the correspondence.

It is also necessary to acknowledge with regret the interesting projects that cannot be covered due to space limitations and that it has not been possible to include illustrations of Disneyland and other Walt Disney entertainments.

Preface

Throughout the world popular entertainment has developed rapidly, stimulated by the social economic changes of the 19th century, the increase in spending power and longer holidays available to ordinary working people. Many social entertainment activities which were at one time regarded as the privilege of the wealthy, have adapted to a wider public – ballet, concerts, ballroom dancing, gaming, enjoyment of parks and leisure sport. Traditional forms of popular amusement such as fairgrounds, circus and carnivals continue to play an important part of seasonal festivities. New entertainment activities such as the cinema, television and audio-visual presentations have developed through modern technology.

These leisure entertainment activities have promoted new design techniques and building types. This book endeavours to explore the context for contemporary entertainment, from the wider aspect of resorts in which entertainment is the primary economic activity to the particular aspect involving spectator or participant. The text aims to provide a general view rather than a detailed analysis of individual building types, so that relationships, trends and common principles can be identified. This book does not set out to be a design guide but a general appraisal of entertainment so that spectator, participant, amateur, entrepreneur or designer can enjoy a common panorama.

The historical background shows the growth of demand for popular entertainment and the way in which entrepreneurs have adapted to changing interests. Resorts and neighbourhoods dependant upon the leisure industry indicate the diversity of activities necessary for full-time amusement, and this diversity is also made available in theme parks and pleasure gardens.

For individual activities the two main aspects of entertainment, spectatorial and participatory, find expression in the design of buildings and equipment. Spectator entertainment represented by theatre, ballet, concert music, revue, cinema and television as well as the performance of circus's and marine parks have been subject to the new developments of electro-mechanics and audio-visual techniques. Changes in social conventions, the performer/audience relationship and public safety have brought new priorities in planning.

Play, which extends from children's creative play to leisure sport and leisure skills, provides both an experience and personal fulfilment. Social dancing venues have adapted to new forms of popular music and dance. Gaming, involving both chance and skill, has achieved an acceptance within legislative controls.

The opportunity for leisure entertainment to improve the environment is an important issue for urban renewal and planning. At the same time the contribution that leisure entertainment can make towards improving the 'quality of life' at a time when much work involvement provides little personal satisfaction, presents a challenge for entrepreneur, designer and operator.

Throughout this book dimensions have been given in SI units, with an Imperial conversion in brackets. These conversions are given for information only, and are not necessarily an exact conversion. Where products etc. are made to a specified size, for example cinema projection equipment, only one set of dimensions have been given as these are the figures specified in manufacture.

An additional feature of this book is a summary of the contents in French, German and Arabic. A summary of chapters is also given in the same language at the end of each chapter.

Anthony Wylson

Contents

Résumé des chapitres

Du point de vue historique, les hommes ont toujours trouvé leur épanouissement dans le travail. Mais avec le progrès industriel, ils devront désormais rechercher cette réalisation dans les activités de loisir (*Chapitre 1: 'Dans le contexte des loisirs'*). Les centres de loisirs sont avantagés par le regroupement. Ainsi plusieurs villes en font leur principale activité et les stations de vacances possèdent des installations de loisir intégrées. (*Chapitre 2: 'Centres de vacances et voisinage'*). Le jeu est à la base de la croissance de l'enfant et permet aux adultes d'explorer des possibilités et des activités nouvelles; il fait partir de la vie moderne (*Chapitre 3: 'L'enfant et le jeu'*). Les jardins publics sont devenus une antidote de la vie industrielle urbaine. Les parcs actuels à thème offrent, à partir d'un concept imaginatif, un ensemble d'activités harmonieux. (*Chapitre 4: 'Parcs à thème et jardins'*). Les foires ont évolué depuis la manifestation ambulante traditionnelle, pour devenir les 'Expos' internationales dans lesquelles les œuvres d'imagination et les présentations audio-visuelles élargissent le contexte des loisirs (*Chapitre 5: 'Foires et expositions'*). L'intérêt, soutenu tout au long de l'histoire, dans les qualités utilitaires et attractives de 'eau, se perpétue de nos jours avec les installations balnéaires, parcs marins, centre de loisirs (*Chapitre 6: 'Jeux d'eau et parcs marins'*). Les cirques, malgré le nombre décroissant d'emplacements réservés, ont trouvé de nouvelles techniques de spectacle et de nouveaux programmes pour combattre la télévision (*Chapitre 7: 'Les cirques'*). Au cours des dernières décades, les limites imposées au manteau de scène ont été remises en question, ce qui a abouti à l'apparition de nouvelles formes de spectacles sur scène et de nouvelles productions créées pour la télévision, le théatre et les restaurants (*Chapitre 8: 'Spectacles de scène'*). Le cinéma a dû s'adapter de manière considérable pour concurrencer les autres formes de loisirs populaires (*Chapitre 9: 'Le cinéma'*). Les discothèques, à l'origine sanctuaires des jeunes, sont maintenant adoptées par tous, alors que les dancing d'autrefois sont devenues des salles 'polyvalentes'. (*Chapitre 10: 'Discothèques et dancings'*). Le jeu est roi dans les hôtels-casinos de Las Vegas, mais aussi dans les casinos européens et les 'bingos' britanniques (*Chapitre 11: 'Le jeu et les casinos'*). Les salles de spectacle et autres établissements de loisirs doivent présenter les normes de sécurité requises pour le public, en particulier, en ce qui concerne la protection contre les risques d'incendie (*Chapitre 12: 'Sécurité publique'*). Les tendances actuelles en matière de design mettent en jeu des techniques variées pour l'architecture des loisirs, ou bien louvrage d'art devient partie intégrante des média de loisirs. (*Chapitre 13: 'Tendances et opinions'*).

Inhaltsüberblick

Das Buch enthält einen historischen Überblick über die Selbsterfüllung. Bei wachsendem industriellen Fortschritt müssen Freizeitsbeschäftigungen diesen Bedarf in Zukunft erfüllen (*Kapitel 1: 'Freizeit im Zusammenhang gesehen'*). Möglichkeit zur Unterhaltung profitier von der Gruppierung. Bei der Stadtplanung steht Freizeitunterhaltung im Vordergrund, und neue Erholungsorte haben Mölichkeiten zur Unterhaltung als integralen Bestandteil (*Kapitel 2: 'Erholungsorte und Stadtteile'*). Spiel bietet die Grundlage für die Entwicklung eines Kindes und den Erwachsenen die Möglichkeit, neue Fähigkeiten und Tätigkeiten in Augenschein zu nehmen, die Teil der modernen Freizeit sind (*Kapitel 3: 'Kinder und Spiel'*). Öffentliche Parks haben sich als Gegenmittel zum Leben in den Industriestädten entwickelt. Modern angelegte Parks beruhen auf einem Konzept oder einer Vorstellung, um den verschiedensten Beschäftigungen Zusammenhang zu geben (*Kapitel 4: 'Nutzbare Parks und Gärten'*). Fachmessen haben sich von traditionellen, mobilen Versanstaltungen zu internationalen 'Expos' entwickelt, bei denen interessante Konstruktionen und aud io-visuelle Präsentationen eine breite Basis für die Unterhaltung bieten (*Kapitel 5: 'Messen und Ausstellungen'*). Das historische Interesse an der Nutzung und Zurschaustellung von Wasser ist noch heute aktuell in Form von Piers an der See, Parkanlagen in Seebädern, Wasserspielplätzen und Vergnügungsparks (*Kapitel 6: 'Spielen in Wasser und Parkanlagen an der See'*). Auch der Zirkus—wenige in permanenter Form—hat zur Bekämpfung des Fernsehens neue Verfahren für die Präsentation und neue Akte gefunden (*Kapitel 7: 'Der Zirkus'*). In den letzten Jahrzehnten wurde die Bescharänkung des Theaters in Frage gestellt, wodurch sich Bühnenunterhaltung eines anderen Formats ergab. Für Fernsehen, Theater, Restaurants und Revue wurden Bünenproduktionen in neuer Form geschaffen (*Kapitel 8: 'Bühnenunterhaltung'*). Auch die Kinounterhaltung mußte sich wesentlich umstellen, um de Wettbewerb mit anderen beliebten Attraktionen standzuhalten (*Kapitel 9: 'Kino'*). Diskotheken, ursprünglich exklusiver Treffpunkt für die Jugend, wurden zum allgemein anerkannten 'Tanzraum', wogegen der Ballsaal zum Mehrzweckraum geworden ist (*Kapitel 10: 'Diskos und Tanz'*). Das Glücksspiel hat Ausdruck in den elegant ausgestatteten Hotel-Kasinos von Las Vegas Gefunden, in Europa in kleinen Spielclubs und im britischen Bingo-Club (*Kapitel 11: 'Kasinos und Glücksspiel'*). Für die Unterhaltung gedachte Gebäude müssen angemessene Sicherheitsvorschriften für die Öffentlichleit erfüllen, insbesondere hinsichtlich des Brandschutzes (*Kapitel 12: 'Öffentliche Sicherheit'*). Bei den derzeitigen Tendenzen in der Ausstattung wird von vielen Verfahren ebrauch gemacht, um die richtigen Mittel für die Unterhaltung zur Verfügung zu stellen, oder die Konstruktion selbst wird integraler Bestandteil der Unterhaltungsmedien (*Kapitel 13: 'Tendenzen und Stellungnahme'*).

موجـــز الفصــول

يشير التاريخ الى أن العمل يهيىء لنا اطار تحقيق المتعة الذاتية ، ومع التقدم الصناعي فلاشك أن النشاطات الترفيهية سوف تشبع هذه الحاجة في المستقبل (الفصل ١ ـ اطار الاستجمام فـي وقـت الفراغ) .

تكون تسهيلات الترفيه أكثر نفعاً عند ربطها ببعضها ، وقد نمت المدن الكبيرة وتطورت على أساس أن الراحة في وقت الفراغ هى النشاط الرئيسي ، كما زودت المصايف الجديدة بوسائل الترفيـه كجزء لا يتجزأ منها (الفصل ٢ ـ المصايف والمناطق المجاورة) .

ان اللعب يهيىء الاساس لنمو الاطفال والفرصة للكبار لاكتشاف مهارات جديدة ، وتكون النشاطات جانباً من وسائل الاستجمـام الحديثة (الفصل ٣ ـ الاطفال واللعب) .

وقد انشئت الحدائق العامة لتكون تريافاً ومتنفساً للحياة الصناعية في المدن ، وتستخدم الحدائق العصرية الفكرة أو التخيل لتحقيق التناسق بين النشاطات المختلفة (الفصل ٤ ـ حدائق الفكرة وحدائق الالعاب) .

وتطورت المعارض من الطراز القديم المتنقل الى «مهرجانات» دولية تبرز فيها الانشاءات البارعة والعروض المرئية السمعية اطار الترفيـه العريض (الفصل ٥ ـ المهرجانات والمعارض) .

استمر حتى اليوم الاهتمام التاريخي باستخدام وعرض خصائص المياه باقامة الأرصفة الممتدة في البحر والحدائق البحرية والالعاب المائية ومراكز الاستجمام (الفصل ٦ ـ الالعاب المائية والحدائـق البحرية) .

وقد اكتشف السيرك ـ الذي لم تبق له سوى بضعة أماكن قليلة ـ وسائل جديدة لتقديم العروض والالعاب الجديدة التي يواجه بها منافسة التلفزيون (الفصل ٧ ـ السيرك) .

جرى التساؤل في الحقبات القليلة الماضية حول تقييدات استخدام قوس خشبة المسرح مما أدى الى ايجاد طرازات بديلة للترفيـه المسرحي ، فابتكرت أشكال جديدة للاخراج المسرحي للتلفزيون والمسرح والمطاعم والاستعراضات (الفصل ٨ ـ الترفيه المسرحي) .

تعرّض الترفيه السينمائي الى تكييف واسع حتى يقدر على منافسة وسائل الترفيه المحبوبة الأخرى (الفصل ٩ ـ السينما) .

أما نوادي «الديسكوتيك» التي كانت مقصورة على الشباب فقط فقد أصبحت مقبولة على أنها «مكان للرقص» على حين أصبحت صالات الرقص الكبرى متعددة الاستعمالات (الفصل ١٠ ـ الديسكوتيك والرقص) .

وضقت المقامرة طريقها الى كازينات وفنادق مدينة لاس فيجاس الفخمة ونوادي الكازينات الصغيرة في أوروبا ونوادي البينجو البريطانية (الفصل ١١ ـ الكازينات والمقامرة) .

يجب أن تهيىء مباني الترفيه مستويات السلامة الكافية للجمهور وخاصة بالنسبة لاحتياطات مقاومة الحريق (الفصل ١٢ ـ سلامة الجمهور) .

تلجأ الاتجاهات الحالية في التصميم الى مجموعة واسعة مـن الطرق الفنية لتزويد وسائل الترفيه أو يصبح الانشاء نفسه جزءا لا يتجزأ من واسطة الاتصال في مجال الترفيه (الفصل ١٣ ـ الاتجاهات والتعليق) .

Chapter 1

Leisure context

As Mr Sleary, the circus personality in Dickens 'Hard Times' remarked, 'People mutht be amuthed. They can't alwayth a learning, or yet they can't alwayth a working, they an't made for it'.

Popular entertainment is many sided and, in this book, the phrase 'leisure entertainment' has been adopted (for the sake of clarity) to identify entertainment associated with leisure. The design aspect is concerned with the specific organisation and accommodation of popular entertainment activities within the appropriate physical and visual environment. The arrangement must allow the spectator or participant to enjoy the facilities provided, by satisfying the functional technical requirements and creating ambience for a specific mood. This book is principally concerned with those neighbourhoods in which entertainment is the primary economic generator, buildings that represent a synthesis of popular entertainment, and equipment specifically designed for amusement. The implications of the greater leisure time that people will have in the future are also examined.

Entertainment as part of leisure has always been a human preoccupation and has reflected basic social values. In recent decades, with the advent of greater leisure time the social economic aspects have been the subject of interest and analysis and the resulting studies assist in understanding the context for leisure activities. Not only is leisure the 'activity remaining after work, family, social and other obligations have been fulfilled' implying the freedom 'to do ones own thing'; it also provides the opportunity for rest, respite, restoration, entertainment, self-realisation, spiritual renewal, the increase of knowledge, the development of skills and the opportunity to participate in community life. The factors which are considered important to personal well-being include novelty, health, dominance, self respect, challenge, freedom, comfort, affection, security, achievement, status and involvement—all of which may be enhanced by appropriate leisure activities and entertainments.

The unsatisfied worker in a restrictive and repetitious industrial context, seeks compensatory satisfaction by his leisure activities and, from this, to obtain desirable experiences, temporary autonomy, self-expression and agreeable status. People who lack an intrinsic involvement with their work will be more likely to use leisure activities as a means of self-fulfilment. Qualities that are insufficiently present in work are pursued and undesirable experience is redressed in the selected leisure context. For others, who find satisfaction in work, leisure is used to facilitate the capacity to gain greater fulfilment. The implications are important both to the works manager and the designer, as both motivation and environment can influence attitudes to work. As labour efficient machinery reduces both working hours and the application of human skills the situation is further accentuated.

The designer must plan for spectator, performer and participant. For the first half of the century, entertainment provided an escapist adventure, and the trend was to entice people into 'boxes' to be entertained (cinema, theatre, dance halls, bowling alleys). Current entertainment is based on greater diversity. Travel, wide coverage by the media of all aspects of life, and moneyed social freedom have given meaning to realism. Dreams have been made tangible by cheap air travel and hire purchase. Furthermore the satisfaction with the way leisure time is spent continues to gain popular expression in the basic human qualities of eating, drinking and sexuality.

In addition the growth of the mass consumer market, open educational and vocational opportunities and youth culture are creating new values independent of historic social patterns; these and other forces could radically change the context in which the individual achieves identity and fulfilment. Status symbols and life styles are becoming ever increasingly expressions of individual taste rather than a reflection of occupation, economic position or social class. Probing mass media, the breaking-up of traditional working-class communities, the greater mobility of skilled workers and the anonymity of urban life has also generated individualism. In the place of the 'work ethos', the quest is for individual self-awareness, new sensations, experiences, skills, new leisure identities, and the questioning of both traditional values and social codes.

The social economic systems of Europe and America have created longer non-productive adolescence, more years of retirement and the repetitious nature of industrial work. At the same time, the value system has not conferred honourable significance to increased leisure even though, in Britain, there is a restrained admiration for the adroit amateur. Whereas in Britain there is a sub-conscious desire to canonise Robinson Crusoe for launching 'do it yourself' almost single handed, in America (as Margaret Mead describes) fun and enjoyment have become mandatory social obligations and work is now regarded by many people as the place where they can relax and escape from the social pressure to derive the maximum possible enjoyment from leisure. Even so, there exists the inevitable reduction in necessary manpower and a move towards the anti-utilitarian, hedonistic rationale.

The present quality of life, as generated by the work ethic, is partly represented by pollution, decaying city centres and precarious human relationships. A leisure aware society that provides moral reinforcement for people to express and act out leisure attitudes and behaviour could give equal importance to leisure styles and cultural tastes as that associated with occupations. Many people feel that in modern society technology subordinates individual human aspirations.

In the classical spiritual sense, leisure provided man with the opportunity to be the sole master, designer and interpreter of life. This would be unrealistic within the disciplines and interdependence of modern living. However, a change in the significance of 'work' must convey to leisure a more acceptable role of providing creative and meaningful self-fulfilment. Educational aims, closely linked as they are with the economic system, must prepare young people with the capacity to use unorganised non-spectator time. At the same time the recreative forces inherent in leisure entertainment could provide a humane contribution to urban living.

Historic background

The cultural ideal of ancient Greece encouraged the citizens to cultivate a balanced way of life which included enjoyment, self-fulfilment, political activity and religious observance. There was little difference between leisure activities and other areas of life. Until the 20th century, the idea of valuing leisure for its own sake was a social privilege virtually unknown by the majority. Over the centuries the work ethic, with the rewards that could be achieved, became predominant.

The United Kingdom

In the agrarian economy of medieval England, holidays were numerous with public festivals including organised entertainments. Trading fairs also brought large numbers of people together to be entertained. The religious drama was an important feature of some festivals. Minstrels formed bands of players and gave short variety and pantomime shows; they travelled in pageant carts, performing in inn-yards and market places. As towns grew larger providing a substantial local population, bands of players replaced the wandering minstrels and purpose-built theatres were created based on the galleried courtyards of inns.

By the 17th century, the tastes of the court and the ordinary citizens began to separate. The aristocrats watched masques and the Court of James I patronised private indoor theatres, while the public theatre lost its appeal. Furthermore, puritanism did much to restrict entertainment and sport. Gambling, horseracing, bull and bear baiting and cock fighting were becoming established in the 18th century. The coffee houses of the Queen Anne period became meeting places for gaming and by 1778 there were 400 lottery offices in London alone.

Pleasure Gardens such as Vauxhall in London had existed since the Restoration but in 1728, Vauxhall was subject to improvements and became the principal park for aristocratic pleasure seekers. Gradually the enjoyment of the pleasure garden was extended to the middle classes and ordinary people. The spas, serving as health resorts also became popular at this time. Places such as Tunbridge Wells and Harrogate provided concerts, promenades, assembly buildings and gaming rooms.

The quest for a health promoting environment away from the grime of industrialisation and urbanisation, promoted the seaside resorts in the early 1800s. Brighton, Margate, Ramsgate and Scarborough developed similar amusements to the spas. In June each year people in society moved to the fashionable resorts where leisure was a full-time occupation. Later in the century Blackpool developed the entertainment suitable for the cotton mill workers of the north-east. Industrialisation continued to stimulate the development of towns which gave an opportunity to promoters of leisure interests to create permanent resort establishments.

For the 'beau monde' in town, coffee houses, fencing clubs, boxing saloons and centres of fashion (such as Holland House) for dances, suppers and concert parties gained in popularity. For the industrial worker life was regulated by the factory routine with repetitive work and long working hours. Housing conditions were overcrowded and thus the public house became the haven for the working man to enjoy his beer and social life. The 'pub' developed as an entertainment centre providing skittles, card games and a dance on Saturday nights. Musical entertainment was encouraged and street entertainers were brought in to provide additional entertainment.

The most popular travelling show was the circus visiting towns in conjunction with festivals and annual gatherings. For the circus, the winter months were spent in the towns and some permanent circus arenas were constructed.

The end of the 18th century saw a revival in the theatres with playhouses being built in the provinces. The Theatres Act of 1843, allowed all theatres to produce plays but prohibited eating, drinking and smoking during the performance yet allowed all three diversions at music hall shows. This encouraged the music hall theatre, in which the working-class public could find 'song and supper'.

A typical music hall had a large stage, an auditorium with fixed tables and chairs and a horseshoe balcony with more expensive seats. The food and drink element was gradually taken out of the auditorium, the audience concentrated on the entertainment. This change of emphasis led to the 'Empires' and 'Hippodromes' of London and the provinces.

The economic boom of the 1860s, the reduction in working hours and increase in public holidays provided the working man both with leisure time and money to spend.

Music and dancing has been a source of popular entertainment since the 1850s particularly in the resorts. The magnificent ballrooms in the Blackpool leisure complexes built at the end of the 19th century and elegant ballrooms included in the large hotel buildings constructed during the same period provided both the working and wealthy classes opportunity to enjoy social dancing. The dancing mania became more universal after the First World War as an expression of relief at the end of a long and miserable war.

In the 1960s, music and dance again gave expression to young people, who with increased spending money and greater freedom, achieved a cultural identity in 'pop' music and discotheques.

Cinema entertainment, originating in the fairgrounds was adopted by the music hall and quickly became independent as a significant form for popular entertainment. However, the escapism afforded by cinema entertainment was eroded by improved standards of living, cheap travel, package holidays, the motor car and home television. The cinema industry was faced with decline in support and many cinema owners had to find alternative uses for their buildings. Although ten-pin bowling was tried, bingo (based on simple 'housey-housey' gambling) has provided the principal use for redundant cinemas and has maintained the community club facility.

The 5-day week established the 'weekend' holiday and the Holiday with Pay Act of 1938, obliged employees to grant at least 1 week's paid holiday each year. Not only was leisure time expanded for working people but the margin of income available for free-spending increased. During the 1920s, the resorts in particular, benefited. By the 1930s Blackpool could accommodate 7 million visitors per year, with Southport $5\frac{1}{2}$ million, Hastings 3 million and Southend 2 million. These resorts provided the popular 'bed and breakfast', mass amusement, family entertainment of films, dancing and funfairs within the context of the seaside holiday. The combination of amusement facilities, entertainment and seaside accommodation was developed with the Holiday Camp system. Billy Butlin's camp at Skegness, housing 2000 people in chalets, started in 1935, followed by further Butlin's Camps and resorts developed by Pontins, Warners and Cooks. Cheap air travel has directed holiday traffic towards the sun, seaside and skiing resorts, with activity holidays utilising 'play' as recreational entertainment.

U.S.A.

The historical development differed initially with the scattered nature of the early settlements. However, with the advent of urbanisation and industrial growth, an interest in both the traditional theatre and less-sophisticated forms of popular entertainment were generated. The American vaudeville, with origins in touring companies, gained a more permanent home in the so-called 'museums' of the large cities that added live entertainment to the inanimate exhibitions. Barnum's museum in New York, established in 1841 was followed a year later by Franklins theatre, advertised as the first variety theatre in the city. By the end of the 19th century, chains of theatres were operated under corporate management. However, the success of the motion picture industry eclipsed vaudeville entertainment and seriously effected straight theatre until the 1930s when the musical shows, revues and folk opera were produced in the same spectacular idiom as the lavish products of Hollywood. The 'star' appeal and scale of productions of Hollywood and Broadway were reflected in the spectacular cinema buildings of the day. The tradition of superlatives has been maintained partly in the resort 'showrooms' (as the MGM Grand, Las Vegas) and partly diversified into the television industry and, in recent decades, the themed amusement parks.

Western Europe

For Western Europe, the 19th and 20th centuries have been a time of radical change towards an industrialised and an urbanised economy, a spread of spending power to working people, entitlement to paid holidays and leisure time. This has prompted an ever increasing variety of leisure and entertainment opportunities ranging from television in the home to the highly competitive 'all-in' holiday with entertainment and amusement provided. The many forms of leisure entertainment include the large supper club providing popular cabaret, the technical refinements of concert hall and experimental theatre, popular bingo and sophisticated gaming, amusement parks, theme parks, marine parks, cinema, competitive dancing and discotheques for all ages as well as traditional fairs, carnivals and circuses.

Thus the context for entertainment today has many aspects. These include greater purchasing power by the majority, greater mobility, liberation in social attitudes providing greater freedom for men and women in their social life, a wide range of spectator and participatory entertainment; and a growing need for self-fulfilment in leisure activities.

Entrepreneurs

Today leisure entertainment is financed both by private individuals and government. As leisure time increases and where governments are elected on service to the community the electorate expects more 'leisure services' supplied by the state. In Western Europe the state has become a major patron of cultural entertainment, facilities for community interests and leisure activities associated with health and sport. There are many situations where public finance and private enterprise work together constructively.

At the same time, entrepreneurs and leisure organisations, such as Rank, Disney and Club Méditerranée, must continually adapt and adjust to changes in public interest. The public continue to look for new and exciting experiences, greater luxury, magic and fantasy, health conservation, acquired

skills, the uncertainty in risk and the reassurance of the evocative.

The Rank Organisation

The Rank Organisation was started by J. Arthur Rank who, with inherited wealth and a desire to show religious films that he had produced, eventually controlled the Odeon Theatre and Gaumont British organisations. Gaumont British Picture Corporation was one of the first cinema companies in Britain. Odeon Theatres, established by Oscar Deutsch in 1932, consisted of a major circuit of cinemas and film production studios at Pinewood Studios.

In 1941 Oscar Deutsch died and Rank acquired control of Odeon Theatres. By 1945 he also controlled Gaumont British and many other companies concerned with film production and distribution. Although 1946 was the peak of cinema attendance in the UK with a total of 1500 million, the subsequent years became more difficult for the film industry. Hollywood, the great film producing machine, came near to collapse. The British government of the day threatened to nationalise the whole cinema industry and many companies fell by the wayside. The Rank companies not only persevered, but incorporated many less substantial organisations.

In 1948 Circuits Management Association Limited was established to run the Odeon, Gaumont and other Rank cinemas. This Association formed the basis of the present Rank Organisation. In the late 1940s there were nearly 600 Rank cinemas. The flow of films was reducing and British film production was finding it difficult to maintain a high standard. In the early 1950s, the BBC Television service made strides into family entertainment, and in 1955 Independent Television was established. The early 1960s saw a spending boom that concentrated on home ownership, domestic equipment and motor cars.

In 1957, J. Arthur Rank retired and John Davis became principally responsible for the Rank Organisation. He recognised that drastic measures were needed in the cinema industry and directed interest to 'rationalisation' and 'diversification'. Rationalisation determined that cinemas should only operate where they needed, and diversification required a spread to other leisure activities and interests other than leisure. The wide range of companies originally acquired by J. Arthur Rank provided great potential for diversification.

The rationalisation programme created a context in which to assess the merits of existing cinema buildings. Some cinemas were closed. Some were converted into other leisure uses such as bowling and bingo. Bowling alleys were compatible with the space available in a cinema, but it was a short-lived 'rave'. Bingo was more appropriate to the auditorium and stage format and it has become established as an important leisure entertainment and socially congenial activity in the community.

Following the initial rationalisation that established the viable base of existing buildings, new cinemas were built in the new towns and developing areas in the form of 1000 capacity, stadium type, planned on one level.

The viability of large auditoriums was undermined by the drop in cinema attendances and a process of twinning (dividing large cinemas into two cinemas) was commenced. On this basis overheads and staffing are shared, and alternative film entertainment is offered. The popular films can run longer whereas the less popular films do not prejudice the success of the cinema in that proportionally less seats remain unoccupied. The first twinning project was the Odeon, Nottingham in 1965.

The process of subdivision extended to tripling and there have been examples of cinemas divided into four, even into five, auditoria. In this context the number of cinemas was increased after the initial need to cull the large uneconomic structures. In 1976 the yearly attendance was 106 million in which the sixteen to twenty-four age groups had the largest representation.

The leisure interest extended to ballrooms (such as Top Rank Suites), ice rinks and subsequently discotheques.

The Rank Organisation had started including ballroom and restaurant accommodation in their cinemas in the 1950s. The Top Rank Suites were constructed to provide dance and ballroom facilities in answer to a popular interest; the number of suites increased to twenty in 1960.

Over the last decade, social attitudes to dancing have changed. Serious competitive dancing has increased in interest, but the main bulk of social dancing has decreased and the discotheque has become the venue for social entertainment. There are now nine Top Rank Suites; reorganisation has modified many establishments, and in Brighton, Sussex, cinema and dance facilities have been brought together under one roof at the Kingwest Leisure Centre.

Ice skating played a minor part as an alternative leisure activity to cinema. Rank constructed two rinks—one at Southampton and one at Brighton. Ice skating as a commercially operated leisure activity suffers the disadvantage of mixing the talented competitive skater who requires space, with the casual and inept. The commercial context has also suffered the unequal competition of local authority subsidised establishments. The Brighton Ice Rink has disappeared in the Kingwest reorganisation. The Southampton Ice Rink remains recharged by the current interest in skating.

Thus of the 141 Odeon Cinemas built before 1939—twenty-five remain unchanged, twenty-five have been subdivided or tripled, fifty-two have been closed, twenty-nine have been sold as cinemas, seven have been sold and converted to bingo, and eight have been converted by Rank into Top Rank (Bingo) Clubs. This is indicative of the adjustments that are made necessary through changes in the appeal of particular forms of entertainment, and the way one company has adapted.

Today the Rank Organisation includes companies not only concerned with the film and leisure industry, but also hotels, Xerox, and Butlin's holiday centres. Rank Organisation has sixteen divisions of which Rank Leisure Services is one. Within this division there is a theatre section with 270 cinemas in 180 separate buildings, Top Rank Clubs with seventy-nine bingo clubs, entertainment and catering within seven Top Rank Suites and forty-three other premises, and the Motorway Services Section concerned with four motorway establishments.

The Disney Organisation

The Disney Organisation has revolved around the skill and imagination of Walt Disney and his capacity to develop and exploit new techniques. The association with animated films portraying a fairy tale or folk hero image is well known.

Disney films inaugurated such new techniques as the sound cartoon, the full length animated feature (Snow White and the Seven Dwarfs), stereophonic sound, 360° screen projection, and new methods of animation leading to audio-animatronics (electronic operated figures that move and speak).

In 1955, Disneyland, Los Angeles, was created as a new concept in family entertainment, capitalising on the successful film images and having much in common with 'Expo' planning. The creative work was an extension of the film making process with adventure rides creating a three-dimensional cartoon presentation through which the public is conveyed. These techniques were used to represent commercial organisations in the 1964–65 New York Fair.

Walt Disney World, Florida (Vacation Kingdom) completed in 1971, endeavours to provide a total leisure resort with theme park and accommodation, and it will include the EPCOT (Experimental Project, Community of Tomorrow) project. Contrary to the original concept, this is to become a mini-'Expo', providing a forum showcase of American Companies and an arena of cultures of individual countries, the Disney Organisation acting mainly as agents for the countries and companies concerned.

In 1977 less than 19% of Walt Disney Organisation income came from film rentals and two-thirds of its revenue from the leisure parks. From an enterprise generated by individualistic creative and innovative skills responding to a particular market, it has extended into theme park entertainment and using entertainment techniques to convey commercial good will in the trade fair context.

Club Mediterranée

Club Mediterranée was started in 1950 by Gerald Blitz and a group of friends, as a sporting club. Gilbert Trigano, who has been responsible for the extensive development of the company joined Club Mediterranée in 1954 as managing director. The first village with tent accommodation was at Alcudia in Majorca, and the first village with straw huts was at Palinuro. In 1956 the first Club Mediterranée winter sports hotel was established in Leysin in Switzerland. In 1967 Club Mediterranée became a limited company and has subsequently increased the number of holiday villages to nearly eighty. These are located in Europe, the Mediterranean and North Africa coast, Polynesia, Antilles, Mexico and the Indian Ocean, development of further villages is anticipated in the Caribbean and the Pacific.

The philosophy of the organisation combines consideration for the site and location of the resort with the facilities and freedom for guests to explore sporting activities, artistic skills and crafts. This leisure entertainment of individual participation is combined with conventional spectator entertainments of cabaret and music, and discotheques. In fact, since its initiation, Club Mediterranée has endeavoured to promote sporting activities including the well-known ocean racing yachts 'Club Mediterranee' and 'Vendredi 13'. The organisation also promotes the Corsican professional football team of Bastia.

In many cases the villages have been developed by other companies and have been taken over by Club Mediterranée as a going concern facing difficulties. All accommodation is based on double rooms and all the villages have restaurants, a theatre and a night club. There are facilities for small children in some villages, but generally the selection of sporting activities and life style is geared to the eighteen to thirty-five age range. Older people with children are catered for more adequately in the Club Mediterranée hotel accommodation. There are instructors in the various sports and such artistic and craft facilities as pottery, painting and fabric printing, so that visitors can explore new skills.

As a company, Club Mediterranée has diversified into hotel management outside their own holiday villages, also into cosmetics, luggage and beach towels. In 1976, the Company employed nearly 13 000 people and had a total of 43 131 beds in the holiday villages.

The qualities that identify Club Mediterranée from other tourist and holiday organisations are the facilities that are made available to the visitors. The freedom, co-operation and self-sufficiency reflects the spirit of 'camping' and exploration 'play' for adults.

1. Dans le contexte des loisirs—Résumé

Le concept des loisirs a subi un changement radical au cours de ces dernières années. Aujourd'hui, par rapport à il y a quinze ou ving ans, un nombre croissant de gens accordent de plus en plus de temps `a la détente. La tendance est nettement orientée vers une forme de divertissement pour toute la famille avec un désir plus prononcé de participation. Les pouvoirs publics, les municipalités, ainsi que les entreprises privées telles que la Rank Organisation, Walt Disney et le Club Méditerranée, fournissent et financent une grande variété d'activités de loisirs.

1. Freizeit—Zusammenfassung

Im Laufe der Jahre hat sich das Freizeitkonzept radikal geändert. Heute haben im Vergleich zu früher, D.H. vor etwa fünfzehn bis zwanzig Jahren, immer mehr Leute Zeit zur Entspannung. Es besteht eine Tendenz zur Unterhaltung für die ganze Familie und einem Wunsch, teilzunehmen, anstatt zuzusehen. Staatliche Stellen, städtische Behörden und Privatunternehmer tragen alle dazu bei, die verschiedensten Anlagen zu finanzieren und zur Verfügung zu stellen. Beispiele sind die Rank Organisation, Walt Disney und Club Mediterrane.

١ - بيئة الاستجمام وقت الفراغ - موجز

ان مفهوم الاستجمام وقت الفراغ قد تغير تماماً في خلال السنوات الماضية ، والكثير منا اليوم يجد لديه وقتاً للاستجمام أكثر مما كان يجده من خمس عشرة سنة أو من عشرين سنة مضت . وهناك اتجاه نحو تهيئة وسائل الترفيه المصممة من أجل الأسرة كلها ، وهناك الرغبة في المساهمة بدلا من الاكتفاء بالمشاهدة . سوف تقوم الحكومات والسلطات المحلية والشركات المستقلة جميعها بالمساعدة في تمويل وتوفير مجموعة واسعة من النشاطات . الأمثلة : مؤسسة رانك - والت ديزني - كلوب ميديتيراني .

Chapter 2

Resorts and neighbourhoods

Entertainment facilities benefit by being grouped together, providing an attractive character and sharing 'spin off'. This is true to the entertainment centres of the large cities, new leisure orientated cities and tourist regions. In some cases the development of the city has been principally based on leisure-entertainment as Blackpool, Las Vegas and Disney World. Blackpool has grown into a substantial resort providing holiday entertainment for the industrial north-east of England. The rapid establishment of Las Vegas as the international casino based resort in Nevada has, in its desert location, the contemporaneous character of a new city in the Middle East. In contrast, Walt Disney World, Florida, is the realisation of one man's aspirations to provide a specific environment for family entertainment.

The majority of large cities such as Hamburg have facilities for business and holiday visitors, but the main leisure activities are directed towards the residents. The concern that leisure needs have far reaching planning aspects (from family house design to city planning) is propagated by such an international organisation as ELRA (European Leisure and Recreational Association).

The rehabilitation of existing entertainment centres is a complex process. To achieve a comprehensive scheme, the individual development of the many interests concerned must be related. In the case of Piccadilly, London, this has proved to be an extremely slow process, resulting in a prolonged blighted appearance in contrast with the popular image as a centre of entertainment.

At the same time, new holiday patterns have provided resorts with entertainment and instruction on leisure activities. For example, in Britain, Butlin's holiday centres provide for 1¼ million people each year and Club Mediterranée Villages have been developed throughout the Mediterranean and sub-tropical locations.

Blackpool, England

By 1870 Blackpool, located on the north-west coast of England, had four inns and several lodging houses. A stagecoach from Manchester provided transport for those who travelled to Blackpool for healthy bathing, fresh air and to drink the salt water. Entertainment consisted of an occasional concert in a barn improvised as a theatre, and a monthly fair on the sands. The first stimulant to development was the construction of a railway branch line from Preston in 1846 which increased the tourist traffic. This was followed by the gradual provision of services, such as street lighting and fresh water, the increase in inns and beach houses.

At first, the entertainment enterprises were modest. It was the 1862 Companies Act (which limited commercial loss to the share ownership) that acted as a catalyst to the entrepreneur. The North Pier was constructed to provide a promenade for the better class visitors. A second pier was constructed and survived competition by providing steamboat trips and popular dancing. Dancing was the social entertainment of the Lancashire working class and the facilities at Blackpool made it attractive to the Lancashire cotton workers.

By the 1870s, development at Blackpool had become entwined in an investment spiral with the local authority providing such basic facilities as the 2-mile-long promenade. Furthermore, the establishment of public holidays provided thousands of people the opportunity to sample the resort on day trip visits.

The entertainment facilities increased. An open air leisure park based on Vauxhall gardens, London, was followed in 1876 by the first stage of the Winter Gardens to provide accommodation for visitors in bad weather. One pier extended its facilities to a 1200-seat indoor pavilion. The principal entertainment enterprises continued to compete for the attention of the visitors.

Blackpool grew increasingly popular with the improvement of railway access but maintained a homeliness that appealed to the working-class Lancashire people. It was referred to as being 'a mill town without the mills but with the sea'. It had a safe beach, an interesting area of cliffs, and managed to escape the epidemics that hit several resort towns in the 1870s and 1880s. In 1876, Blackpool became a Borough and its Council was able to implement services and improvements conducive to further development. In fact, improvements such as the electric lighting to the promenade and the improvement to the railway service assisted to maintain the popularity of the town during the economic depression of the 1870s. In 1885 an electric tram system was established more as an entertainment feature than an effective form of transport.

In the 1880s the spending power of the working classes increased and continued to the end of the century. Development of Blackpool was activated—an opera house, a theatre, and all day entertainment at the Winter Gardens. The new buildings captured an opulence far removed from the home environment of the average visitors.

In 1890, the Tower was built with the idea that it would be possible to signal to a similar construction to be built on the Isle of Man. An entertainment building was constructed in conjunction with the Blackpool Tower to provide a multi-entertainment complex including circus, dance pavilion and restaurant. The project was a bold use of a limited liability company with £300 000 contributed by 3000 individuals, and proved a commercial success. It remains today, a building combining several aspects of popular entertainment. The opulent decor that entertained the Victorian visitors remains none the less effective as a popular place today.

In the wake of the success of the Tower, a great Ferris Wheel was constructed at the Winter Gardens to counteract the competition but proved unsuccessful. Another entertainment complex, the Alhambra was built in the 1890s, but the enterprise was launched on exaggerated land values and the

Blackpool Tower Ballroom looking towards stage

project nearly foundered. It was refurbished and re-opened as the 'Palace' and remained a popular entertainment centre until 1961.

The season of entertainment was extended by the autumn feature 'the illuminations', the brilliantly illuminated decorations of the promenade and trams.

By the end of the century the number of holiday visitors to Blackpool reached 3 million, with over 400 000 visiting during one Whitsun weekend. The tram transport system was improved and a private tramway was established along the promenade. The facilities of the town increased with flying, air pageants and a racecourse. The Pleasure Beach was opened by 1904 and increased attraction year by year.

Thus Blackpool was established by the access provided by the early railway link, competitive entrepreneural showmanship and a local authority providing basic services to enhance the resort. The main structure was established before the First World War, and it has continued to build on its reputation as a holiday resort with popular entertainment. For over a century, it has had entertainment facilities and tourist accommodation as the primary economic activity. In recent years, accessibility by car has been improved and the effect of this on the centre of the town and the promenade has been a major issue in the town development plan. The proposals aim to extend pedestrian areas and rationalise car parking.

Today the entertainment centre of Blackpool consists of the 3 km (2 mile) promenade from the Pleasure Beach at one end to Uncle Tom's Cabin, with the Tower, Winter Gardens, three piers and

Blackpool Golden Mile promenade (Photo: Anthony Wylson)

many individual buildings. The town population is approximately 150 000 with a growing proportion of elderly people over sixty. Seasonal unemployment is natural to a resort, but there is a higher percentage of unemployment in Blackpool than the average for the north-west. Tourism is the principal source of employment with over 10 000 people employed in associated activities, and a revenue of £150 million. There are $16\frac{1}{2}$ million visitors each year of which $3\frac{1}{4}$ million stay longer than 4 days.

The car traffic flow into the town on the principal access road (Preston New Road) averages 15 000 per 24 hours two-way flow from mid-November to mid-June (with an increase at Easter) rising to 30 000 cars each weekday and peaking at 40 000 per weekend day between July and mid-November. The airport handles 50 000 arrivals a year that range in monthly rate from 1500 in January to 8000 in August. The local authority provides nearly 10 000 parking spaces and accommodation for tourists is provided by 2712 guest houses, 140 hotels and 6000

Blackpool Illuminations (Photo: H. A. Hallas, Blackpool)

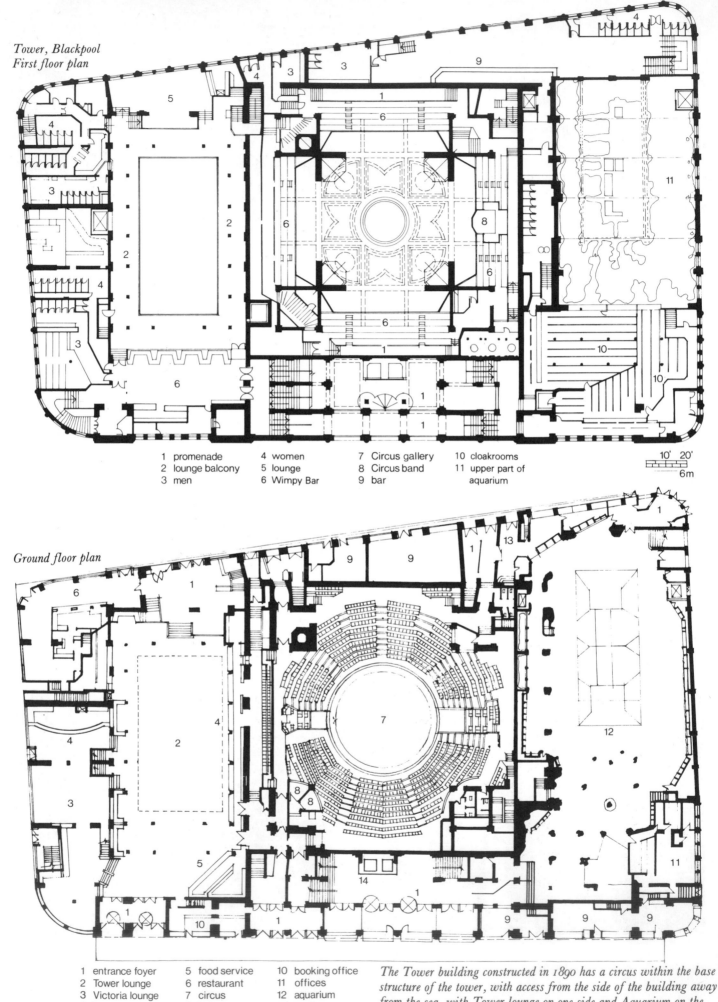

Tower, Blackpool
First floor plan

Ground floor plan

1 promenade	4 women	7 Circus gallery	10 cloakrooms	
2 lounge balcony	5 lounge	8 Circus band	11 upper part of	
3 men	6 Wimpy Bar	9 bar	aquarium	

10' 20'
6m

1 entrance foyer	5 food service	10 booking office	
2 Tower lounge	6 restaurant	11 offices	
3 Victoria lounge	7 circus	12 aquarium	
4 bar	8 box	13 staff	
	9 shops	14 lifts	

The Tower building constructed in 1890 has a circus within the base structure of the tower, with access from the side of the building away from the sea, with Tower lounge on one side and Aquarium on the other. The ballroom is at first floor level with access from the sea side.

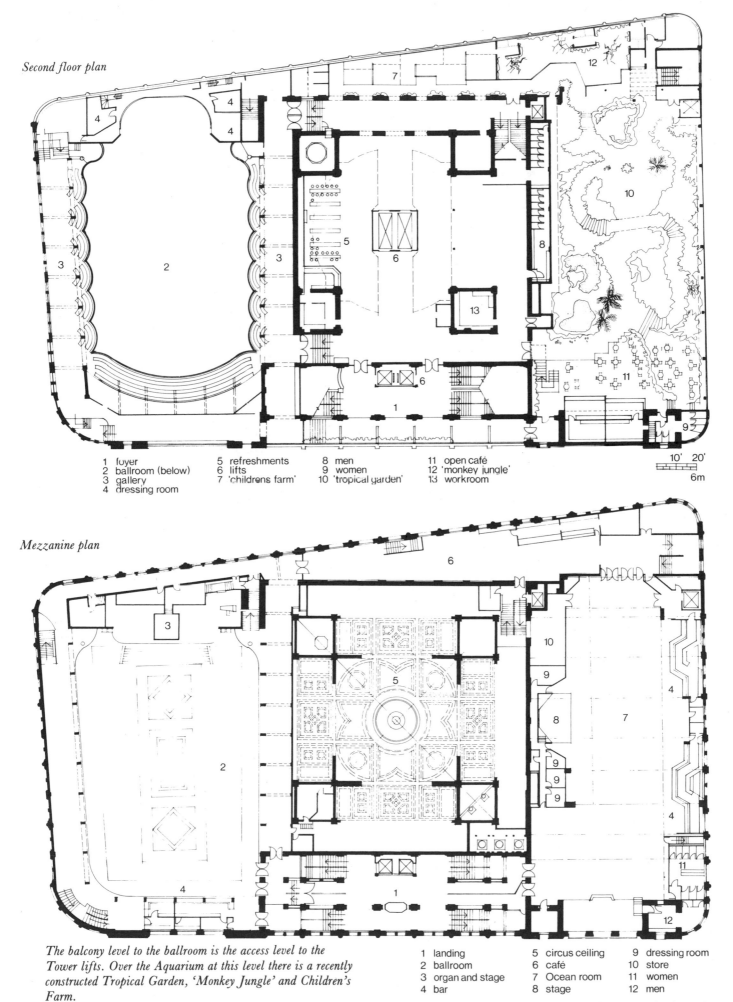

Second floor plan

1 foyer	5 refreshments	8 men	11 open café
2 ballroom (below)	6 lifts	9 women	12 'monkey jungle'
3 gallery	7 'childrens farm'	10 'tropical garden'	13 workroom
4 dressing room			

Mezzanine plan

The balcony level to the ballroom is the access level to the Tower lifts. Over the Aquarium at this level there is a recently constructed Tropical Garden, 'Monkey Jungle' and Children's Farm.

1 landing	5 circus ceiling	9 dressing room
2 ballroom	6 café	10 store
3 organ and stage	7 Ocean room	11 women
4 bar	8 stage	12 men

Tower, Blackpool

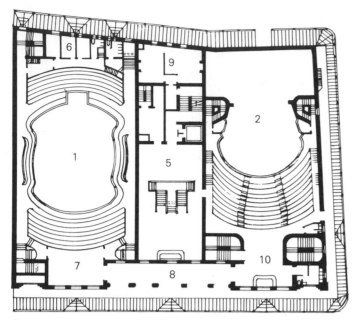

Lower balcony level

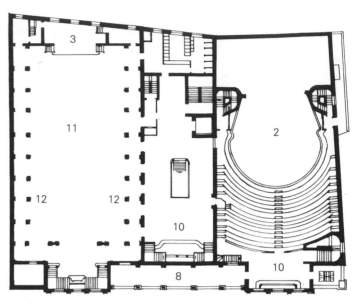

Ballroom level

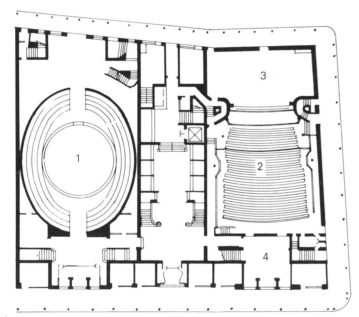

Ground floor plan

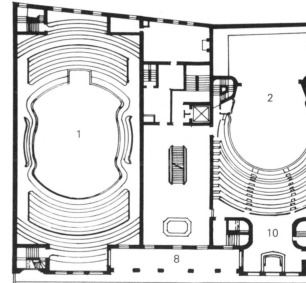

Upper balcony level

1 circus	5 restaurant	9 offices
2 theatre	6 dressing rooms	10 lounge
3 stage	7 buffet	11 ballroom
4 vestibule/foyer	8 promenade	12 balcony

Alhambra, Blackpool
The Alhambra was designed by Wylson and Long, Victorian Theatre Architects, and was completed in 1899, replacing the Prince of Wales Theatre and a Hall of Aquatic entertainment.

The new building consisted of a four level entertainment centre with centralised access. One side of the building consisted of a 2000 seat circus with two levels of balcony seating, and a 3000 capacity ballroom at third floor level. The other side of the building consisted of a 3000 seat theatre with three tiers of seating. The central area had a restaurant at one level, café at second floor and a conservatory on the third floor. At each level there was access to promenade balconies overlooking the beach and sea. At roof level, there was a promenade with kiosks, shooting gallery and other small shows. The basement housed kitchens, horses stables and mechanical services. The total capacity of the building was 12 000 visitors. The interior decor for circus and theatre included velvet drapes, Utrecht Velvet upholstery, and carpeting throughout. The lighting consisted of large gas 'sun burners', electric arc lamps and incandescent lamps. The ballroom had a sprung parquet floor and carpeted balcony promenade.

1 Theatre proscenium
2 Circus
3 Ballroom stairs to gallery
4 Exterior of building
5 Ballroom looking towards orchestra
(Photos: Anthony Wylson)

separate holiday flats. Besides the illuminations, the holiday season has been progressively extended as a quarter of a million visitors a year go to Blackpool for conferences and trade exhibitions.

The Council has also embarked upon a progressive programme of pedestrianisation and renewal within the central area to improve the main shopping environment. The central area is served with over 5000 off-street car parking spaces. Aware of the changing trends in the holiday and leisure market, the Council maintains a policy to allow the private sector maximum flexibility for investment and innovation across the spectrum of leisure, entertainment, shopping, commercial development and industrial development. Recently, there was substantial investment into leisure and entertainment facilities.

At the same time, the town is encouraging industrial growth with comprehensive community development including office development to provide for the dispersal of government offices from London. A natural gas discovery 20 miles west of Blackpool has provoked speculation as to the possibilities of oil beneath the Irish Sea. Thus it is the policy that Blackpool should continue to develop on a diversified industrial base but with entertainment providing a principal attraction.

Walt Disney World, Florida, U.S.A.

The idea of Disneyland, the forerunner to Walt Disney World, started as a result of Walt Disney's dissatisfaction with conventional amusement parks of the 1930s when he made visits at the weekends with his two small daughters. He considered that an amusement park should be a place where parents and children could enjoy themselves as a family. In the 1950s the idea became a reality with the creation of Disneyland, a 160-acre theme park in Annaheim, Los Angeles, was opened in 1955.

The isolation of Disneyland was soon destroyed by surrounding development and thus in siting Walt Disney World, a far larger area ($113 \cdot 0$ km^2 43 square miles) was acquired, sufficient to allow for an entirely self-supporting complex. Walt Disney World is a massive and continuing enterprise. The project aims to provide a holiday resort that caters for everyone, providing a choice of accommodation, with a range of recreation facilities from the Magic Kingdom theme park, to boating, riding, water fun, and golf; also the Lake Buena Vista community, and an experimental project (EPCOT) originally to enable new urban systems to be tested in practice.

The Orlando location was chosen because of the prolific tourist traffic (20 million through Florida at the time the project was assessed) with the majority both travelling through central Florida and resident east of the Rocky Mountains. In this respect the new project would not be competing but it would be complementary to Disneyland in Los Angeles, California. The land was purchased by October 1965 at 5 million dollars. The project set out to be a complete environmental exercise with an imaginative conservation and land improvement programme, to provide a complete vacational and theme park with resort and camp site accommodation. Stage one, which consists of theme park, resort accommodation, land reclamation and community centre, was complete in 1971 for a cost of 400 million dollars. The EPCOT project is to follow.

The environmental programme is a significant land engineering achievement since the land was originally aboriginal wilderness with wild life, ancient stands of cypress, wild orange and other colourful flora and fauna. Florida had suffered over-drainage. The project commenced in 1967 with a land improvement and water reclamation programme sympathetic to the natural ecology. The authority to proceed was achieved by special legislation to establish the Reedy Creek Improvement District to implement the project area with building codes, zoning regulations, planning, and to provide public services necessary for the future tourist and residential population. When the ground had been shaped and compacted, the location, height, and size of all the major elements were marked by balloons, ranging from 180 ft above the ground representing Cinderella's Castle, to a rectangular space for the Contemporary Resort Hotel. This provided a preview of the projects skyline on the flat Floridan landscape.

In the development of the project, the aim was to set an example of good development in planning, uses of space, water control, prevention of pollution, building codes, land improvement, conservation, etc. It was to demonstrate that man and technology can create a new urban area without destroying the natural environment. The technology includes water purification, solid waste disposal systems, a central energy plant, a comprehensive transport system, and a total integrated communications system linking computer, telephones, automatic monitoring and control devices.

The total family entertainment complex, as completed in stage one, consists of two lakes and numerous waterways, two lakeside resort hotels (Contemporary Resort and Polynesian Village Resort) and a Golf Resort Hotel, the Magic Kingdom theme park, a camping ground resort (Fort Wilderness) with a water fun park (River Country)

Polynesian Village Resort (Photo: Anthony Wylson)

residential buildings with the Lake Buena Vista shopping centre. One island on the lake, Treasure Island, has been developed with a tropical garden and bird sanctuary. The complex has a comprehensive transportation system from the extensive car park area, the resort hotels, the camping and residential areas.

Las Vegas, Nevada, U.S.A.

The rapid growth of Las Vegas as the 'Mecca of Leisure Entertainment' is unique and development continues even though similar facilities are being established in Reno, Nevada and will be stimulated in New Jersey through recent laws permitting gambling. Las Vegas is the largest of four incorporated communities in Clark County which has an estimated population of 375 000.

Tourism and retail trade form the principal base for development followed by military and scientific installations of the Federal Government, manufacturing mining operations and power generation. Las Vegas is accessible to the large population centres of Southern California.

Las Vegas (the meadows of the Las Vegas valley) was discovered by the Spanish who were looking for a westward route from Santa Fe to California in the early 1800s. At the end of the century, a group of Mormons settled in the valley to provide for and protect the US mail route between Los Angeles and Salt Lake City. The road and rail communications were stimulated by prospectors for gold and silver in the 'Meadows'. A new railroad to the south-west coast and passing through Las Vegas was constructed in 1905. The Railroad Company auctioned off the surrounding land which became the original town site. A temporary tented town was established.

A statute in 1931 permitted gambling in Las Vegas and a further significant impact in the development of the town was the construction of the Hoover Dam in 1933. This is 40 km (approximately 25 miles) from Las Vegas and was built to control the Colorado River. Lake Mead, formed as a result of the dam, is 185 km (115 miles) long.

In 1941, when people went to Reno to gamble, Las Vegas town was still relatively undeveloped and respectable, a smart hotel El Rancho Vegas was built, initiating the luxury hotel casino pattern in the Freemont Section of the town. This attracted Hollywood stars and a year later the Last Frontier Hotel was constructed a mile farther along Highway 91. In 1946, Benjamin 'Bugsy' Segal opened the Flamingo Club (named after fiery red-headed friend, Virginia Hill, who he called 'the Flamingo') in the desert away from the existing town and initiated the development of the 'Strip' along US Highway 91 or Las Vegas Boulevard. The casino business soon became a matter of concern to the authorities in Las Vegas and the Las Vegas Gaming Control Board introduced a law making it compulsory for all casino owners to operate under licence.

The 'Strip' became the location for new large casino hotels with leisure and entertainment facilities, and in 1966 the property investment aspect was stimulated by the involvement of Howard Hughes. To Howard Hughes, the favourable tax base, the 24-hour operations and the open space were appealing and finance released through the sale of TWA was directed towards buying Las Vegas properties. The involvement of Howard Hughes brought further development.

The present architectural characters of the 'Strip' and downtown Las Vegas are noticeably different. The older pedestrian scale streets of 'downtown', create the conventional urban enclosure but with spectacular night time illuminations. The lighting level is so high that daytime light meter readings are registered. The 'Strip', that has developed in the last few decades consists of 4·8 km (3 miles) of wide dual carriageway that has the character of a jetty projecting into the desert, with the massive hotels and illuminated carousels moored either side. It is not a pedestrian scale but the continuous movement of traffic and the vast car parks associated with each of the large hotels represents, not only the principal method of transportation from casino to casino, but also the context in which buildings are appreciated. The initial development gave priority to illuminated

Downtown Las Vegas (Photo: Anthony Wylson)

MGM Grand Casino area, 140 yards long

signs (some, as in the case of the Dunes Hotel and Stardust, are twenty storeys high) with low rise hotels or motels spread out behind. In recent years the hotels have expanded and tower above the carousels creating a greater enclosure to the highway.

Today the hotel complexes enclose their individual terraces and gardens, protecting carefully established landscaping from wind-blown sand and extraneous distractions. The basic components of the hotels consist of a large casino area (measured in acres) dominating the hotel entrance, with bars, restaurants, 'show' rooms (which vary in size from the large auditorium of the Aladdin Theatre of the Performing Arts, the large theatre restaurants of MGM and Stardust to the more intimate lounge theatres and night clubs), shopping arcades, convention rooms, health and beauty salons and bedroom accommodation. At the rear of the hotels, protected from the noise of the road and the blatant casino atmosphere, there are the pool terraces where water and rich landscaping exist in contrast to the desert. In addition there are specialist items as the Jai Alai at MGM and Circus entertainment at Circus Circus. The principal luxury hotels aim to provide a complete holiday of gambling, sport and relaxation.

The casino space is windowless and by tradition without clocks. Each has rows of fruit machines (with over 900 in one casino) with players, mainly women, directing suspended animation towards the moving parts. Besides slot machines there are craps, blackjack, roulette, baccarat and keno. The casinos are staffed by women with coin change and uniformed armed security men.

Hotel Casinos
The MGM Grand (at present the largest hotel in Las

Dunes hotel and illuminated Carousel, Las Vegas

Vegas), does not have an extravagant illuminated carousel but the entrance canopy and architectural massing is impressive. The hotel, costing 120 million dollars, was opened in December 1973 on a 17 ha (43 acre) site. The building is twenty-six floors high and provides for 2100 rooms and suites. The casino area is 50 000 square feet (over an acre*), with 930 slot machines, ten crap tables, sixty-one blackjack or '21' tables, six roulette wheels, three big six wheels, three baccarat games, ten card games and a keno lounge seating 200. The complex includes three theatres; the 1200-seat Celebrity Room theatre restaurant for star shows, the 900-seat Ziegfield room for musical spectacular and the 300-seat cinema (see also Chapter 8). There is also a Jai Alai arena for 2200 spectators, restaurants and cocktail lounges, swimming, tennis and health club, a 1524 m (145 000 ft) convention area and a shopping arcade with forty speciality shops. Size conveys a security in

the very scale of the building and the number of people involved is indicated by the continuous paging.

An example of the sequence of development of the hotel-casino is the Dunes Hotel. This was opened in 1955 with 194 bedrooms. A wing was added in 1960 with 256 rooms and a twenty-four-storey tower with 446 guest rooms was added in 1965. A further two towers are programmed to provide another 1000 rooms and increased convention and theatre accommodation, parking and sports facilities. In addition the hotel has two pools, an eighteen-hole golf course, a driving range, large casino, restaurants (with a restaurant and cocktail lounge on the 24th floor of the tower block), bars, ballroom and a 710-seat showroom for dinner show.

The Dunes has one of the largest carousels in Las Vegas costing half a million dollars, 180 ft high, 80 ft wide and weighing 1·5 million pounds. The word

* 1 acre=0·4 ha.

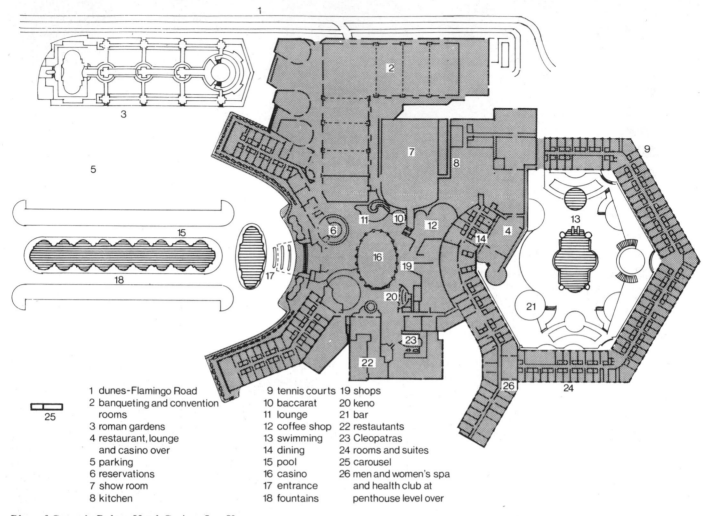

1 dunes-Flamingo Road
2 banqueting and convention rooms
3 roman gardens
4 restaurant, lounge and casino over
5 parking
6 reservations
7 show room
8 kitchen
9 tennis courts
10 baccarat
11 lounge
12 coffee shop
13 swimming
14 dining
15 pool
16 casino
17 entrance
18 fountains
19 shops
20 keno
21 bar
22 restautants
23 Cleopatras
24 rooms and suites
25 carousel
26 men and women's spa and health club at penthouse level over

Plan of Caesar's Palace Hotel Casino, Las Vegas

'Dunes' is 6 m (20 ft) high and the sign has a rating of 624 683 watts and consumes 625 kilowatts per hour costing 240 dollars per day to run.

Caesar's Palace enjoys the Roman connection. The building and impressive entrance use classical themes and features with entertaining exuberance. The layout consists of an entrance forecourt with a sweeping arcade either side, a central line of fountains, ample reproduction of classical sculpture and a triumphal carousel that would have done justice to any Emperor not given to humility. Unlike the cavernous casino entrance halls of many of the Las Vegas hotels, Caesar's Palace has a variety of spaces, identifying the various gaming areas and hotel services. The entrance hall also provides access to the convention rooms, the ballroom and banqueting room, showroom (theatre restaurant), shops, coffee shop restaurants and Cleopatra's Barge which rocks gently to give the impression that it is afloat.

At the rear of the hotel there is a hexagonal court with pools, garden and outdoor bar. A sweeping multi-storey block and the building enclosing the pool terrace provide hotel accommodation. In addition, there are health clubs, solarium, gymnasium, massage, sauna and tennis courts. It is referred to as a 'Palace of Pleasure' and the architecture is in the spirit of calculated pastiche aimed to provide amusing and elegant decor.

The Landmark provides an interesting modern architectural solution for a hotel-casino, with a roof-top bar and restaurant providing a panoramic view of the 'Strip' and a pool terrace with a water cascade.

Circus Circus Casino was opened in 1968 with a unique arrangement of circus entertainment as an almost continuous performance over the main casino area. The architectural appearance combines the tented shape of a circus marquee of the casino, a multi-storey hotel block, a forecourt with parking and

Caesar's Palace; Cleopatra's Barge, Las Vegas

Landmark,
(above) rooftop restaurant (hotel)

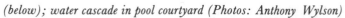

(below); water cascade in pool courtyard (Photos: Anthony Wylson)

(above) The 'Strip' with Stardust Hotel Casino illuminations
(Photo Las Vegas Bureau)

(below) MGM Grand

Circus Circus; forecourt pool (Photo: Anthony Wylson)

fountains and carousel representing a clown. At the rear of the hotel there is a pool terrace.

Las Vegas is accessible to the recreation attractions of many National Parks including Lake Mead and Death Valley, and the city has expanded from the original agricultural, mining and leisure activities to a wider industrial base.

'Off Season' conventions have added to motel and hotel occupancy to achieve a year round average of 80%. Hotel occupancy reached a maximum average of 94% in August 1976. The Las Vegas Chamber of Commerce report in 1977 states that Nevadens enjoy one of the highest capital incomes in the U.S.A. of over 7100 dollars per person.

For those living in Nevada there are no state or local personal income taxes. The turnover of sales is rapid so that direct taxation is held at a low level and the personal property tax is one of the lowest in America. There are many tax advantages for various

Circus Circus; casino marquee in front of hotel block (Photo: Las Vegas News Bureau)

business activities, including no state tax on corporate income and the 'Freeport Law' that permits storage without inventory taxes and custom duties.

The tourist traffic into Las Vegas is by air, road and rail. In 1977 there were 10·1 million visitors of which 56% was by air, 1% by bus and 43% by car. A recent visitor profile study carried out for the Las Vegas Convention Visitors Authority sets out an interesting review of visitors of Las Vegas. The enjoyment is more from entertainment than gambling, although the reason for going was in the

Circus Circus; carousel (Photo: Anthony Wylson)

reverse order. A high proportion return for several visits with an average of two trips each year and average four-day stay each trip. An analysis of these visitors has found that they:

'spend 72·75 dollars per day exclusive of gambling, to be male, to be over forty years of age, to be married with one or more children, to have completed some college education or beyond, to be earning from 15 000 to 25 000 dollars, to be self-employed and to reside in the western region of the U.S.A.'

In March 1978, there was a total of 40 350 hotel and motel rooms. The revenue for Las Vegas in 1977 was approximately 3000 million dollars, with one-third from gaming and two-thirds from other activities and represented 19·4% increase on 1976.

Hamburg, W. Germany

Hamburg, originally established by Emperor Charlemagne with a Christian missionary church on the meeting point of the rivers Alster and Elbe in 810, has developed through its advantageous trading position and political independence. A fire in 1842 destroyed a large section of the city, and a century later, the Second World War was the cause of substantial parts of the city being demolished. Since 1945, there has been reconstruction into a modern city and in 1949 the 'Free and Hanseatic City of Hamburg' became one of the states of the Federal Republic of Germany. In 1976 there were 765 600 dwellings of which 532 700 were built after 1945. Eighty per cent of the port has been replaced by modern facilities.

As a commercial metropolis (and the West German federal structure provides no capital) Hamburg is placed fourth in importance after London, Paris and Stockholm. The GNP for 1976 was DM 53 400 m (DM 31 290 per capita compared to the West German average of DM 18 476) and Hamburg's budget for 1977 was 10 000 million DM. The working population in 1976 was 912 000, 40% being manual workers, and 60% of the white collar workers are self-employed. Thirty-one per cent of the working population is engaged in manufacturing, 33% in commerce and transport and the remaining 36% in other occupations including agriculture. There is now diversification supplementing shipping and trading activities with manufacturing services, allowance for future industrial development, modern communications with a new airport (intended to extend from the present 3·6 million passengers to

Planten un Blomen Park, Congress Hall and Alster Lake, Hamburg

Oriental garden Hagenbeck's Zoological Gardens (Photo: Anthony Wylson)

ultimately 30 million passengers a year) and new railway marshalling yards. The high standard of housing, entertainment and educational facilities are put forward as significant to its economic development.

The way in which the city has grown organically, bringing together long established villages, focusing the city centre around the Lake Alster and the important role played by the harbour has provided Hamburg with a rich balance of water, parkland and urban spaces. The historical development of the city has transformed fortifications into a continuous series of parks stretching from S. Pauli landing quay on the Elbe to the Alster lake. The park system extends into the residential areas beyond. The remaining historic canal system provides a further urban component, penetrating the old city and the surrounding residential areas.

Poseldorf (Photo: Anthony Wylson)

Residents

In the residential areas, leisure facilities include recreation parks and adventure playgrounds. There is a recent policy decision to develop traffic-free zones particularly in the inner city. This is to achieve 'a recovery of peace and quiet for the inhabitants, immediate freedom of movement for pedestrians, a reduction of accident risk particularly for children and old people, less damage to health through exhaust gases and a more friendly setting for the

surroundings'. Some residential areas as Poseldorf and Eppendorf, are being 'Chelseafied' for the tourist providing evocative cafes and meeting places, antique shops and boutiques. However, for both the residential neighbourhoods and city centre there is a strong feeling that development has been directed towards the quality of life for the inhabitants. To protect the smaller shops, services and restaurants from the universal trend of large-scale city centres, a new 120 hectares (under 50 acres) office zone has been established 6 km ($3\frac{1}{2}$ miles) from the heart of the city to provide spacious office accommodation for large firms. This has preserved the scale of central Hamburg even though there are few historic original building groups to set the parameters.

The concern for children, young people, the handicapped and the elderly is reflected in the special provisions including day centres, playgroups, youth group centres and play centres. Nearly 20 000 young people of Hamburg are members of the Youth Circle of Culture and Artistic Affairs providing 'theatre passes' giving entry to theatres at reduced prices. One in five citizens belongs to a sports club. The diverse education facilities includes pre-school, primary, secondary and grammar, day and evening schools, vocational and technical colleges. The university has 26 702 students and the polytechnic approximately 6000 students. There are also colleges of art, music, economics, politics and a Federal Armed Forces College, and research organisations concerned with maritime, forestry and industrial matters, museums and galleries.

There are eighteen theatres in Hamburg ranging from the State Opera House, theatres for classical drama to the light-hearted operetta and musical. There is an awareness of the importance of communication. For the young people, communications centres are based on specific art

(left) Pedestrian shopping, Hamburg (Photo: Anthony Wylson)

(below) Bandstand and dance area in Planten un Blomen Park (Photo: Anthony Wylson)

topics fulfilling an important role with art patronage through prizes and scholarships. There is also a wide range of 'Jazz' and 'Pop' concerts in unsophisticated surroundings, as well as a traditional interest in classical music.

As a convention centre Hamburg has developed a substantial Congress Hall with sixteen public rooms of various sizes from 30 to 3000 person capacity (see also Chapter 8). The city has become the home for international fairs, and the hall is also used for popular concerts. In 1975 there were nearly 700 000 visitors to Trade Fairs in Hamburg.

The tourist population is modest in comparison with other comparable European regions. In 1976 there were over 1·4 million visitors of which approximately one-third came from outside West Germany. The hotel accommodation consists of 400 hotels of all classes providing 16 000 bed spaces. For the tourist, tours of Hamburg include both coach parties and boat trips. From the design aspect, the problem of transporting an audience is of particular

Reeperbahn; nighttime (Photo: Hamburg-Information Bassler)

Jungfernsteig (Photo: Hamburg-Information/Hasse)

Congress Hall and t.v. tower, Hamburg (Photo: Anthony Wylson)

Tour of Hamburg docks (Photo: Anthony Wylson)

interest. The 'audience' becomes spectator to the commercial and industrial activities of the city, and an explorer of the city's historic roots. This is not an escape into fantasy, but an entré into the life of a city. Evening boat trips on the Alster Lake include dancing and entertainment on board. Another form of spectator entertainment is provided by the television tower. It was a specific decision of the City Council to permit a luxury restaurant at the top of the TV tower that has a panoramic view of the city, on the condition that the ordinary public would be permitted in the afternoons for 'tea' at normal prices.

The S. Pauli area with the Reeperbahn (notorious for its sex entertainment) presents a particular curiosity of urban management. The modern version of 'red light' quarters common to international cities, are often degenerate areas with brash touting, key chinking soliciting and furtive communications. The remarkable German logic and the liberal traditions of Hamburg have turned a sailor's haunt into a licensed and medically controlled industry in which stage acts cover many aspects of erotic behaviour and brief encounters are pre-selected by shop window or showroom style display. The atmosphere of Reeperbahn (which operates more as a specialist market than a theme park) is made less salacious by the close proximity of respectable entertainment, restaurants and showroom display of such healthy activities as sailing and water sports. Furthermore, the explicit display is not encouraged during the daytime and the well-maintained street in which women appear in 'boutique' windows is discreetly screened from the normal pedestrian routes.

Without judging the social implications, and assuming that sex entertainment (apart from the theatre, ballet or cinema) is a feature of the modern international city, each country has its own attitudes and laws controlling the level of acceptability and the planning context is a reflection of the corporate licence to the activities concerned. The tourist brochures are candid in presenting the attractions of Reeperbahn, but suggest that visitors should be cautious. The planners have influenced Reeperbahn so that it exists as a curiosity with its specialised entertainment but without the furtive character that new attitudes and licence has brought about in other cities.

Another aspect of tourist Hamburg that merits attention is the lack of a central space that conveys the spirit of the city, a Piccadilly or Champs-Élysées. The lakeside Jungfernsteig with visual contact with the City Hall, quality shopping area and the Alster, nearly provides a 'popular place'. But the tourist and entertainment interests, well recorded in the excellent guide book 'Hamburg Von 7 bis 7' (Dr Walter Stahl), are dispersed throughout the central area. There is no resort area with hotels geared to leisure although the luxurious Intercontinental hotel, with its enclosed pool and surrounding sun terrace overlooking the Alster, suggests a quality for leisure accommodation if Hamburg developed further as a cultural tourist or convention centre.

The forces that will influence the future leisure entertainment will be a balance between maintaining a 'city for Hamburgians' and providing, in competition with other major European cities, new sources for employment, means of attracting industry to Hamburg and ways of securing the use of the Congress Centre and the projected new international airport. The planners must balance the environment for the people against the possible change of character that would occur if too great an emphasis were placed on convention visitors facilities and tourism. Alternatively, commerce and industry based economic growth may be given less importance with the acceptance of greater leisure time and the need for more leisure entertainment facilities. Whatever the course, the natural features on which the city has developed provide tremendous opportunities and past achievements could be equalled.

Leicester Square and Piccadilly Circus, London

Piccadilly Circus has gradually deteriorated since the 1950s into a circus of traffic congestion during the day and a venue for 'drop-outs' at night. However, if the proposals now under consideration are put into effect, the image hopefully associated with Piccadilly Circus, a centre of fun and entertainment, could be restored with family entertainments as a primary attraction.

The pedestrianisation of Leicester Square and Coventry Street to provide an area less effected by traffic, has been put into operation starting with Leicester Square. Carrying out alterations to the public highway in central London creates immense legislative problems involving government departments at all levels. The pedestrianisation of the north of Leicester Square was carried out between December 1976 and May 1977 for a cost of £150 000. The space is designed not only to improve the facilities for pedestrians but also to provide an area for casual outdoor entertainment. The paving has been extended to south and west of the Square and in front of the Swiss Centre. The paving does not exclude traffic but technically limits use and psychologically excludes traffic.

The extension of a pedestrian environment to include Coventry Street and Piccadilly Circus has been approved by the Greater London Council. The redevelopment and restructuring of buildings in this area will radically increase the entertainment content which will give meaning to the pedestrianisation and traffic reorganisation.

In January 1976, the Central Area Board of the Greater London Council approved in outline a road and pedestrian scheme for the Piccadilly Circus area incorporating a pedestrian piazza on the south of the Circus. This will require reorganising traffic in Great Windmill Street, between Shaftesbury Avenue and Coventry Street, and arcading on the Trocadero side of Great Windmill Street. A restructuring of the London Pavilion Theatre would also provide an opportunity to include a further arcade.

The more detailed report, prepared jointly with Westminster City Council in February 1978, includes arcading on both sides of Great Windmill Street. The proposals comprise the creation of a pedestrian piazza on the south side of the Circus, the moving of the 'Eros' statue into this piazza, extending the pavement areas around the Circus and providing additional carriage width in Great Windmill Street and Jermyn Street.

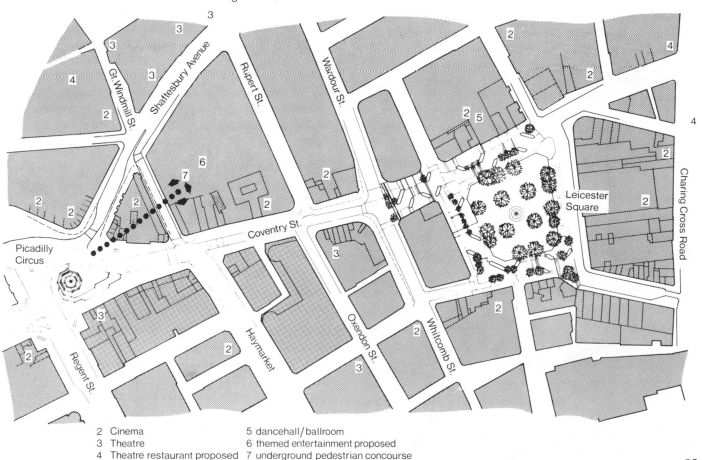

2 Cinema
3 Theatre
4 Theatre restaurant proposed

5 dancehall / ballroom
6 themed entertainment proposed
7 underground pedestrian concourse

Proposed scheme for Leicester Square/Piccadilly circus

The piazza on the south side of the Circus would form a visual part of the partly pedestrianised Piccadilly/Coventry Street/Leicester Square area, with the repositioned 'Eros' as a feature visible along the axes of both Coventry Street and Piccadilly. The repositioning of Eros is also to maintain traffic capacity around its west and north sides. The existing pavements around the Circus would be improved on the north and east sides. The widening of the footways in Coventry Street would create a pedestrian link with Leicester Square. The closing of Glasshouse Street is undecided but would be to the advantage of pedestrian movement from Regent Street to Shaftesbury Avenue.

The scheme depends upon restructuring or redevelopment proposals of the Criterion, London Pavilion and Trocadero sites being carried out, and also the declassification of the metropolitan road and extinguishing vehicular rights to pave over the carriageway to form a pedestrian piazza. The repositioning of the 'Eros' statue, being a listed building, requires approval from the Department of Environment and planning approval. There is also the possibility of both parliamentary involvement in the exercise and consultations with the Crown Estate commissioners as it is believed that the ground on which the enclosure of the statue is sited, and part of the ground where it is to be resited, are vested in the Crown.

The reorganisation of the roads (Great Windmill Street, Jermyn Street, Coventry Street and Glasshouse Street), requires the formal agreement of Westminster City Council and the Department of Transport. It is also necessary to realise the effect of the proposals in redevelopment or restructuring of buildings adjoining the Circus and roads concerned.

London Transport (in respect to the effect on bus routing), the Fire Brigade and the Metropolitan Police are all involved in discussing the merits of the scheme.

The Greater London Council proposals are included in a programme in which the work would commence in 1981–82, a budget cost of £1 million with £90 000 for York Stone pavings, £50 000 for signals and £200 000 for work in connection with gas, electricity and water services.

Thus to progress a major improvement to a central area in London, it is not only necessary to obtain approval from the statutory bodies concerned and to satisfy the legalities relating to the land and buildings affected, but the development proposals of the owners of properties affected must be consulted so that the street improvements are incorporated into their own proposals. In this particular case, arcading which is necessary to achieve road widening in Great Windmill Street may be carried out by the owners of the buildings affected.

Activity resorts

The rise of 'all-in' holidays and low cost travel has resulted in the extensive resort development both in European countries, America and in selected exotic locations. The architecture has developed along various trends. The early holiday camps of the 1950s were geared to the family market and to achieve low costs the buildings and landscapes were utilitarian. During the 1960s the competition for 'sea, sun and socialising' resulted in the multi-storey hotels and holiday accommodation of Palma, Torremolinos and Miami. Few resorts were part of an overall concept, such as la Grande Motte (S. France).

The effect of such a scale of development stimulated a reaction in favour of regional 'evocative' style to maintain both a sympathetic scale and continuity in character with existing buildings. Although many such developments in Tunisia and Spain are remote from existing towns and villages, the designs have set out to 'interpret' the regional tradition as applied to a holiday complex and in both France and Spain a 'mediterranean' style has been adapted to create modest but imaginative surroundings to holiday accommodation and marinas.

Few holiday organisations incorporate entertainment to the same extent as Club Mediterranée with activities geared mainly to the mentally and physically agile, and Butlin's who provide for family interests.

London. Leicester Square pedestrian area (Photo: Anthony Wylson)

Butlin's holiday centres

Butlin's holiday centres in the UK were started in 1936 when a camp was opened in Skegness on the Lincolnshire coast to house 1000 people in chalet accommodation. The founder, Sir William (Billy) Butlin, had experience in the running of seaside amusement parks and was aware of the conflict between holidaying in England and the English climate. The holiday camps that he started were based on an 'all-in' tariff to include indoor and outdoor amusements and entertainment. The success of Skegness was followed by the opening of a second camp at Clacton-on-Sea in Essex. The camps were reopened in 1946 and the company extended its interests to acquiring hotels (Brighton, Margate and Blackpool).

Besides developing a further seven holiday camps, Butlin's have also developed smaller 'Freshfields' self-catering holiday centres. The nine holiday centres each accommodate from 8000 to 10 000 people and in 1977 the total number of visitors to Butlin's holiday centres was approximately 1·30 million, with an annual turnover of £48 million.

The Butlin's formula has been to provide a holiday package (principally for the family) not affected by the weather and at a weekly cost of not more than an average 1-week's pay for each visitor. Entertainment and activities are provided although the close proximity of such licensed uses as bingo and bar with entertainment, dancing and children's free use of the camp, creates problems of demarcation. There are also problems of fire compartmentation that interfere with the open planning. However, generally the entertainment and amusements buildings provide large clear spaces for flexibility of use, running one use into another, to give a relaxed and communal atmosphere. Most camps (as at Minehead) comprise a reception building, an amusement centre, one or more theatres, buildings housing food stores, restaurants, cafes, bars, ballroom, amusement arcade and launderette. Outside activities include a swimming pool, boating lake, horse riding, tennis, funfair rides, and a grassed space for football and sports. Some camps have indoor swimming pools, indoor bowls, table tennis and billiards. The accommodation blocks consist of one- or two-storey chalet type buildings providing family and self-catering accommodation. The reception buildings house reception and information counters, a lost property office, guests' mail room, post office and private safe deposits.

The restaurant and dining facilities cover a wide market. Identifiable 'fish and chips' is provided in a comfortable cafeteria ambience geared to family use.

Butlins holiday centre at Minehead—amusement area

In the evenings there is a grill service in more sophisticated surroundings.

The licensed components within a centre include a quiet classical decor bar with background music or a pianist, a club bar open at lunchtime and evenings with late night stage entertainment, a sing-song bar in public house style and with high powered entertainment, and finally a cabaret bar which can be used for other activities. The dance facilities would include ballroom space (for old-time dancing), discotheques for young people and dancing space in the club bar.

Butlin's are hosted and run by 'Red Coats' who keep the fun moving. Red Coats are twenty to thirty year olds, carefully selected, who are able to turn their hands to most activities provided for the guests. The organisation is instrumental to promoting entertainment, ballroom and sports talent, and in this respect the buildings and visitors spaces must provide a standard compatible with the star artists and professional sports trainees that take part. One camp has a 2050-seat theatre, and visitors stage talent is selected for 'finals' at the London Palladium.

The outdoor activities are to provide for all ages and include funfair rides (monorail, cable car, miniature railways, roundabouts). In most cases, the sea is close by with the added attraction of sea bathing and beach activities.

In 1971 Butlin's developed additional smaller centres (the Freshfields Centres) mainly in the West Country and with caravan and camping centres in France. In 1972 there was a merger with the Rank Organisation.

Playa Blanca (left and right) holiday village (Photo: Club Mediterranée)

Club Mediterranée villages

The development and organisation of Club Mediterranée has been outlined with an indication of the basic approach to resort planning (see Chapter 1). Of the three types of 'Club Med' resorts, the 'bungalow villages' have provided most scope for imaginative design. Generally, the concept is in sympathy with the local tradition and character.

In Marrakesh the medina-village is adjoining a historic square and adopts a courtyard plan; in Tunisia there are low rise whitewashed buildings; in Senegal the village consists of a terraced development.

At Playa Blanca (Mexico) the accommodation extends up the sides of a valley at the point where it opens out to the sea. The central feature is the pool with restaurant adjoining and a nearby auditorium

Playa Blanca—plan

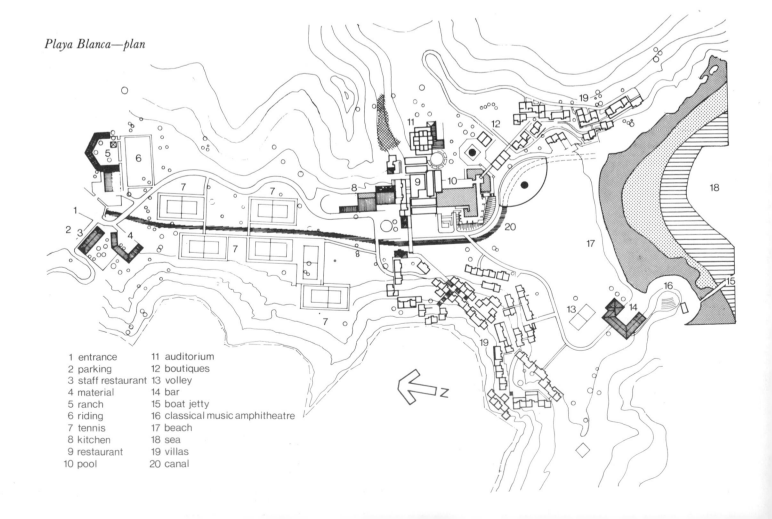

1 entrance	11 auditorium
2 parking	12 boutiques
3 staff restaurant	13 volley
4 material	14 bar
5 ranch	15 boat jetty
6 riding	16 classical music amphitheatre
7 tennis	17 beach
8 kitchen	18 sea
9 restaurant	19 villas
10 pool	20 canal

Holiday village Assinie (Photo: Club Méditerranée)

Les Almadies

and boutiques. The two-storey accommodation extends around the slopes where the valley opens to the beach. At one side of the beach there is an open-air theatre, volley ball, 'bar de plage' and jetty. Farther inland there are tennis courts and stables.

The holiday pattern at Club Méditerranée starts with the activity leaders being introduced to the guests so that the guests can decide which sports, hobbies or skills to support. The activity leaders put on a musical show (in which they take part) on the first evening to create an opportunity for socialising. The routine of the following days depends upon the selection of activities, if any, chosen. Opportunities are available for a visitor to be introduced to new activities, and these facilities form an integral part of the design of the villages.

2. Centres de vacances et voisinage— Résumé

Il est plus avantageux de regrouper les aménagements de loisirs. C'est le cas par exemple des stations balnéaires et de quelques grandes villes: Blackpool, dans le nord-ouest de l'Angleterre, Las Vegas aux Etats-Unis et, en particulier, Hambourg, en Allemagne, dont les ressources d'ordre éducatif et culturel profitent à la fois aux habitants et aux touristes.

2. Ferienziele und Nachbarschaft—Zusammenfassung

Auf Unterhaltungsstätten wirkt sich die Gruppierung günstig aus. Dies ist der Fall bei Ferienzielen an der

Theatre space seating and dance space, Club Med. Marbella (Photo: Anthony Wylson)

See und in manchen Großstädten. Beispiele sind Blackpool in Nordost-England, Las Vegas in den USA und Hamburg in Deutschland. Die kulturellen und Bildungsstätten der letztgenannten Stadt sind für den Touristen und ihre Einwohner gleichermaßen interessant.

٢ـ المنتجعات والمناطق المجاورة ـ موجز

تتهيأ أقصى الفائدة من وسائل الترفيه اذاكانت مجتمعة قريباً من بعضها البعض كما هو الحال في مناطق الاصطياف الساحليــة وبعض المدن الكبرى . والمثال على ذلك مدينة بلاكبول وشمال شرقي انجلترا ومدينة لاس فيجاس في الولايات المتحدة ومدينة هامبورج بالمانيا ، وتتوافر الخدمات التعليمية والثقافية في الأخيرة للزوار وأهل البلاد على السواء .

29

Chapter 3

Children and play

The reappraisal of the significance of 'play' and 'play environment' by such organisations as the International Playground Association and the European Leisure and Recreation Association is of extreme importance to child development, adult leisure and urban planning. Urban planning and urban renewal must provide for a 'quality of life' that gives priority to a humane environment. This must accommodate the growing need for leisure activities that reflect the qualities inherent in enlightened education.

Individualistic and spontaneous creativity can provide both an appreciation of and a stimulant to corporate values. The city of the future must accommodate the growing demands of leisure by providing a context for creative play and learning for all age groups, complimentary to or as an extension of work commitments. Furthermore, the context of creative play identified as for example in the adventure playground philosophy, can provide an area of cohesion in a diverse society. Children in an urban environment can benefit by the qualities of adventurous, creative and co-operative activities, contact with nature and animal life—the fundamentals of 'living' that have been overshadowed by urbanisation.

Context for play

Play for children is a continuous activity that is not only a release of energy but also the context in which children learn and develop. Play extends from the individual's protected activities in the home, to the group activities outside home; from journeys to and from school to a wider discovery of the neighbourhood.

City life with traffic imposing on the older urban fabric has limited the space in which children can play safely near their homes. Modern urban life is dominated by traffic in which personal mobility by car and easy vehicular access have priority. With multi-storey flats, planning has denied children an easy freedom between indoors and outdoors. Garaging a car has achieved greater importance than providing space for leisure activities in the home. Traditional formal playgrounds deny children creative involvement.

Even where family life has easy access to the outdoors, the pedestrian, children's activities and landscaping are too easily in conflict. The elderly pedestrian or pram-pushing mother does not want to be harassed by the daring young skateboard rider or cyclist. Planting is particularly vulnerable to disrespectful treatment. Immovable formalised play equipment has not the backyard magic which involves the creative and constructive abilities of the children. There is a conflict between the creative, experimental and temporary and the permanent, ordered and visually acceptable environment.

As implicit in the ELRA Children's Charter there is

Play area, Jardin D'Acclimatation Paris, with rock climb for zoo animals adjoining

a case for urban renewal not only to retain existing houses (and thereby to retain existing communities) but to limit traffic and thus revive the safe and casual use of the street for pedestrians and children. New housing schemes can apply the correct priorities. The problem is maintaining, in the existing urban structure, the leisure use of public space by children and adults.

The rehabilitation of existing housing means not only improved standards of plumbing and heating, but also the reduction of conflicts that have arisen. Within the house, a diversity of ages promotes a diversity of activities. This requires space and sound insulation. Convenient play spaces as a line of 'communication' between the homes and schools are as relevant to leisure as the more specialised adventure playground, enclosed hard surface play areas and protected areas for toddlers. These could be an integral part of a community rehabilitation scheme with landscaping and organised car parking. The project for the London Borough of Camden relocated the traffic and parking on to the noisy and

sunless side of the estate, allowing the existing road to become a pedestrian route on the south side, giving access to the proposed community room, playgrounds and football area.

Also in Kentish Town, London, Inter-Action, an organisation concerned with community and self-help projects, have developed a centre with nearby adventure playground and the first UK 'city farm' (started in 1972).

City farms aim to give children and adults in urban areas a first hand experience of rural activities. With Government support, Inter-Action provide free advice and services to help the setting up of 'city farms'. The wasteland utilised sometimes entail a short term licensing arrangement on a 'three months notice' basis. The activities of a city farm can extend from a garden club for the elderly, kitchen gardens, household and auto repair shops, and pony clubs. School parties would visit the hand reared animals. The activities aim to provide for all age groups so that families can share a common interest.

London Borough of Camden (plan of environmental improvements scheme)

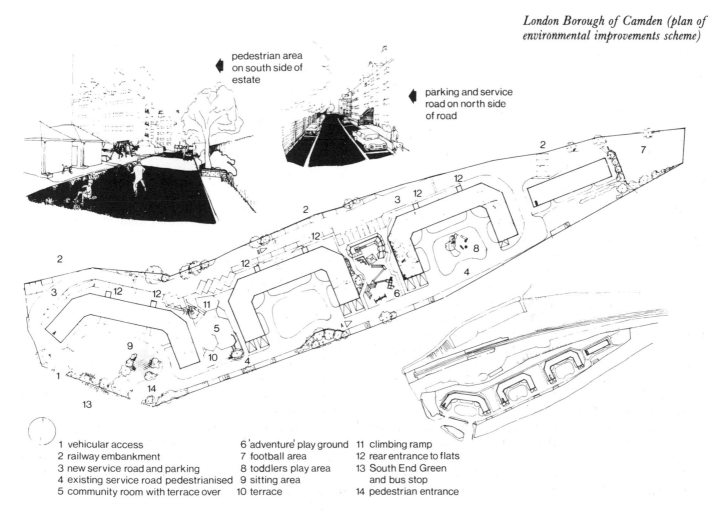

1 vehicular access	6 'adventure' play ground	11 climbing ramp
2 railway embankment	7 football area	12 rear entrance to flats
3 new service road and parking	8 toddlers play area	13 South End Green
4 existing service road pedestrianised	9 sitting area	and bus stop
5 community room with terrace over	10 terrace	14 pedestrian entrance

Pro Juventute Robinson playground, Volta Basel (Photo: W. Bommer, Zurich)

Theory of play

A theory of play outlined by Leo Jago in 'Play on Adventure Playgrounds', which fits the practice of adventure playgrounds emphasises that the growing child's behaviour stems from his feelings and needs. This is always appropriate to himself even though it is not appropriate to the adult world. The child playing out his own needs is able to satisfy those needs, and his play will arise spontaneously. Play is an experience, always a creative experience (creative of the child's personality as well as external objects), a basic form of living.

An analysis by Dr M. J. Ellis, University of Illinois, looks at the biological significance of play reflecting the consistent curiosity concerning new elements and the emission of new responses being integral to survival. Play can be characterised as adaptive behaviour and as new responses and new experiences are accumulated, the 'animal' is better qualified to adapt to further unpredictable situations. Novel interactions are created for their own sake, but over time, convey a selective advantage.

Play is the way children learn about themselves and the world they live in. In the process of mastering familiar situations and learning to cope with new ones, their intelligence and personality grows as well as their bodies. The environment for play must be rich in experience, and it must be, to a significant extent, under the control of the children. It must allow each child to exercise choice and grow at his own rate. Play can be a socialising factor, structures within society are reproduced in miniature. Thus the context of children's play can promote social values.

These ideas extended into adult life would confront conventional culture and traditional creative roles.

Play and creativity in adult life could encourage the individual's interest in the immediate environment, not just 'do it yourself' proficiency, but a meaningful creative involvement. A need to democratise the creative and cultural life may be in conflict with control exercised by 'professionals', as the quality of corporate life style is largely determined by the quality of the environment. The 'alternate architecture' expressed in the Californian communities are relevant and provide the experimental side to home building and an independence in living patterns, apart from 'pioneering' camping.

Design is based on the creative interaction between the individual and his environment. Environmental education is concerned with the development of a common set of values of creativity. Creative participation in the environment will involve more than just comfort giving and visual quality applied by others. The experiental side could be developed within the framework of a common set of values to provide the individual with a meaningful involvement with the community.

At the same time, adult play in which an opportunity is provided for adults to explore new knowledge, skills and activities in a leisure context, underlines the basic philosophy of such holiday organisations as Club Méditerranée. In a relaxed, non-competitive, non-obligatory context, the individual can explore new skills and activities with expert instruction. Leisure centres based on popular activities, such as Butlin's, the community leisure centres as those developed in Switzerland, the community leisure centres of Britain, local amateur activities and adult education, specialist vacations based on music and drama, exhibitions (as Evoluon in Eindhoven); all these provide children and adults with the opportunity to expand their interests and capabilities.

Adventure play

Adventure play is one of many aspects of a wider understanding of child development and education, which extends from the particular provision for play in the home to the organisations that cater for specialist skills and interests. However, adventure play represents an important new element in the play environment.

The idea of the playground with materials for construction had been advocated since 1931 by the Danish landscape architect Professor C. T. Sorenson.

His project near Emdrup, near Copenhagen, was opened in 1934 and was followed by many 'junk

(above) Robinson adventure playground, Zurich (Photo: Jurg Wolfensberger)

(right) Pro Juventute adventure playground, Zurich. (above) suspended net; (below) slide

yard' playgrounds in Denmark and 'building site' playgrounds in which children with a play leader were allowed to utilise scrap material and the corner of a construction site during building operations. 'Robinson' playgrounds in Switzerland developed on the same basis catering for all ages and providing for a wide choice of creative games and activities. One particular Zurich playground aims to provide a leisure time centre for the whole district which makes parents, grandparents and children 'real neighbours' again and lifts them out of the cold anonymity of the big town. These leisure centres aim to complement the recreational and cultural institutions of city centres. 'Red Indian' playgrounds were developed in Germany as at Mannheim, with caves, tunnels, camp fires, ponds and shrubs. The German jugend farm is a playground predominantly based on animals and animal care.

In the UK, public play parks have been within the scope of local authority activities from the middle of the 19th century as a response to the effect of industrialisation upon the urban environment. Grounds for recreation were provided following the First World War and the legislation of the 1930s reflected the need for improvement in physical and mental health. Since 1945, recreation in the widest sense has been given great importance. Public parks and amenity areas have multiplied and play areas have been provided with an increasing variety of fixed play equipment. This includes both conventional swings, slides and roundabouts and also less orthodox shapes, play sculpture and climbing structures in concrete, metal and timber. Adventure playgrounds started in Britain in the late 1940s.

In London since 1959, the Parks Department of the Greater London Council have concentrated on three types of play facility through the Council's Play Leadership Scheme; One o'clock Clubs; Play Parks and Adventure Playgrounds.

The 'One o'clock Clubs' are for children under five accompanied by adults. These clubs provide for creative play with opportunity for the adults with them to relax or be involved. Most 'One o'clock Clubs' are in GLC parks, but there are also a number in housing estates, catering for areas where older properties and overcrowding limit the recreational facilities for small children.

The GLC Adventure Playgrounds, staffed by play leaders, differ from the play park in that they are usually situated outside park boundaries, on housing estates or in heavily built up older residential areas. They are not subject to normal parks bylaws as to hours of use. Fire, barbecues and record music, not normally allowed in parks, can be enjoyed by young people. The playgrounds fulfil a significant role within the community life and most playgrounds have a charitable association running alongside them organising further activities as weekend camping and summer holiday schemes.

The Play Park is a special area within a public park set aside for the adventurous and creative play of school-age children, with unobtrusive leadership to assist the children. Play parks are an acre or more in size and include a heated building approximately

12 m×6 m for indoor activities. Some play parks are used in term time by schools, including special schools for handicapped children who thereby gain the opportunity to enjoy adventurous games under the direction of their own teachers.

Also in London, the London Adventure Playground Association and the Handicapped Adventure Playground Association sponsor and supervise numerous projects. All age groups are catered for but generally the adventure playgrounds are geared to the five to fifteen year old, for whom little is provided by Youth Service. London Adventure Playgrounds have supervised play groups for the under fives in the mornings and afternoons during term time.

Adventure playgrounds

The concept of the playground has been radically changed by the Adventure Playground movement that extends children's play from the use of standard equipment to the personal and creative involvement of the children in the playground environment. The freedom of the backyard, that corner of a garden away from interfering tidying adults, where a child can enjoy his adventure of constructing his own play-environment, provides an educational experience in the widest sense.

Children are impelled to explore, to test and to discover the world around them. Play for children can provide the means to relate to and understand the adult world. In an urbanised environment the escape into the countryside for exploration is not available. A space must be provided where children can be free to live out the process of discovery,

GLC Play Park—Battersea: building and play equipment

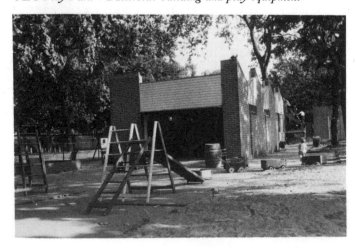

GLC Play Park—Battersea: interior of building (Photos: Anthony Wylson)

GLC adventure playground. Glamis Road, Wapping

(left) suspended walk
(right) ramps   *(Photos: Anthony Wylson)*

imagination and fantasy that their emotional and social development requires. The initial interest shared by the children and the play-leader role create a framework for co-operative and practical human relationships.

The London Adventure Playground Association describes an adventure playground as a place where children are free to do many things that they are not free to do elsewhere in our crowded urban society. In an adventure playground, which can be any size from 0.4 Ha to 1 Ha, children can build houses, dens and climbing structures with waste materials, have bonfires, cook in the open, dig holes, garden or just play with earth, sand, water and clay. The atmosphere is permissive and free, and this is especially attractive to children whose lives are otherwise much limited and restricted by lack of space and opportunity.

The design of a playground is based on the premise that intelligence and learning consist of a creative interaction between the individual and his environment. The environment must provide an adequate range of experience and must allow a measure of control by the individual. In this way, the child has the experience of effecting his environment with the opportunity to achieve change and to see the effect.

The playground should provide as many materials as possible to be shaped and manipulated, and a series of challenges, ranging from simple individual

experiences to problems that must be resolved by co-operating with others. Children must find in the playground an opportunity for experience and they must have an opportunity to control that experience.

The overlooking of an adventure playground will determine the extent to which equipment is formalised. Whereas 'junk' may provide unique objects for the children to assemble, a selection of components (sleeper-like timbers, tyres, drums and mounds) that provide a reasonable appearance is more appropriate to the majority of urban sites. The buildings should at very least provide lavatory facilities for the children, storage space, a utility area for the play leaders, and an indoor area for play in bad weather.

Provision for handicapped children

The need for free activity for handicapped children is particularly important. The aim is to arrest the deterioration of existing abilities, to strengthen the skills that are imperfectly developed and to provide alternate compensatory skills to replace those not available.

The Handicapped Adventure Playground Association in London started as a research committee set up by Lady Allen of Hurtwood in 1966, to investigate the possibility of creating specially designed playgrounds for handicapped children. The first project was set up in the garden of a rectory in Chelsea and this has been followed by playgrounds in Fulham Palace, Wandsworth Common and Islington. The association deals with most kinds of disabilities—physical, mental or emotional—and an age range from three years to young adults.

The opportunity for handicapped children to go to

35

specially designed, equipped and staffed playgrounds, allows them to attempt and achieve all kinds of physical and mental activities at their own speed, and without the competition of more able children. It is through unstructured play, play that is freely chosen and enjoyed for its own sake, that children learn new skills, gain confidence, sort out fact from fantasy and extend their knowledge of the real world. The playground's aim to provide handicapped children with the same possibilities of limitless adventuresome play as those enjoyed by non-handicapped children. Different disabilities require a different design approach. For example, the child in a wheelchair requires play equipment at an accessible level and freedom of movement whereas blind children should be able to explore safely. Handrails are needed for some as an assistance to walking, and non-abrasive surfaces are necessary where children are likely to fall.

HAPA's recommendations for the development of an adventure playground for handicapped children are well covered in their publication *Adventure playgrounds for handicapped children*. The site should be accessible within the built-up area it serves, at least 0.4 Ha in size, ideally situated within an open space (a park, common or garden) and enclosed by a wall or fence for privacy and security. Within the site, trees, grass and space create a feeling of freedom in addition to hills, slopes, hollows and rough terrain. A hard surfaced open area is necessary for games for children dependent on vehicles. A tarmacadam path should wind around the perimeter and to give access to tree areas and the main play spaces. The provision of running water in the forms of artificial streams (circulated by a pump) can provide an item of interest for sailing boats, damming, splashing and paddling.

Sandpits should have at least a 1.5 m (5 ft) depth of sand to allow deep digging, and should have ramped sides to allow access by wheeled chair. Play structure should be flexible to allow improvised extensions and alterations. The look-out tower or high climbing

frame, about 3.3 m (11 ft) high, would be approached by a simple ramp, steps or rope ladder. An ordinary pulley device from the top deck allows the children to haul equipment up and down. Additions to the tower could include slides and additional steps.

A jumping frame with a sorbo of foam rubber as a landing area is suggested by HAPA. To partially sighted or the physically handicapped child who is normally afraid to fall, dropping through space on to a soft landing brings a great feeling of release. Similarly, the large inflated mattress for jumping and rolling is an important item.

The building within the HAPA adventure playground should be single storey with tough and durable finishes and a ramped entrance wide enough to admit wheelchairs. The office should be positioned to overlook the main entrance, grounds and playroom. Sill levels should be low. There should be ample storage within the office and a wall safe for petty cash, a space for a desk, filing cabinet, first aid kit, and space for at least two chairs. There should be a staff cloakroom with lavatory and shower cubicle.

The cloakroom and lavatory accommodation for the children should be separate. The cloakroom should be near the entrance with space for drying clothes, a supply of protective clothing, lockers, washing machine, tumble dryer and airing cupboard. Children's lavatories, depending upon the size of the playground, should have five or more cubicles with wide doors and changing plinth in one cubicle and basins in all cubicles.

The building would include an internal play space with several exits to the garden. This should be a flexible room, subdivided with screens, low sill levels, good daylighting, ample shelves and cupboards, a quiet area and a climbing structure or slide in the main area. An additional 'noisy' room is recommended with a low level sink for filling buckets, paint pots, etc.

The quantity of play equipment necessitates ample storage, some of which should be lockable and not easily accessible to children. There should be a workshop with bench and space for tools and

Adventure playground for handicapped children Chelsea, established by HAPA. (Photos: Anthony Wylson)
(left) Swinging mattress; (right) Swinging rail

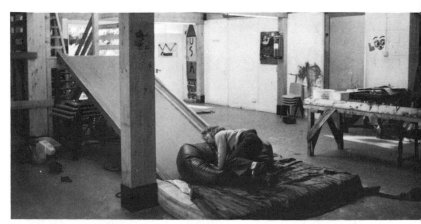

Adventure playground for handicapped children. Fulham Palace established by HAPA (Architect: Stephen Gardener)
(left) exterior of building and paddle pool (right) slide and mattress
(below) plan (Photos: Anthony Wylson)

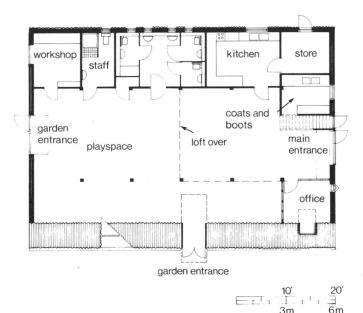

3. L'enfant et le jeu—Résumé

Laprise de conscience de l'importance du jeu dans le processus de croissance et d'éducation de l'enfant est maintenant particulièrement manifeste dans le contexte urbain. La théorie du jeu a montré la nécessité d'aires de jeu et a trouvé son expression dans l'aménagement de terrains de jeu entièrement équipés de manière imaginative et remplaçant les anciens espaces de récréation. Le concept de l'aventure dans le jeu se révèle d'une importance capitale lorsqu'il s'agit d'enfants handicappés. Les meilleurs exemples d'application sont certainement les terrains aménagés selon les besoins particuliers des enfants.

3. Kinder und Spiel—Zusammenfassung

Das Bewußtsein, daß die Bedürfnisse von Kindern beim Heranwachsen und Lernen mit dem Spiel verbunden sind, ist von besonderer Bedeutung in der Stadt. Die Spieltheorien sehen die Verfügbarkeit von Platz zum Spielen als eine Notwendigkeit an und fanden ihren Ausdruck in Abenteuerspielplätzen und die Vorstellungskraft anregenden Anlagen als Ersatz für die formelle Erholung. Das Konzept des Abenteuers beim Spiel ist für behinderte Kinder von großer Bedeutung. Beispiele sind Abenteuerspielplätze, die besonders auf die Bedürfnisse von Kindern ausgelegt sind.

٣ ـ الاطفال واللعب ـ موجز

ان ادراكنا ان الاحتياجات الأساسية للنمو والتعلم عند الاطفال ترتبط بنشاطات اللعب هو أمر مهم بصورة خاصة في البيئة المدينية . وقد كشفت نظريات اللعب عن الحاجة الى توفير مساحة اللعب ووجدت الاستجابة لذلك في ملاعب المغامرات للاطفال والتسهيلات الخيالية لاستبدال الالعاب الرسمية . ان فكرة لعب المغامرات مهمة جداً للاطفال المعوقين . الأمثلة : ملاعب المغامرات المصممة خصيصاً لمواجهة حاجة الاطفال .

construction projects, a kitchen with space for four children (some may be in a wheelchair) and an adult to gather around a table. The kitchen should include various worktops with allowance for wheelchairs, ample cupboards, refrigerator and gas cooker. It is recommended that there should be no distractive view from the windows.

An adventure playground will accumulate materials for use: basic timbers for construction, rubber off-cuts, tyres, ropes, old cushions, seats, curtains, old domestic equipment, ball games, conventional games, painting equipment, musical instruments and useful junk—all of which has to be accommodated. The children find their own fun amidst junk and create their own use and order. The playground would be run by a play leader with two or three assistants.

Chapter 4

Theme parks and pleasure gardens

In England the development of Pleasure Parks has reflected the process that made urban life more democratic. Hyde Park in London was opened to the public by Charles I in 1635 and the large public parks of London were used for great public occasions.

Many public gardens were essentially tea gardens. Some were associated with springs and spas and some were the gardens of public houses. Some of these public gardens included entertainment, such as a small zoo, performances by acrobats and fireworks displays.

In London, the gardens at Marylebone, Ranelagh and Vauxhall were known for music and dancing. Ranelagh opened in 1749, was set out as formal gardens with gravel walks which were illuminated at night. There was also dancing around the maypole, a variety of grandstands throughout the park, a decorated gondola on the canal, shops with shopkeepers in masks, an illuminated amphitheatre, booths for tea and wine, gaming tables and provision for dancing. The facilities altogether provided for about 2000 people.

Vauxhall garden which was first opened in 1661, by 1751 included five pavilions, shaded groves, delightful walks, illuminations, a temple for the musicians surrounded by seating for the public. A gothic temple 'ruin' was added and a dance pavilion. During the years of the greatest popularity, there was a spectacular impression of a sea-engagement which was later followed by a grand spectacle 'the Battle of Waterloo'.

Vauxhall eventually faced competition from a park at Cremone which was between the river and the King's Road, Chelsea. Cremone was designed to attract the new type of patron and in 1843 it became exclusively a pleasure garden with a banqueting hall, theatre, pagoda with orchestra and a circular platform that could accommodate 4000 dancers. In 1843, an American bowling saloon was introduced and a circus, a theatre, a marionette theatre, a maze, ballroom ascents and aquatic tournaments were added. However, by the 1870s the commercial pressure to sell the land for building became too powerful and the park was closed. In 1846, in response to the effect of industry upon the urban environment, a Parliamentary Bill was passed to give local authorities the powers to provide public parks.

In the USA, the family amusement park has achieved particular significance. The first parks were built at the turn of the century, by traction companies as picnic areas at the end of the trolley line. Gradually rides and amusements were added. Coney Island in New York started in 1895 as a trained sea-lion show.

Although there are many small parks still being established, in recent years the traditional family operated American amusement park has become a market for investment. The improved highways, increased spending power, and an improved image provided by the new and imaginative theme parks have given significance to the regional parks. These draw their patronage from an area of approximately 150-mile radius, and each park has established a particular identity.

Disneyland, completed in 1955, brought a new approach to amusement parks with cleanliness, attractive presentation, the use of college students, theme attractions, food sales and the familiar Disney characters. Knott's Berry Farm which was started in 1920 with a Ghost Town theme has added new themed and amusement areas. The Busch Gardens, Tampa, opened in 1959, developed an African theme featuring wild animals. The Busch Gardens in Los Angeles focuses on an environment of rocks, birds, trees, cascading water as well as rides and shows. Busch Gardens in Virginia has an old country theme presenting images of France, England and Germany. Opryland, completed in 1972, concentrates on music and live entertainment. The three Sea World marine parks which started with the park in San Diego in

1964, have developed on the basis of marine animal research and education along with exhibitions and entertainment.

The 1970s saw significant investment into large-scale theme and amusement parks, encompassing a wide range of activities including animal parks, bird gardens and marine parks. By 1974 there were in the order of 900 amusement parks in the USA with an annual attendance of 470 million visitors and revenue in excess of 150 million dollars.

The pay-one-price admission giving access to rides is a popular entrance policy, with additional revenue provided from the sale of food, beverage and gifts. The average American regional park has a ride capacity of 20 000–35 000 visitors per hour. One of the largest parks has a ride capacity of 90 000 visitors per hour.

Feasibility considerations for leisure parks include low depreciation (compared with manufacturing machinery), ability for revenue to keep pace with inflation, and the relatively slow obsolescence of rides. Attendance level is dependent upon catchment area population, income level, type of facilities, number of days of operation, and the nature of competing attractions. When a park reaches a maturity level, it is found that continued popularity depends upon both effective marketing and the development of new attractions within the park. The cost involved in regional amusement parks (capital cost of 40–60 million dollars at 1974 prices) could only be considered by Corporation finance.

Today, urban planning acknowledges the need to provide usable public gardens in urban areas with recreational and leisure facilities. Cities such as Hamburg take particular pride in the quality of such amenities. The historic pattern of parks has been developed to impose a pedestrian and leisure structure across the city. As in Hamburg, the land originally used in Copenhagen for protection (the city wall and moat) has been gradually transformed with the Tivoli Gardens, creating a break between new business and residential areas and the old city centre. On the other hand, the Pleasure Beach at Blackpool represents the fairground tradition. The American theme parks as Knott's Berry Farm and the Disney 'Magic Kingdoms' provide an evocative theme in a country with little incentive for historic conservation. The Hot Spring Theme Park, Arkansas is representative of the American family amusement park.

Historic sites in Europe, through conservation and the demands for maintenance, have become an important part to leisure and have sought supplementary activities to encourage tourists.

Historic buildings such as the Tower of London

(with 2·5 million visitors each year), maintain a sense of history with ceremonial display and exhibitions. To provide a wide range of attractions for visitors, British country parks have also established supplementary activities such as the Safari parks and amusement areas at Longleat, Windsor and Woburn and the specialist museums as at Beaulieu. The numerous historic buildings and parks in Europe fulfil an attraction with an inherent evocative theme similar in appeal to theme parks, in each case aiming to attract visitors of all ages. The historic base is clearly identified and supplementary exhibitions, displays and shows aim to reconstruct historic context.

Peacock Theatre, Tivoli Gardens. The screen that covers the proscenium opening has a large peacock motif (Photo: Anthony Wylson)

Tivoli Gardens, Copenhagen

The Tivoli Gardens, situated in the centre of Copenhagen between the Central Station area and City Hall, reflect the character of the traditional European pleasure parks popular in the early 19th century. Tivoli was established by Georg Carstensen (a contemporary of Hans Christian Andersen), in the same decade that the Danes achieved their free constitution and a time when industrial growth created a need for popular entertainment. In his negotiations for the Tivoli site, Carstensen had suggested to the King that 'When the people are enjoying themselves, they have no time for politics!'

Georg Carstensen had experience in the entertainment business, having arranged festive parties, and had travelled extensively in Europe and America. In 1841, he applied for permission to start a permanent amusement park in Copenhagen and he acquired open land from the military authorities outside the walled city. The site included part of the ancient fortifications, the pattern of which is still evident today, and the present lake was derived from part of the old moat of the city. The gently

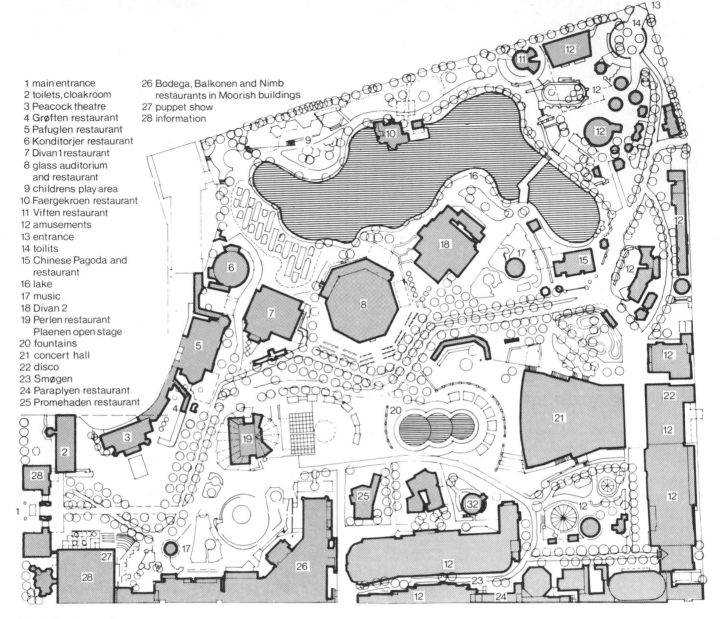

1 main entrance
2 toilets, cloakroom
3 Peacock theatre
4 Grøften restaurant
5 Pafuglen restaurant
6 Konditorjer restaurant
7 Divan 1 restaurant
8 glass auditorium
   and restaurant
9 childrens play area
10 Faergekroen restaurant
11 Viften restaurant
12 amusements
13 entrance
14 toilits
15 Chinese Pagoda and
    restaurant
16 lake
17 music
18 Divan 2
19 Perlen restaurant
   Plaenen open stage
20 fountains
21 concert hall
22 disco
23 Smøgen
24 Paraplyen restaurant
25 Promehaden restaurant

26 Bodega, Balkonen and Nimb
   restaurants in Moorish buildings
27 puppet show
28 information

Tivoli Gardens—plan

Tivoli Gardens. Pagoda and Lake (Photo: Anthony Wylson)

undulating ground provided scope for a layout of wide avenues that follow the zigzag of the old bastion walls.

At the time of the opening, the central building in Tivoli was the concert hall, in which, by candlelight, two orchestras played music inspired by Johann Strauss and Joseph Latner. There was also a less dignified pavilion with chorus girls. The Chinese Peacock Theatre was opened in 1874, housing the pantomime and Tivoli Ballet Company. Candlelight is still used today in the stage wings to provide light for the performance. The Pagoda tower was constructed in 1900. The last decade of the 19th century saw the craze for ballooning which became well established at Tivoli, with ascents (of a captive balloon) of 3000 m (9840 ft) retrieved by a 20 hp steam winch.

The dismantling of the ramparts started in 1872 as

Wall street signs in Smogen

External lighting to the Moorish bazaar (Photo: Anthony Wylson)

Sunshades during the day and (right) illuminated forms at night (left)

Pagoda at night (Photo: Anthony Wylson)

Plaenen stage—the roof immediately over the stage opens and closes as a fan (Photo: Anthony Wylson)

the area was surrounded by a rapidly expanding city. The Tivoli Gardens eventually came under the ownership of the City Council.

Buildings of the early 1900s were in the Moorish style such as the 'Bazaar' that remains today. Many buildings were destroyed in the fire of June 1944, but new buildings have been constructed that maintain the character and scale of the park. The new concert hall was opened in 1956, and the children's playground corner was completed in 1958.

The main entrance from Vestergrogade leads into the avenue system that zigzags through the park tracing the line of the old fortifications. The main route taken by visitors leads to the central space with a large open-air auditorium, fountains and the concert hall. This central space is surrounded by areas of individual character.

The first space has the open stages of the Chinese Peacock theatre (with pantomime and ballet), and the children's Punch and Judy show, restaurants and band platforms. The second space is dominated by the Bazaar, a large Moorish style building with restaurants, pool and gardens; a distinct sense of enclosure is provided by Danish Street Scene Smøgen close to the Central Station entrance to the park. The next space provides an amusement and funfair corner with a roundabout. The broad arcade that passes under the stage end of the concert hall gives access to slot machine saloons and a discotheque. Finally the lake area with the pagoda and other restaurants, sensitive landscaping and the playground for small children provides the quieter sitting areas and scenic views.

The character of each area is distinct, the generous central space with large fountains in scale with the broad façade of the concert hall contrasts with the narrow busy traditional shopping street of Smøgen. The relaxed atmosphere of the gardens around the lake contrast with the jazzy activity of the discotheque and 'fruit machine' corner. There is a horticultural tradition that is evident in the care taken over the gardens. Each single tree of importance is catalogued and the growth is closely observed. Approximately 150 000 flowers are planted over the course of each year.

About 5·5 million people visit Tivoli every summer with an average of 38 000 per day with 113 000 as a 1-day maximum. One in six visitors are children. There is something for all age groups and no one age group predominates. There are twenty-six restaurants and five open stands for orchestras providing a range of music from classical, popular, folk to beat music. The concert hall has played a

Tivoli Gardens: amusement ride (Photo: Anthony Wylson)

significant role in the music life of Europe. It is claimed to be the largest concert hall in Scandinavia with seating for 1800. There are eighty-two leases in Tivoli and seventeen faculties under Tivoli management. The company employs forty-two people on administration and sixty-five in maintenance.

Tivoli Gardens provides within close proximity of the city centre the variety and intensity of landscaped urban life without the traffic and noise. It is made accessible by the modest cost for entrance and its historic development reflects humane European qualities and sensitive design.

Blackpool Pleasure Beach

The Pleasure Beach at South Shore, Blackpool has developed over a period of 80 years. The Company was founded at the turn of the century by two men with interests in the entertainment business, W. G. Bean and John Outhwaite. It has remained a family business and the present Managing Director,

Blackpool Pleasure Beach 1910

Ferris Wheel (Photo: Anthony Wylson)

Blackpool Pleasure Beach 1920's

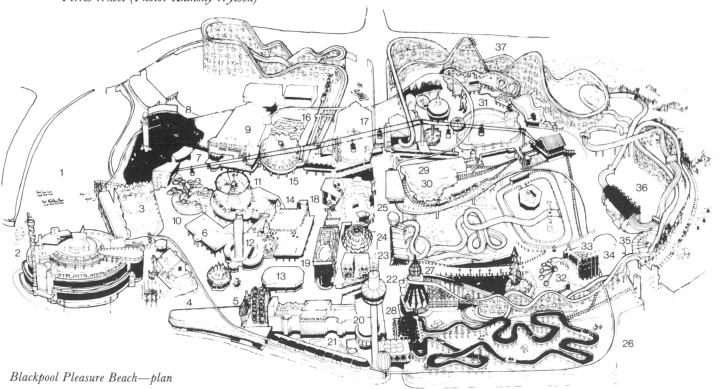

Blackpool Pleasure Beach—plan

1 parking	9 fun house	17 ice drome	25 gold mine	33 giant slide
2 casino building	10 monster ride	18 ghost train	26 monorail	34 vintage cars
3 reel	11 flying machine	19 wild mouse	27 big dipper	35 caterpillar
4 Noah's Ark	12 Grand National	20 planetarium	28 log flume	36 steeple chase
5 Ferris wheel	13 whip	21 go-karts	29 model railway exh.	37 roller coaster
6 autoscooter	14 Alice ride	22 space tower	30 pleasure beach express	
7 cableway	15 Derby racer	23 river caves	31 kiddies amusement park	
8 speed boats	16 maze	24 astro whirl	32 turtle chase	

Geoffrey Thompson is a grandson of W. G. Bean.

The character of Blackpool Pleasure Beach is in the funfair tradition. It replaced a fairground on South Shore when the 16 Ha site was acquired as an amusement park in 1896. During the last decades of the 19th century, visitors to Blackpool had enjoyed the facilities of an amusement park at Raikes Hall, but this was closed in 1901.

In acquiring the site at South Shore, it was the aim of W. G. Bean to create an American style amusement park on the lines of the permanent pleasure ground (similar to that at Earls Court in London), 'to make adults feel like children again'. The two men saw the need to supplement the attractions provided to Blackpool visitors by the Tower, the Alhambra (later the Palace) and the Winter Gardens, with outdoor amusements. Rides and amusements were imported from America. The first ten years of development included the following: the Hiriam Maxim Flying Machine (1904) designed by Sir Hiriam Maxim (whose lack of success with a steam-engined aeroplane had encouraged an interest in captive flying machines); the Lighthouse Helter Skelter (1905); a scenic railway 'The Rivers of the World' (with travel through enclosures each depicting a different country); a roller coaster; a water chute; and a Naval Spectatorum providing a

Hiriam Maxim's Flying Machine (Photo: Anthony Wylson)

Giant slide (Photo: Anthony Wylson)

General view with Ferris Wheel (Photo: Anthony Wylson)

River caves (Photo: Anthony Wylson)

360° projection and mechanised device to represent a naval battle. In 1906 an electrical supply was established and the park was made into an attractive evening entertainment.

The accommodation of the South Shore amusement park into the community life of Blackpool had its critics and supporters. The local residents were not keen to have the residential qualities of the neighbourhood impaired, but some of the more business-like councillors saw the advantage of an agreeable rate revenue.

The second decade of development following the First World War included more elaborate rides; the Big Dipper with 18 m (60 ft) drops and a 910 m (3000 ft) run and constructed in pitch pine; Noah's Ark; Virginia Reel; Skooter cars (dodgem cars); an Indian style 'casino' built in 1913 and lavishly illuminated at night and containing a restaurant, billiard room, cinema, theatre and company offices.

The site remained part of the beach until the 1930's when it was separated from the sea by the extended south promenade.

By the 1930s the owners became aware of the mixed character of the buildings and decided that it should develop as one architectural entity in the

Astro Swivel (Photo: Anthony Wylson)

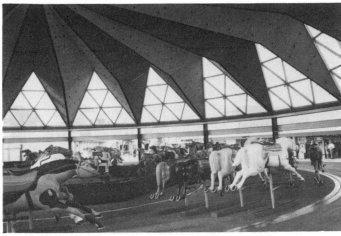

Derby Racer (Photo: Anthony Wylson)

modern style. This task was entrusted to Joseph Emberton. Thus in 1938, a cubistic style was applied to the features. The 'River Caves' rocks and Noah's Ark animals were remodelled. The original flying boats of the Maxim Flying Machine were replaced by rockets as reality had overtaken the original fantasy. The Indian style casino, although robustly constructed, was considered an architectural anachronism and was replaced by a circular three-storey casino with a spiral feature tower. The new casino building was opened in 1939 and represents a fine example of the 'modern movement' in pre-war English architecture.

Since 1945 there has been a succession of International Exhibitions in which engineering skill has been employed to provide new forms of

Space Tower (Photo: Intamin AG, Zurich, Switzerland)

transportation and amusement structures. There was also the influence of the Walt Disney theme park in Los Angeles. In 1956 Jack Radcliff, one of the Festival of Britain designers, was commissioned by Blackpool Pleasure Beach to create a 'New Look' for the amusement park. The desire to regain the unity of the original sets that had been divided by the construction of Watson Road, was achieved with an extended platform over the road and a monorail based on the 1965 Lausanne Expo monorail. The Monster Ride and Astro Swirl was inspired by Expo '67 Trade Fair at Montreal. The 48·7 m (160 ft) high Space Tower built in 1975 with its circular capsule that spirals as it ascends and descends, was based on a 122 m (400 ft) tower also at the exhibition in Lausanne. Since 1974 the Consultant Architect has been Keith Ingham.

The layout of the 16 ha (40 acre) area has maintained a fun fair character with attractions competing for attention rather than the spatial planning of theme parks. Pleasure beach empties the 'toy box' in front of the visitors, and each toy has its own magic and excitement. There are three car parks and three points of access. There are no dominant vistas, routes or areas within the park. The principal activities are concerned with the dynamic excitement of the various rides, the individual theme buildings (Noah's Ark, Alice Ride, Ghost Train, River Caves, Gold Mine, Magnolia Cafe, Grotto, Tom Sawyer Ride, Yellowstones Park, Gaslight Bar and Diamond Lil's saloon) and the spectacle entertainments of the ice rink and cabaret show. There is an area for small children with 'little dipper', special rides and a supervised enclosed playground. This area is identified by the giant figure of Gulliver.

The unifying character is the historic growth and the familiarity enjoyed by regular visitors. To a newcomer, there is much to absorb. There are 8 million visitors a year, arriving by car, coach, and train both as day visitors and holiday guests. A day capacity would be in the order of 50 000 visitors with a full car park of 600 cars. The growth of Pleasure Beach is an interesting record for designers, indicative of the continual necessity to respond to the changing demands of popular entertainment. The trend at Blackpool has been for longer and more exciting rides with the fantasy or evocative element secondary. Possibly, no contrived unifying theme could have withstood the 80 years. It is 'all go' and activated fun synonymous with the tradition of Blackpool and the ingenuity of the English funfair.

Knott's Berry Farm, Los Angeles

Knott's Berry Farm is a 61 ha (150 acre) three-part theme park with a leisure area and shopping area. It is in Buena Park near Los Angeles. The three themed areas are the 'Old West Ghost Town', Fiesta Village and an amusement area 'the Roaring 20's'. There is extensive car parking surrounding the park. This accommodates forty-five buses and 10 000 cars.

The park started from an original boysenberry stand on the 4 ha (10 acre) farm of Walter Knott in the 1920s. It was extended in the 1930s to include a chicken dinner restaurant and, in the 1940s, the first structures of the Old West Town were constructed to provide a diversion for dinner guests. The buildings were reconstructed from authentic stores and saloons of the period, and were developed as a replica of a gold prosperous town, with mine, traditional craft buildings, stores, printers, assayer's office, laundry, barber, saloon, sheriff's office, town jail, blacksmith and post office, church and chapel. Walter Knott wanted to preserve the historic buildings of America's

Knotts Berry Farm—aerial view

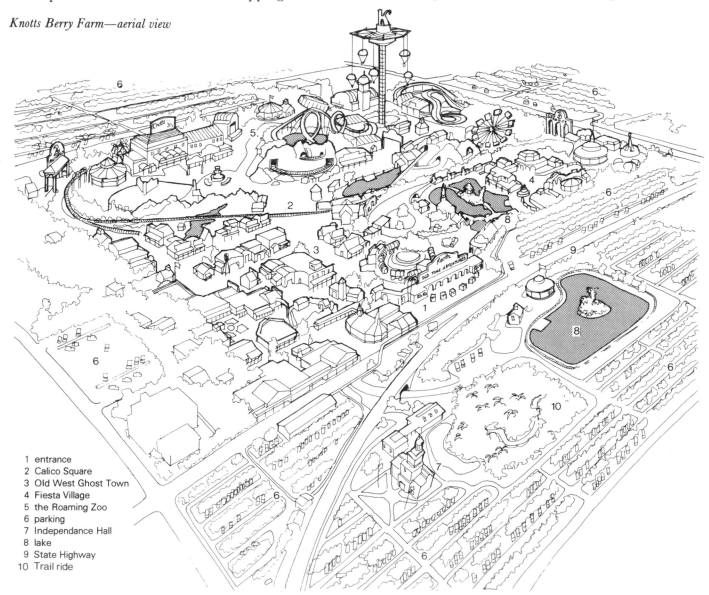

1 entrance
2 Calico Square
3 Old West Ghost Town
4 Fiesta Village
5 the Roaming Zoo
6 parking
7 Independance Hall
8 lake
9 State Highway
10 Trail ride

Covered Wagon Show

pioneering days and many of the buildings continue
both to be used for their original function, and to
maintain traditional crafts.

In 1966, an exact replica of the Independence Hall,
Philadelphia was built on the east section of the park.
The building houses a copy of Liberty Bell and
visitors can hear presentations of historic debates.

In 1970, Fiesta Village was completed, based on
Spanish settlers' villages in California. In 1975, the
'Roaring 20's' park was opened, including a
corkscrew ride, and Starlight Pavilion Theatre. This
venture increased annual attendance to 4 million. In
1976, the 'Roaring 20's' airfield was completed,
dominated by the twenty-storey Sky Tower, with
revolving Sky Cabin and Skyjump for twelve
'parachutists'. The theme is further developed by the
display of antique aeroplane parts and 'aeronautic'
rides.

Corkscrew ride

The number and size of stores in the shopping area
has gradually increased the number of shops to a
total of thirty-nine, with an emphasis towards gifts,
food and casual wear and each themed around the
particular area in which it is located. For example,
Old West Ghost Town has the Western Wear shop,
general store and bottle house; in the 'Roaring 20's'
area there is a magic shop, Cordy's Variety Corner
with 1920s type merchandise and a Candy Cottage.
In Fiesta Village, there are exotic imports in Casa de
la Modesta and Mission Trails Market.

The layout of Knott's Berry Farm achieves
continuity from one theme to another through unity
of scale and the interesting spatial sequence. The
main contrast between the areas with evocative
themes and the active amusement park is separated
by the mountain-like forms of the Calico flume log
ride and the Calico mine ride. There is also the
railway line and stagecoach stop in Calico Square
that prelude activity. Transportation around the park
includes authentic stagecoaches and a narrow-gauge
passenger steam train.

Much of the character of the period is conveyed in
exhibitions and museums within the Old West Ghost
Town. There is also a wagon camp open-air stage
which creates a suitable setting for hill-billy slapstick.

Fiesta Village is separated from the pioneer
buildings by the stagecoach route and a small lake.

Calico Square, stage coach, train and flume ride

(above) Wagon Camp, outside stage and seating

(right) Parachute jump and sky Cabin Parachute Gyro tower
(Intamin AG Zurich, Switzerland)

(Photos: Anthony Wylson)

The Mexican style shops and patios overlook the water, and the village centre has a dance plaza. There is an Animal Park small amusement area as part of the Fiesta Village, 'Montezooma's Revenge' a 23 m (76 ft) diametered loop ride incorporating a 42·3 m (139 ft) tower), and a 180° screen cinema.

The 'Roaring 20's' amusement area is clearly separated. It has various rides, including the loop trainer, log ride, mine ride, impressive corkscrew ride extending over well-designed landscaping, parachute jump creating a tall feature visible outside the park, whirlwind ride and propeller spinner. These attractions are interspersed with restaurants and cafes, a dance pavilion, landscaped areas, a large amusement arcade, a bumper car pavilion and the Good Time theatre that can seat 2098.

The leisure area on the east side of State Highway 39 and connected to the main park by a pedestrian underpass. This area includes the marketing offices, replica of Independence Hall, two lakes and a children's adventure trail, in which they explore 'Jungle Island' on burros.

The reconstruction of the 'Old West Ghost Town' and the Spanish settlers' village has an interesting parallel with conservation in Europe. The imperative desire to realise new ideas and the rate of development in America since the turn of the century, has not permitted the retention of many historic communities. So there is this reconstruction, reminiscent of the legend implicit in many Western films of pioneering young America.

The authenticity of the buildings give it a reality. Visitors could be in a genuine old western town, and there are suitably costumed characters appropriate to the function of the various buildings to animate the concept. The visitors are sometimes drawn into the act—the 'gun fighters' will often pick guests out of the street and involve them in a 'street show' (which usually ends in a shoot-out). The staff associated with the principal buildings are also there to provide historic information about the origins and use of the structures, and in some cases continue historic crafts. The total presentation has the universal interest of the movie tradition but also conveys the real components of the historic American way of life.

As a leisure park, its popularity confirms the balance of amusement activities to the nostalgic re-creation of pioneering days. The surrounding extensive areas of parking, interspersed with lines of trees, are appropriate to the climate, avoid the otherwise monotonous appearance of acres of parked cars, and provide a landscaped zone to protect the park from adjoining development. The number of visitors per house has registered a maximum of 17 000 with a maximum of 37 000 visitors in one day.

48

Disneyland/Walt Disney World Magic Kingdoms

The Magic Kingdoms of Disneyland and Walt Disney World have much in common. Disneyland in Annaheim near Los Angeles was opened in 1955 and Walt Disney World in Orlando, Florida was opened in 1971. In both cases the main layout is based on a radial plan with a single point of access. This is connected to the central plaza of the park by 'Main Street'.

The transportation systems are similar in each case. The visitors are taken by open carriages (drawn by a motor tractor) to the ticket booths and then by either monorail or by paddle steamer to the access point.

The variety of transport systems is an important element in the theme parks, ranging from renovated historic steam engines (now converted to oil), horse-drawn trams, to high-level monorails, skyway cable cars and the WED transport system. Within the attractions further transport methods are used, from the boats through 'Adventureland', the rail boats in 'Pirates of the Caribbean', rail 'submarines' of '20 000 Leagues Under the Sea', open roller cars of the 'Haunted Mansion' and the fast moving roller cars of 'Space Mountain'.

The circulation within the parks consist of a central 'Main Street' extending from a civic square (at the entrance to the 'Magic Kingdom') to a central plaza from which routes radiate out into the adventure areas. The civic square with 'City Hall' and 'Fire Station' provides a terminal point for the horsedrawn trams. 'Main Street' is lined with shops (confectionery, crafts, cameras, gifts, etc.), cafes and a cinema. The central plaza confronts the 'Cinderella/Sleeping Beauty Castle' and is separated from it by a bridge and a moat.

Individual routes extend to the theme areas; 'Adventureland', 'Frontierland', with a visible water context, 'Bear Country' in Disneyland and 'Liberty Square' in Walt Disney World, 'Fantasyland' (with access through Cinderella's Castle) and the futuristic 'Tomorrowland'. Each provides a variety of features including the principal themed 'rides'.

For example in 'Adventureland' the four features, 'Swiss Family Island Tree House', 'Enchanted Tiki Birds', 'Jungle Cruise' and 'Pirates of the Caribbean', each has a distinct method of conveying the visitors through the experience. The visitors find their own way across a bridge on to 'Swiss Family Island' and climb the steps into the various rooms of the tree house. The 'Enchanted Tiki Birds' is a fantasy created within an auditorium in which visitors sit, watch and listen as the decorative birds are presented. The 'Jungle Cruise' is an open air river boat journey through hazardous tropical scenery and archaeological fantasy where 'wild animals' lurk in the pools and undergrowth. The 'Pirates of the Caribbean' is a rail-controlled boat ride in a vast studio space with visitors travelling in a line of open boats through a sequence of stage set experiences, with animated cartoon characters, also lighting and sound effects. It is, in effect, a journey into a Disney film.

In each case the buildings have an impressive point of entry appropriate to the theme, and a large enclosed activity space or studio behind. The movement through the space is at various levels with a commentary, background music, or voices from the animated figures, and lighting effects to dramatise the experience.

In both parks the 'Space Mountain' building provides an architectural landmark with the marquee and feature pinnacles. It forms an enclosed space for a high-speed twisting and turning ride through 'space' apparently in darkness with high illumination at 'lift off' and during occasional space fiction situations. The travelator exit from the side provides an exhibition of futuristic ideas. 'Tomorrowland' gives scope to imaginative building forms, Disneyland provides an open-air auditorium and in Disney World, the contemporary style buildings include restaurants overlooking a pool.

A point of particular interest in the adventure area is the management of entry and egress by the large numbers of visitors. The entry queueing pattern is usually on a zigzag basis. Visitors are able to see others waiting instead of a line of featureless backs.

Much of the design is an extension of Disney characterisation but the façade of 'It's a Small World' at Disneyland is a decorative abstraction of particular appeal. It conveys a mood of the attractive animations inside. The 'It's a Small World' ride had appeared as part of the Pepsi-Cola Pavilion in the New York 1964–65 World Fair.

The philosophy behind the designs avoids contradictions by providing the continuity in the theme parks similar to scenes in a film. The themes are different in character. Adventureland is fantasy; frontierland is nostalgic. These two are separated by a modest enclosed street scene with distinct location character, with bazaars and shops, landscaping and snacks (retail commodities are obtainable—the fantasy and nostalgia are transmitted). In fact, the impact of the individual theme areas is preserved by the less demanding character of the 'circulation' spaces between. Fantasyland itself is separated from

Main Street by the imposing Cinderella Castle with its bridged moat and the central plaza. There are vista views of Cinderella Castle from Tomorrowland, the scale of each provides a common link.

There are also various methods of presenting shows to seated audiences. In 'America Sings' and 'Carousel of Progress', the audience is seated in a segment that rotates around a circular stage divided into stage sets. The auditorium stops at each set and the performance is played through. The auditorium then moves on. Circle vision 360° in which nine screens form a continuous picture around the audience, is used in both parks. The audience stand between rails, to which some of the visitors cling when the travel scenes become hazardous. The Circlorama tradition conveys space and speed effectively.

The standard of maintenance, repair and

cleanliness is such that the Disney parks always look fresh. The litter is removed to underground service tunnels, which are also used for storage, supplies and services. The Cinderella Castle at Walt Disney World accommodates the communications equipment. The technology is there but it is only shown when it is displayed as part of the overall concept. Modern technology is used to operate the theme parks, but without destroying the fantasy.

The actual attractions are computerised and the entire shows are recorded on tape and magnetic systems controlled by the Disney Audio-Animatronics Control System. This combines and synchronises voices, music and sound effects, and activates the physical movements of the performing figures. The magnetic tapes have thirty-two channels and control as many as 438 separate actions.

The human side of the Disney theme parks is

American Family Park Magic Springs (Leisure and Recreation Concepts Inc.)

important in conveying attitudes and respect by both visitors and staff for the parks. The young attendants, mainly students, have a distinct 'good will' disposition that reflects the image associated with Walt Disney. The visitors (four adults to every child) are reliving an innocent and undemanding pleasure, rediscovering old images, and savouring expectations for the future.

Magic Springs Family Fun Park, Hot Springs, Arkansas, U.S.A.

This family amusement park near Hot Springs (designed by Leisure and Recreation Concepts Inc., Dallas) is a 30-ha (75-acre) park with a feature fountain display resembling the original 'hot springs'. It includes seventeen major rides, more than a dozen craft shops, the provision of food and refreshments, and it is divided in three major themed areas; County Fair, Mill Town and River Town.

County Fair represents a turn of the century rural fair and includes a theatre (to be used for a multi-media presentation about Arkansas), a puppet theatre, an arcade, a giant wheel, a carousel and other 'fair' rides. Mill Town has active craftsmen producing confectionery and gifts and includes such major rides as the 384 m (1260 ft) run log flume (the final down chute drops 13.4 m or 44 ft), and the 55 m (181 ft) high Sky Hook that originated in the Brussels Expo and served at the '64 New York Expo'. River Town, based on a 4½-acre lake has more craft shops, a children's zoo, and various rides including coin-operated Remoto-o-boats.

Magic Springs is within heavily wooded landscape, and the park is served by a 5 ha (13 acre) car park. Hot Springs is a resort town within a National Park, and it has extensive hotel, motel and camping facilities for visitors.

Longleat Safari Park, Wiltshire, England

The impressive Elizabethan house and extensive parkland has been subject to elegant modification since it was constructed in the 16th century, including park landscaping by Capability Brown. The most radical change has been in recent years when its use has been directed towards popular appeal support. The 'Safari park' and the 'Lions of Longleat' were initiated by Jimmy Chipperfield (with his lifetime experience of working with animals and interest in African Safari parks), and the owner of Longleat, the Marquess of Bath. Today, the 'drive through' wildlife park with lions, tigers, elephants, rhino, buffalo, antelope, ostrich, monkeys, consists of discreetly fenced enclosures, and there is a picnic area free from carnivours with giraffe, zebras and camels. The park includes a lake on which there are safari boat rides amongst hippos and sea-lions and an island inhabited by gorillas. Visitors use their own cars or coaches to drive through the enclosures. The park's five pay boxes, road system and staffing is geared to a maximum of 4500 vehicles in one day. The number of visitors has peaked at 1 million a year with 350 000 visiting Longleat house.

The historic theme of the house is developed with a mixture of 'in use' impressions (rooms prepared for visitors and life-sized figures as the staff in the Victorian kitchens), exhibitions and collections associated with the owners. Close to the house there is a leisureland, children's amusement area, a maze and a garden centre. The house has also served as the setting for cinema and television drama with historical themes.

Theme Park Planning

Throughout Europe and America, amusement and theme parks have been developed to create a protected fantasy environment with provision for entertainment and relaxation.

In cases as Knott's Berry Farm and the folk farm of the Jardin d'Acclimation in Paris, an authentic image is reconstructed. In the Disney parks, a film image is extended into a three dimensional experience. De Efteling conveys a 'life size' picture book of fairy tales with appropriate buildings and images. The Danish 'Legoland' provides Lego models of historic buildings, ships and trains as well as

Longleat Safari Park (Photo: West Air Photography)

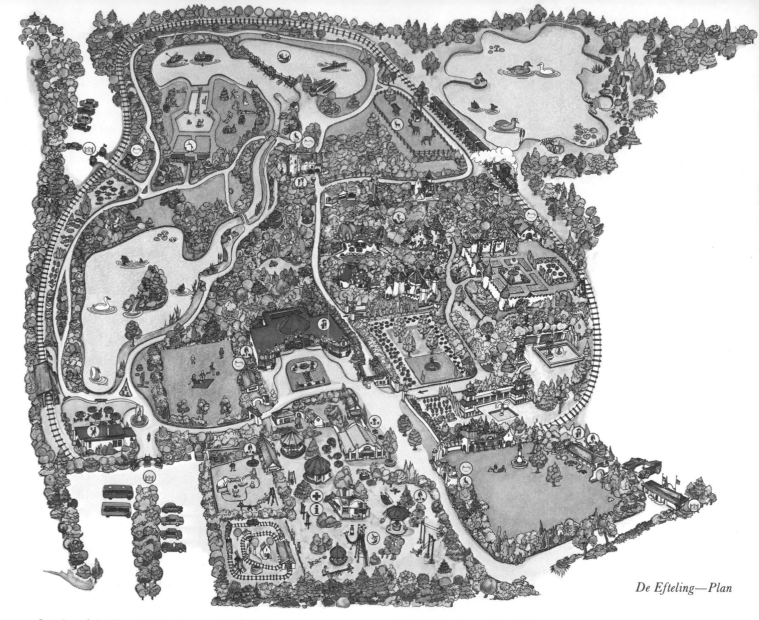

De Efteling—Plan

Interior of the Haunted Castle scene, De Efteling

Snow White scene, De Efteling

52

providing amusement rides and a 'Wild West' fortified town. The active fun and fantasy of the fun fair tradition is developed at Blackpool, and the 'Wild West' fun heroics is the theme at Fort Fun, Wasserfall, W. Germany. Tivoli achieves a vital contact between pleasure park and city centre. The planning of theme parks has much in common with

the themed International Expositions. The pedestrian visitor, group or family is the customer and spectator to be conveyed, enticed or guided through the attractions without becoming overawed, confused, bored or lost. Some of the main issues to be considered are the theme, presentation techniques, transportation, circulation and spatial concept. The

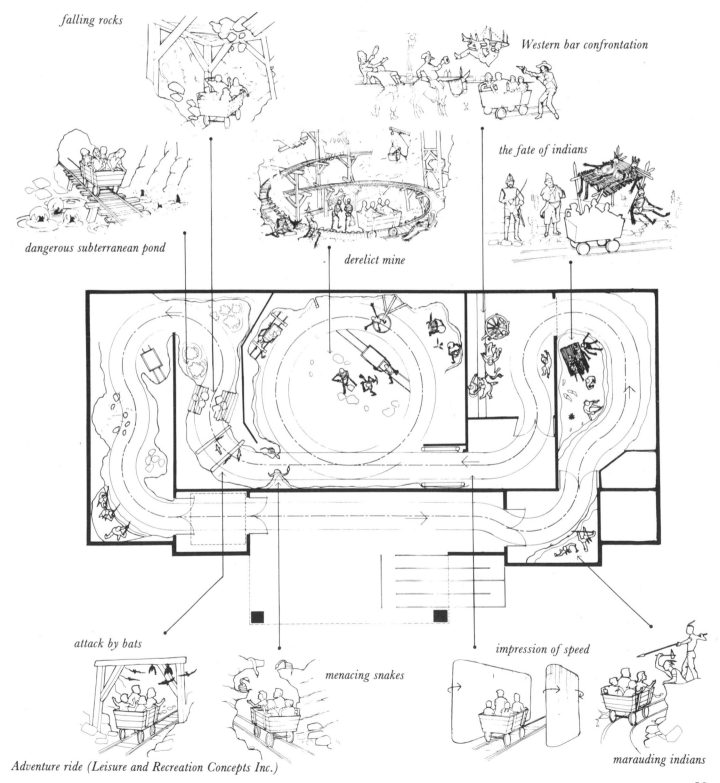

falling rocks

Western bar confrontation

dangerous subterranean pond

the fate of indians

derelict mine

attack by bats

menacing snakes

impression of speed

Adventure ride (Leisure and Recreation Concepts Inc.)

marauding indians

capacity of rides, transportation and attractions must be assessed in relation to the anticipated attendance.

The theme must be strong enough to give a unity of concept. For many parks, there is an abstract main theme as the Expositions, with individual and more comprehensive themes developed within specific areas. In this case the relationship between specific areas is important and particularly difficult where pavilions set out to be competitive or visually individualistic. A continuity of landscaping, water element, scale, spatial sequence or transport circulation patterns can assist to provide cohesion, but a sense of unity within the park is essential to sustain the experience. In some cases, such as Knott's Berry Farm, a visually dominant theme is developed over an extensive area into the components and activities related to the central idea.

Presentation techniques must be appropriate to the feature. With electronics and audio-visual techniques, the technology of presentation can confuse reality with fantasy. Many parks are geared to family groups combining the entire age range. Thus the relationship between convincing presentations of reality (as the Disney 'Hall of Presidents') and fantasy are important.

If the theme park provides an 'escape' it would be prudent to identify the object from which the visitor wishes to 'escape'. With their high proportion of adult attendance, the Disney theme parks could be seen as an escape from other more lurid and violent forms of entertainment. There is a human instinct to

Jardin D'Acclimatation—Multi-use theatre

fantasise an idyllic past, to project the image of a promising future or to make real the substance of folk culture.

The transport system must provide a comprehensive method of transporting visitors from outside public transport or car park to the theme park or to locations in the park within walking distance of the attractions. It must be related to pedestrian movement, either separated by different levels (e.g. cablecar, monorail, WED transport system), or by separate routes (e.g. train, boat). Several theme parks have slow vehicles moving through the pedestrian areas (e.g. horse drawn trams, electric cars) but these are generally small scale, low on the ground, quiet, fumeless, and keep to the wider pedestrian routes where side attractions keep the visitors away from the centre of the road. At Expo 70 a travelator system was used but, as with escalators, the point of discharge must be carefully planned to avoid dangerous congestion.

The movement of large numbers of people through the site, requires clear circulation routes so that the attractions can be easily identified. It is important that visitors are not overcome or confused by an apparent complexity and vastness of the park. The predominant central walk, boulevard, piazza or 'main street' can provide a 'datum', giving access to specific areas. An elevated viewing platform can assist to obtain an image of the park layout, as the central walk at Pleasure Beach, Blackpool.

Alternatively a system of clearly visible landmark features, good signposting, coherent guide maps, can all assist to make the visitor confident. The movement of people can also be influenced by the ticket system as shown by the scheduled programmes of Marineland and Sea World. Access and exit points of individual attractions is important not only to the

Diagrammatic layout of Magic Kingdom Theme Park

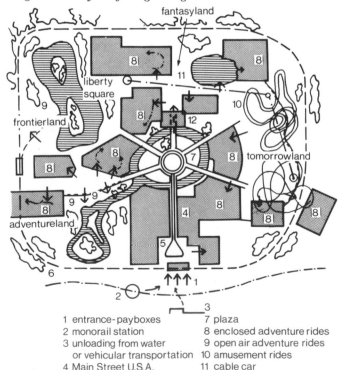

1 entrance-payboxes
2 monorail station
3 unloading from water
  or vehicular transportation
4 Main Street U.S.A.
5 horse drawn tram
6 railway
7 plaza
8 enclosed adventure rides
9 open air adventure rides
10 amusement rides
11 cable car
12 'Castle'

rate of flow through the attractions, but to the basic 'dynamic' of the park. The movement of people in urban spaces can reflect national characteristics. In general people are gregarious; they go to a park to see other people as well as to enjoy the park attractions. They respond to the opportunity to explore, and the opportunities to view from different levels.

Within the park the sequence of spaces and location of relaxation nodes is important to the circulation pattern. Introvert and outward looking relaxation areas, continuity of vistas, total enclosure to capture a particular ambience, the use of neutral areas or scenic features to bridge from one ambience to another—are all significant to the total character. Sound and light patterns are equally important; the quiet areas, the movement of crowds by creating an attraction such as a performance of music or an outdoor show; dynamic lighting, appropriate to activity areas that can enhance spaces and buildings in a manner synonymous with leisure; the night scene of a park in which the character of particular zones are re-created through the effect of artificial lighting. Although the ultimate in manufactured themes is a vast range of transistorised hardware with which visitors can work out their fantasies, large-scale theme parks include interesting planning solutions.

4. Parcs à thème et jardins—Résumé

L'aménagement de parcs au sein de la ville est une manière de rendre plus démocratique la vie urbaine. En Europe, les parcs traditionnels tels que les jardins de Tivoli à Copenhague, offrent détente et divertissement à proximité du centre ville. Blackpool offre un parc d'attractions. Aux Etats-Unis, l'accent porte davantage sur les parcs d'attractions pour toute la famille et les parcs régionaux à thème. Ainsi le parc Knott's Berry Farm, à Los Angeles, est une reconstitution d'une ancienne ville fantôme du Far-West avec boutiques artisanales et personnel en costume d'époque. Les parcs Magic Kingdom de Disneyland et Walt Disney World présentent une nouveauté en matière de conception car ils introduisent non seulement la technologie de l'électronique telle qu'elle est appliquée dans les studios de cinéma, mais maintient également un très haut niveau de qualité de l'aménagement environnant. Magic Springs, dans l'Arkansas, est le type même du parc familial américain. Dans le parc De Efteling, aux Pays-Bas, on retrouve le monde irréel des comtes de fées. Les Safari Parks établis sur les propriétés domaniales anglaises, tels celui de Longfleat dans le Wiltshire, sont une source supplémentaire d'intérêt pour les visiteurs des demeures hidtoriques.

4. Stadtparks und Vergnügungsparks—Zusammenfassung

Der Stadtpark gestaltet das Leben in der Stadt demokratischer. In Europa bieten traditionelle Vergnügungsparks wie das Tivoli in Kopenhagen Möglichkeiten zur Entspannung in der Nähe der Stadtmitte. Im 'Pleasure Beach' vom Blackpool in England kristallisiert sich die Jahrmarkttradition. In den USA haben Vergnügungsparks für die ganze Familie und regionale Naturparks an Bedeutung gewonnen. Knott's Berry Farm, Los Angeles beruht auf einer zu diesem Zweck gebauten 'alten Geisterstadt des wilden Westens' mit Personal in entsprechenden Kostümen und Kunstgewerbeläden. Die Parks mit dem Thema 'im Reich der Magik' von Disneyland und Walt Disney Worldverleihen der Parkform eine neue Norm und verbinden nicht nur die Filmstudio-Technik mit Elektronik, sondern gewährleisten auch eine erstklassige Möglichkeit zur Entspannung. 'Magic Springs' in Arkansas ist ein Beispiel für den Vergnügungspark der amerikanischen Familie. De Efteling in Holland vermittelt ein lebensgroßes Bilderbuch mit Märchen. Die 'Safari-Parks' auf einigen großen englischen Gütern, zum Beispiel Longleat in Wiltshire, bieten neben historischen Gebäuden zusätzliches Interesse.

٤ ـ حدائق الموضوع وحدائق الملاهي ـ موجز

ان حديقة المدينة تمثل عملية جعل الحياة في المدينة أكثر ديموقراطية ففي أوروبا تهيىء حدائق الملاهي مثل حديقة تيفولي في كوبنهاجن تسهيلات الاستجمام وقت الفراغ قريباً من وسط المدينة . ويبلور شاطئ الملاهي في بلاكبول فكرة المهرجانات التقليدية . أما في الولايات المتحدة فقد نمت أهمية حدائق ملاهي العائلات وحدائق الموضوع الاقليمية . تقوم مزرعة نوتس بيرى فارم في لوس انجلوس على شكل «مدينة مهجورة من عهد الغرب القديم» وفيها المضيفون والمضيفات بالزي التقليدي وفيها حوانيت الحرف القديمة . تعبر حدائق الموضوع مثل «المملكة السحرية» في ديزني لاند ، وفي عالم والت ديزني عن مستوى جديد في تصميم الحدائق ليس فقط بجمع الوسائل الفنية لاستوديوهات الافلام مع تكنولوجيا الالكترونيات بل والمحافظة على أرقى نوعية لجو الاستجمام . وتمثل حديقة «ماجيك سبرنجز» في اركانساو حدائق الملاهي العائلية في أمريكا ، بينما تبدو حديقة ايفتلنج في هولندا وكأنها كتاب بحجم الحياة من كتب قصص الاطفال الخيالية . أما حدائق «سفاري» القائمة داخل الضيعات الانجليزية مثل «لونجليت» في مقاطعة ولتشاير فهي تهيىء المتعة الأضافية الى جانب مشاهدة المباني الأثرية المجاورة لها .

Chapter 5

Fairs and Expos

The variety, ingenuity and overt competition that animates showmanship within the traditional fairs have initiated many forms of popular entertainment. These characteristics have also found expression in trade fairs and the prestigious Expo exhibitions. Imaginative architecture is used to attract attention, to symbolise national character, and to convey trade or cultural information through entertaining format. The host country also makes provision within the fair, for the relaxation and amusement of the visitors with imaginative features and popular attractions.

The investment into the international trade fairs has permitted the promotion of new ideas in localised transportation, communication media (in particular audio-visual techniques), and auditoria planning and amusement hardware. Crowd control has much in common with theme parks and there is an obvious close connection between the Walt Disney World project EPCO and the planning of expositions.

Traditional fairs

The original trade fairs of pre-industrial Britain had to adapt their character to the urbanising changes of the 19th century. The mobile wagons that transported the amusements and provided the homes for the people concerned, shared their attractions with communities throughout the country, using a calendar of established festivals and fairs and

Roundabout at Traditional Fair at Tunbridge Wells, Kent. (Photo: Anthony Wylson)

adopting established sites. The site would be the market place, a common or open land accessible to the community.

The fairs initiated many techniques for amusements; the bioscope, music hall, circus, bingo. Each of these entertainments has found a permanent home in the large cities, but the fairs have re-charged with new attractions and continue. Over 7000 fair events are held in the UK each year and the fairground continues to provide an entertainment environment in which participation is of primary importance.

Fair entertainment has always been concerned with four aspects: human curiosity, display of skill, competitive games and the desire for excitement.

In conjunction with those aspects there is the traditional visual presentation of fairground entertainment: the 'Baroque' decoration, surrealistic images, the creative fantasy, the brilliant illumination and compulsive demand to attract the attention of the visitors.

Fairs reached a peak of splendour in the 18th century with satirical theatre, fire-eaters, menageries, bell ringers, Punch and Judy shows, moving waxworks, puppet shows, impersonators, jugglers and comedians. In the 19th century, engineering skill gave the fair a new dynamic; not only was steam power being harnessed for traction, transportation, agricultural and industrial machinery, but it also provided the means of generating electricity. There was immense inventive confidence, applying engineering skills to all aspects of life.

People were becoming more urbane and losing their interests in plebeian entertainments. Their interest in fairs was derived from the characteristic 'gallopers' and roundabouts of the 1850s and it was necessary for the new mechanised rides to maintain people's desire for novelty. The 1850s saw projects that anticipated the 'Waltzer' with cars travelling in a large circle, whilst moving to the right or left on their own axis similar to a dancer waltzing. The decade includes such innovations as the Tunnel

Railway, the Razzle Dazzle, and the steam-driven 'big wheel'. The helter skelter towers arrived in 1905 and the steam-driven switchback (derived from traditional 'gallopers' and roundabouts) and utilising gear manipulation under each boat, to provide pitching and rolling, was launched in 1908. In 1910, the adoption of electrical power to drive a 'Scenic' ride was a significant move towards the next stage of machine design. The smaller engine under each car in the 'Scenic' allowed space for more elaborate decoration.

Projected animated pictures were first shown in London in 1896, and the fairs were quick to adopt and develop the bioscope as popular entertainment. The first cinema booths held fifty to sixty people, limited by the level of illumination to project the picture. By 1900, electric lighting and carbon burning arc lamps gave a much brighter picture and seating accommodation in the shows increased. One particular bioscope had seating for 600 and standing room for 400.

The scale of rides and audience accommodation up to the 1930s was a reflection of the tremendous haulage capacity of the steam traction engine. These tractors, sometimes pulling seven or eight trucks, would cover distances of 250 miles between fairs at an average speed of 5 mph. Diesel and petrol engines, with the advantages of speed and mobility, eventually replaced steam. Quicker, more exciting rides and lighter equipment took over from the elaborate steam-driven components.

Nowadays the associations and fantasies have been modified. The Chairoplanes of 1888 gave a sensation of flight, a topical fantasy (the Wright Brothers succeeded in flying in 1903) whereas the rides of today are associated with the simulation of speed and aeronautics. The fantasy element has also changed from the romantic gondola and mythical beasts to the car and aeroplane theme and in recent years to the current space travel images.

The traditional fairground is a combination of engineering and fantasy, in the UK it is a by-product of industrial ingenuity and, in Europe, a continuation of mechanical toy making. The relatively shorter history of American fairs has resulted in culturistic associations with Hollywood and the use of lighter functional machinery.

The fair has become a playground of machines in which mechanical toys provide mystery, fantasy, excitement and thrills. The ornamentation is geared to popular appeal to communicate the spirit of the entertainment concerned. The exciting image, by day and night, is an essential quality. Even at a simple level the fair must imbibe the fantasy and myth of the age to which it belongs. Fairgrounds represent the

'The Monster' combines the outward forces of spinning cars, the circular motion of the entire ride and the up and down movement of each arm to produce multiple sensations of weightlessness. Four cars rotate on the six main rotating arms. The 24 cars each with two to three passengers, have a capacity of 1200 passengers per hour. (Eyerly Inc. Oregon U.S.A.)

most flexible and adaptable form of entertainment environment, and have survived standardisation and many restrictions. The capacity for urban life to be able to respond to the flamboyant traditions of showmanship is very important to leisure entertainment.

The typical layout of a fair locates the big rides in the centre, with 'joints', stalls and shows creating an enclosure permeated by lanes. The perimeter is formed by the lorries and wagons. Site conditions vary from the open common with generous space, to the limited small town market place where the traffic must be re-routed during the occasion of the fair. Sloping sites add a further complication to setting-up the big machines. The size of operation varies from the simple village fair, to the extensive street fairs (as the Kircal Links Market that stretches 2·4 km ($1\frac{1}{2}$ miles) on both sides of an esplanade) and parkland fairs such as the Newcastle Town Moor Festival covering 12 Ha (30 acres). Mobile trading fairs are rare today, but charity carnivals such as the Peckham Rye Carnival in London play an important part in raising money for deserving causes.

Sinda bounce ride constructed of polyester based fabric. (Sinda Industries Inc. California U.S.A.)

Amusement hardware, machinery and games

Certain mechanical features are a familiar sight at most fairgrounds.

Traditional machinery

Roundabouts or 'Gallopers' were the first machines to be driven by steam having a crank action which was devised in the 1850s. The original roundabouts had an organ in the centre with appropriate music issuing forth. The visual appearance entails a decorative fantasy element.

The Dodgem operates by electric current taken from the top metal netting to the motor in the 'car' and earthed through the floor plates. The usual 'set' consists of twenty cars and the machinery was first introduced in 1928. The self-steering and intentional bumping provides a harmless outlet for violent play and retaliation.

Noah's Ark consists of a circular ride with carved animals rotating on an undulating track. It was first introduced in the 1930s. It is a smaller but faster version of the switchback or scenic railway.

The Helter Skelter is basically a chute or slide. It needs only a coconut mat, gravity and an intrepid spirit. The form often consists of a slide spiralling down the outside of a lighthouse tower.

The Big Wheel, probably the original, was created for the Crystal Palace Exhibition in 1851. It is generally 12–15 m (40 ft or 50 ft) high and governed by limitations of transport up from site to site.

The Waltzer consists of cars moving in a circular path, up and down on an undulating track, and also spinning on their own axis. The motion was compared to dancers waltzing.

The Caterpillar is formed by a tram of cars on a circular, undulating track with a canvas hood which enfolds the cars when the tram has gathered speed. A refinement that is designed to compromise the dignity of the riders (in the pre-jeans era) consists of a gale of wind directed below the passengers' legs.

Jet Planes with hydraulic-powered rotating and elevating arms. The rider controls the lift of his plane by the use of a joystick. Additional lift in the Super Jets is provided by the rise and fall of the main vertical shaft.

Dive Bombers and Space Ships have twin cars revolving vertically and also twisting on their axes. This gives a sensation of diving and looping as in aeronautics.

Stalls and games

These would include housey-housey (or bingo) and old-established fairground entertainment such as coconut shies, shooting, hoopla pintables, fruit machines and many other small amusements.

Rock-o-Plane with a capacity of 600 passengers per hour, has a circular motion with individual car control. (Eyerly Inc. Oregon, U.S.A.)

Sideshows

Shows of the early fairground included boxing (exhibition bouts and local amateurs) and wrestling. The 'rotor' which is part ride and part show (riders are suspended against the inside wall of a rotating cylinder) was introduced at the Festival of Britain in 1951.

Shows would also include small circuses or menageries, motor cycle acrobatics in the 'wall of death', flea circuses and live shows of music hall and revue tradition.

'Expo' International Trade Fairs

The thematic trade fairs since the Crystal Palace have provided the opportunity for experiment both in architectural design and communication techniques relevant to entertainment. It is a requirement of the International Exhibition Bureau that a universal exhibition must express a master idea so as to assure a unity of concept in the diversity of presentation. The themes have focused on 'man' and the aim has been to intensify, dramatise and animate the exhibition; to involve and impress the visitors.

The communication techniques have initiated ideas for multi-screen projection presentations with environmental effects to provide a total audio-visual experience.

Brussels, New York, Lausanne, Montreal

The Philips' pavilion at the Brussels Exhibition of 1958, designed by Le Cerbusior set out to be 'an electronic poem in which light, colours, images, rhythm, sound and architecture will be seen to fuse together in such a way that the public will be subject to all the things that Philips does'. The building consisted of a tent form rising in three peaks. The performance was 'son et lumiere' with a continuous movement of pictures, dramatic lighting effects, optical illusions, images and sound effects to give an audio-visual experience. At Brussels, there was also the 'Dia polycran' projection System consisting of a projection screen made up of 2 ft square blocks each equipped with two automatic slide projectors which were electronically controlled so that in the space of 14 minutes, 15 000 slides were shown forming a mosaic of continually changing picture compositions.

The 1964–65 New York Expo reflected show business traditions and incorporated a state pavilion with space for parades, a 76 m (250 ft) observation tower and a variety of water display features; the electronically programmed Fountain of the Planets with fountains, water curtains, and water jets creating various patterns synchronised with colour lights, music and fireworks. There was also the Astral Fountain which included a 70 ft high column of water enclosed in a star-studded rotating open work cylinder.

The Expo at Lausanne in 1964 was planned as a thematic exhibition covering social and industrial life.

In the 'Joy of Living' section there was 'Polyvision' consisting of a polyhedral dome with fifty-seven projectors simultaneously throwing coloured pictures on to the polygonal surfaces. The public stood on a central platform to witness a hemispherical panorama of moving pictures and stereophonic sound. The 'Communications and Transport' section included 'Circarama' projection in an 86 ft diameter theatre with nine synchronised projectors. There was also 'Rotorama' with audio-visual demonstrations on four stages enclosing a rotating dais seating 600 people which stopped at each stage in turn.

The section also included 'Aerovision' that created the illusion of an aircraft taking off and landing. This was achieved by light and sound effects and two screens either side of a luminous stage show. 'Globovision' in the section 'Exchange of Goods and Services' provided another comprehensive audio-visual spectacle within a circular cinema with forty projectors and over 350 coloured lighting effects. The 'Spherama' cinema provided a picture on a hemispherical surface by a system of back projected individual colour pictures on to hexaforal translucent vinyl screens. Each unit was approximately 14 ft square and was mounted on a supporting steel frame 81 ft in diameter and 49 ft high.

The Lausanne Expo included leisure areas; the harbour area with restaurants, casino, cabaret, circus, bearpit, fairground, amusement equipment, miniature railway and helter skelter was designed to provide a colourful area for relaxation and fun. The architectural unity was achieved by the use of 'sail' form roofs of different colours which could be seen across the water in a marina setting, and providing an attractive waterside feature at night. Also at Lausanne the 230 ft high tower lift with elevating

viewing platform has subsequently become a popular feature in theme parks. The exhibition ground included a children's garden where as many as 2000 children could be accommodated daily.

The Expo 67 at Montreal had the theme 'Man and His World' and was located on two islands (one enlarged and the other specially constructed for the exposition) and a promontory. The river setting gave an opportunity for water activities and entertainment, in particular 'Dancing Water' consisting of a 210 ft wide spectacle of water jets programmed to create patterns and cascades with music and coloured lighting.

Interesting structures at Montreal included the Gyrotron, brainchild of Sean Kenny, consisting of a space frame programmed with a 'space' ride. The impression conveyed to the passenger was a journey from space orbit into a hissing, spitting volcano, to be swallowed by a huge monster, supporting the old saying that 'life is not a spectacle or a feast: it is a predicament'. The 312 ft tower of La Spiracle had a two-level cabin holding sixty passengers; the cabin rotated as it ascended the tower. Other interesting structures included the 'Buckminster Fuller', a twenty-storey high geodesic 'Biosphere' containing a controlled environment landscaped park; and the German pavilion consisting of a great tent-like structure with masts rising 120 ft.

'La Ronde', a 135-acre amusement park (dedicated to the 'diversion and delight of man'), the reconstruction of an old west, gold rush town and a safari park provided amusement feature areas at Montreal. The original Expo site continues as a cultural and entertainment park.

La Ronde, Expo 67, Montreal

Expo '70, Osaka, Japan

The theme of the Osaka Expo, 'Progress and Harmony for Mankind', aimed to express solutions to the contradictions confronting present-day society and the need to recover the lost humanity in living. Thus the integration of entertainment into an exposition was particularly evident, with the Festival Plaza providing an arena for festivals, national day events, folk dancing, performances and music, with the national and trade pavilions expressing achievements and technological progress.

The individual pavilions used imaginative structures, symbolism, display and a variety of audio-visual techniques to provide attractive and entertaining features. There were over 64 million visitors during the 183-day Expo season.

The site was divided by a highway and underground train route so that the main gate was centrally positioned within the exhibition. The north side of the highway accommodated pavilions with the Festival Plaza and Symbol Zone as a central structure extending from the main gate to the Japanese garden and lake on the north boundary. The south side of the highway was used for administration buildings, coach park, and a Expoland recreation area. At the most southerly point of the site (and the highest ground) there was a

120 m Landmark Tower representing a futuristic aerial module for urban control. The structure provided an observation platform, lounge and restaurant.

It was estimated that there would be a daytime population of 400 000 visitors. Circulation was based on moving pedestrian walks for visitors to move among the pavilions and exhibitions, and a monorail around the periphery of the pavilion area. Within the site there were seven sub-plazas each with provision for relaxation and information. These also provided points of departure to various pavilions.

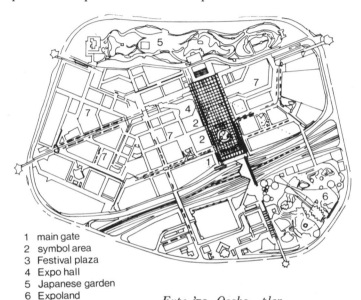

1 main gate
2 symbol area
3 Festival plaza
4 Expo hall
5 Japanese garden
6 Expoland
7 pavilions

Expo '70, Osaka—plan

Aerial view of Expo '70

The structures of particular significance were the air supported and pneumatic structures (the pavilions of the United States, the Fuji Group and the Electric Power organisation), and structures integrating audio-visual techniques, conveying a direct expression of its use.

The US Pavilion provided an elliptical enclosure 142 m × 83·5 m (466 ft × 271 ft), with a translucent air-supported roof of vinyl-coated glassfibre fabric spanning between a diamond grid of steel cables. The cables were anchored to a concrete edge beam. As the domed roof was shallow, the external expression of the building was that of the enclosing tile faced earth work bank. The plastic membrane roof was supported by raising the internal air pressure by 0·2% of atmospheric pressure. Precautions against failure of the support included standby generators for the fans and skeleton steel frames around the exhibit areas.

The enclosure to the Fuji Group Pavilion consisted of double skin type inflated structure with sixteen closed tubes each 4 m (13 ft 4 in) diameter constructed of nylon synthetic rubber sheet. The Electric Power Pavilion floating theatre consisted of three widely spaced tubes supporting an external cover of nylon rubber sheet and an internal lining,

Electric Power Pavilion Expo '70, Osaka

both sealed, with a negative pressure between the two surfaces. This had the effect of drawing the two surfaces together over the inflated tubes on the outside and to a profiled ceiling inside. The space enclosed was 23 m (74½ ft) in diameter. The potential of the air roof for spanning vast space areas is tremendous, providing a simple, economic and light structure with the ventilation system integral with structural support.

The stylised tree sculptured in aluminium that dominated the Swiss stand with electronic music broadcast from loudspeakers inside the structure, represented the imaginative, abstract symbolism that can provide visual entertainment. The Netherlands stand, incorporating fifteen film screens and ten slide screens on walls, floors and ceilings with synchronised audio effects in a spatially sculptured building, provided a synthesis of display and structure. For pre-entertainment experience, the Toshiba I.H.I. Pavilion consisting of tetrapods carrying a domed cinema roof, had an auditorium floor that was raised from ground level, 5·5 m (17 ft) into the

Swiss Pavilion

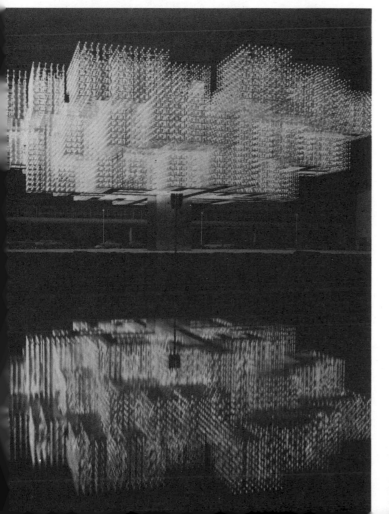

Toshiba I.H.I. Pavilion

Takara Beautilion

film production with a screen 360° horizontally and 210° vertically. Projection used five cameras each with a wide range 133° lens. Stereophonic sound was achieved through 515 speakers.

The flexible use of public space for entertainment could not be better expressed than the impressive Symbol Zone and Festival Plaza. The extensive space frame, 100 m × 150 m (328 ft × 492 ft) and 30 m (98½ ft) ceiling height, was punctuated by the Tower of Sun that extended through a void in the roof structure and with the two smaller towers (the Tower of Motherhood and Tower of Youth). The Plaza had a capacity of 10 000 and the lighting and sound systems, screens and robots were computer operated. The illumination consisted of general lighting, special effects mobile lighting carried on booth trolleys suspended on rails beneath the great roof, and hand-operated special lighting equipment used from

U.S. Pavilion

elevated auditorium dome. Within the tetrahedron framework, the Global Vision Theatre with a diameter of 40 m (131 ft) had a 360° screen. The audience platform 26 m (85 ft) in diameter seated 500 spectators.

The Takara Beautilion was a prefabricated structure of hexahedron capsules. These supported a theatre with rotating and lifting seats for forty-eight people. During the performance, the seats gradually elevated 2 m (6½ ft) within an audio-visual presentation based on twelve globular screens. The Midi-Kan 'Astrorama' provided a hemispheric vision

floor level for close up lighting. The sound equipment took into account the size of the space concerned, the seating conditions for the spectators (similar to an outdoor theatre), and the opportunity for spectators walking around the Plaza to listen to the performance. Echo conditions were carefully considered and provision was made for electronic music with synchronised light and sound effects.

The ground equipment included one mobile stage, six mobile viewing stands, a VIP sitting area, eight wagon stages, eight stage setting units, five projector stands, three screens, four screen stands and two tractors. The vast space was mechanically ventilated and the total accommodation consisted of 2160 seats

Netherlands Pavilion

1 Tower of Motherhood   4 fountain, pond and floating stage
2 Tower of the Sun   5 café terrace
3 elevated viewing stand   6 main viewing stand

Festival Plaza, Osaka—section

in the main viewing stand, 400 on the cafe terrace, 1020 on the elevated viewing stands and 1200 on mobile viewing stands. Technical control included two robot machines, one of which was particularly concerned with entertainment operations with a control room, adjustable stage and mobile dressing-rooms. The concept of this multi-use public space by Kenzo Tange, is particularly relevant to the possible city leisure-entertainment centre of the future.

Expoland was the amusement area covering 170 000 m². It was divided into six sections each with a particular character. The selection of amusements aimed to provide novelty in human experience 'to expose the visitor to new forms of involvement where the sensory organs are in direct contact with the

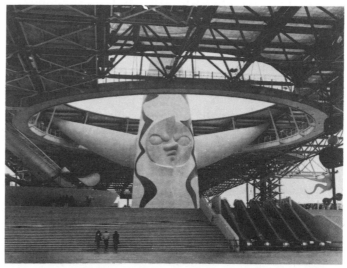

Festival Plaza, Osaka; stairs and escalators leading up to arena

Festival Plaza, Osaka; Space frame structure with 'Tower of the Sun' rising through the structure

surroundings and the sense of living is felt'. The entrance was symbolised by five large inflated vinyl mushroom shaped umbrellas (the largest 30 m in diameter and 26·8 m high) to protect visitors from rain and sun. The umbrellas were red and orange and were illuminated from below at night. The section also included a minirail and woods of poles (consisting of sixty-six glassfibre poles with spatial lighting effects for the evenings). The Daidarasaurus jet coaster ride in the Central Plaza provided a dominant attraction with varied and intertwining routes on which the cars moved reaching up to 65 km/h.

The third section, 'Gameland', consisted of an indoor playground equipped with 357 devices (180 different kinds) including rides suitable for small children. The section 'Land of Ones Self' had a glass castle made of hexagonal units with numerous mirrors, which, with light and sound effects, created a 'world of visual and psychological illusions'.

Expoland also included an amphitheatre, a creative playground with water adventure equipment, a maze, a little stage for children's 'ad lib' dancing, a 'Ride Centre' with a full range of funfair hardware (speeding, jumping, gyrating and floating), and the 'Woods of Recollection' with an assortment of classic amusement facilities. Specific entertainment buildings at Osaka Expo included the Festival Hall, Expo Hall and a floating stage.

Transportation to the site consisted of road and rail access with parking facilities for 20 000 cars, 1500

excursion buses and 1800 business cars. There was a bus shuttle from car parks to the respective gates, a peripheral monorail (with selected elevated sections to provide good views), thirty-seven moving walks, a cablecar and two hundred electric cars used as sight-seeing vehicles within the park.

The moving walks were accommodated in a tubular construction (made of transparent synthetic resin) with a deck 5 m (16½ ft) wide comprising two conveyor belts travelling in opposite directions. The longest single stretch of moving walk was 189·75 m (622 ft) and the belts moved at 2·4 km/h. These proved satisfactory except when occasional rainy weather caused confusion by visitors being reluctant to move away from the discharge point in the open. The cablecar 'Rainbow Ropeway' was a high level tour moving at 30 m above ground, from the Westgate to Expo Hall.

Comment

Apart from the international goodwill and opportunity to realise new technique, expositions represent a major capital investment for a short-term activity. Some benefit is gained from advertising individual national attributes and trading activities and there is revenue from the visitors and possibly from the exhibitors.

In most cases, the long-term advantage can be seen as an opportunity for urban redevelopment in and around the Expo site, or the establishment of a permanent cultural and amusement park. At the

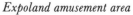

Expoland amusement area

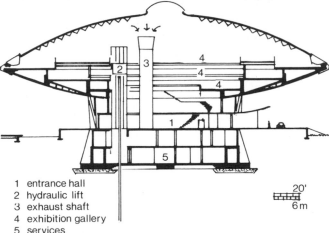

1 entrance hall
2 hydraulic lift
3 exhaust shaft
4 exhibition gallery
5 services

20'
6 m

Evoluon, Eindhoven, Holland. (Above) view of elevated spheroid, (below) sectional view of spheroid

same time, expositions have had a direct effect upon the development of entertainment, amusement equipment and communications.

Evoluon Eindhoven, Holland

An interesting outcome of Exposition experience is the Evoluon building in Eindhoven. This provides a permanent exhibition of 'human ingenuity'. A process of continuous innovation expresses human society in evolution and the important part played by science and technology. In the context of elaborate but temporary exhibitions prepared for various 'Expos', NV Philips Gloeilampenfabrieken of Eindhoven decided to establish a permanent exhibition within a building of distinctive form. The exhibition embodies the human story of people working together to create technology distributing its benefits to those who have need of them.

The building consists of an elevated spheroid 76·8 m (252 ft) diameter (with a highest point 31 m (103 ft) from the ground) with exhibition space for

twenty subjects and room for between 500 and 1500 visitors at any one time. It is designed as one large exhibition space to allow visitors at all times to be aware of the movement and interest of other visitors in the building.

5. Foires et expositions—Résumé

La foire d'attractions traditionnelle ambulante est à l'origine des différentes formes de divertissement qui ont trouvé une implantation permanente. Mais les foires continuent à apporter leur divertissement saisonnier avec stands, spectacles, jeux et loteries. Au cours du siècle dernier, les expositions internationales ont pris l'habitude de colporter les informations industrielles et commerciales par le subterfuge d'une présentation à la fois attrayante et divertissante. Ce sont des foires comme celles de Montréal, au Canada, et d'Osaka, au Japon, qui ont permis d'innover dans la construction de superstructures, oeuvres d'imagination, et de lancer les techniques d'audio-visuel et dispositifs électro-mécaniques.

5. Jahrmärkte und Expos—Zusammenfassung

Der traditionelle Jahrmarkt war für die Einführung verschiedenster Vergnügungsformen verantwortlich, die eine ständige Bleibe gefunden haben. Jahrmärkte sind auch weiterhin eine saisonbedingte Unterhaltung mit Vergnügungsanlagen, Buden, Veranstaltungen und Spielen. Im letzten Jahrhundert wurden internationale Ausstellungen zur Vermittlung von Informationen von Industrie und Handel benutzt, und hierzu wurde eine unterhaltende, attraktive Präsentation verwendet. Sie förderten einfallsreiche Konstruktionen, audio-visuelle Verfahren und elektromechanische Vorrichtungen. Beispiele sind Montreal, Kanada und Osaka, Japan.

٥ ـ المهرجانات والمعارض ـ موجز

كانت المهرجانات المتنقلة التقليدية هي السبب في نشوء عدد من وسائل الترفيه التى احتلت مكانها الدائم . ومازالت المهرجانات تقدم الترفيه الموسمي ويشمل الات اللعب والمنصات والعروض المسرحية والالعاب . وقد جرى استغلال المعارض الدولية في خلال القرن الماضي في نقل المعلومات التجارية والصناعية بوسائل شيقة جذابة ، وقد شجعت على ظهور المنشئات البارعة التصميم والفنون المرئية السمعية والاجهزة الكهربائية الميكانيكية . الأمثلة : معرض مونتريال في كندا ومعرض اوساكا في اليابان .

Chapter 6

Water play and marine parks

Allegory and display

Throughout the ages water has been used to express aspirations and to convey allegorical meaning being a material with both kinetic and tranquil characteristics. The historic Greek Shrine of Delphi was significantly at the source of the Castalian Spring at the foot of Mount Parnassus, and the temple of Sybil that rises above the one time turbulent water cascading over the rocks in the chasm of Tivoli, conveyed a serenity above worldly turmoil. In modern architecture, the cantilevered floors of 'Falling Water', the house designed by Frank Lloyd Wright, creates a similar contrast between dynamic nature and the controlled forces that sustain the structure.

The Renaissance garden, based on classical Roman landscaping, expressed man's attitude to nature by transforming water from a natural source to a feature integrated with the architecture, conveying the reconciliation between man's 'order' and the energy and organic forms of nature. This use of water in landscaping reached an extravagant scale in the baroque palaces of Europe to express princely opulence and to provide a context for prestigious entertainment. The 2-mile vista of water cascading down canals and steps, fountains and changes of level at the Palazzo Reale, Caserta; the Chateau Chantilly near Paris and the Villa d'Este near Rome illustrate the imaginative and expansive constructions of the day.

Baroque exuberance also found expression in civic fountains as the Trevi Fountain in Rome where the wall cascade, fountain, pool and sculpture provides a fusion of mythology, rock forms and ebullient water. The combination of display in baroque fountains, substantial sculpture and inventive mechanics extract the kinetic and volatile qualities of water in its architectural context.

Although there are several 20th-century water fountains designed as kinetic art form, the modern West German state capitals in particular, have

Caserta. Gruppo di Diana (Italian State Tourist Office)

Villa d'Este. Fontana dell'Organo (Italian State Tourist Office)

patronised water display and water play in the civic gardens as at Stuttgart, Hamburg and Dusseldorf. In the 'Planten und Bloomen' gardens in Hamburg, water is used to provide entertainment both through the expansive water organ (where fountains are activated, synchronised to music) and the play devices that use high-pressure jets and cascading water. There are additional water features nearby; a bucket fountain and a transparent water wheel set on an inclined plane to reflect the sunlight.

The play use of water is developed further in children's playgrounds as at Frakenplatz, Dusseldorf, the 'Spray Pool', Frankfurt, and the WeiBenburgpark, Stuttgart. The decorative and evocative display of falling water is captured in the artificial waterfalls of Kassel-Wilhelmshohe.

The circumferential seaside of Britain has promoted water-based leisure with particular expression in the seaside pier. The underlying salubrity instituted the family seaside holiday and the pier provided (and some continue to provide) a characteristic location for entertainment, amusements and relaxation. Today, enclosed leisure centres provide a 'seaside' facility protected from the British climate.

In America, the warm climate of the tourist populated southern states has promoted water gardens, water play and parks for marine life and water-based entertainment. The activity attraction of the Walt Disney World 'River Country' and 'Wet 'n Wild' (both near Orlando, Florida) respond to the desire for a fun use of water apart from orthodox swimming.

This aspect is also developed in the Jaya Ancol Complex, Jakarta and the indoor leisure centres in the UK and West Germany. The marine parks of Florida and California, besides permitting zoological research, capture the interest in marine animal

performance. There are also entertaining displays of man's own aquatic skills.

Piers

The English climate had not deterred an interest in social entertainment based on water activities. Hypochondria was a popular pastime to the wealthy sectors of British society in the 1800s and the 'spas' (as Harrogate, Tunbridge Wells and Bath) prospered as health resorts professing curative powers through their mineral springs. As a result the resorts were well provided with entertainment and cultural buildings. The 'Spa' popularity was challenged by the seaside and drinking seawater was thought to be a cure for many complaints.

By the early 19th century, such places as Scarborough, Weymouth and Margate grew in popularity as exclusive seaside resorts, and the advent of the steam passenger boat increased the amount of traffic to the coastal resorts. The seaside 'pier' grew out of this situation, providing at first, a means of conveying passengers ashore, and then gradually adopting the importance of a promenade. This facility was not just an extension to the beach side walk, but captured the magic of being 'on the sea' without the hazards of being afloat.

The first pier was constructed at Ryde in the Isle of Wight. It was completed in 1814 and extended 38 km (1250 ft) into the sea. The famous chain pier at Brighton (designed as a series of small suspension bridges) was completed in 1823 and piers were constructed in many English coast towns where tidal conditions did not permit passenger boats to dock at low tide.

The pier attraction grew in popularity as the seaside resorts were made accessible for day trips by

Water play. Planten un Blomen Park. Hamburg (Photo: Anthony Wylson)

Eastbourne Pier (Photo: Anthony Wylson)

Bletchley Leisure Centre—Tropical pool (Photo: Anthony Wylson)

Leisure centres

The traditional sports building was utilitarian, stark, and gave little consideration to the spectator or to relaxation. In recent decades, the popular holiday has associated water-based leisure with exotic surroundings and a social atmosphere.

In 1967, the Billingham Forum in northern England was completed, promoting the community leisure centre idea through a multi-use building with ice rink, swimming pool, theatre, bowls and squash, to provide something for everybody. Subsequent projects have developed the leisure ambience with tropical evocations and wave pools, overlooked by sophisticated restaurant and bars, to provide a relaxed leisure environment for all the family. These entertainments are in a controlled environment, and not at the mercy of the climate. In such conditions sport is placed in a leisure context alongside other community activities.

At the Herringthorpe Leisure Centre, Rotherham (also in northern England), designed in 1967, the first free form wave pool was constructed and set in a tropical seaside ambience. The concept of the centre provides several types of area within one multi-purpose complex. Each area is suited to a particular activity but also there is the possibility to permit adaptation to changes in leisure interests. The

the less wealthy through the development of railway transport. Working people became entitled to leisure time and seaside holidays became a social institution. By 1910, there were nearly seventy piers around the coast of England and Wales. Southend pier (Essex), the longest, was 6600 ft ($1\frac{1}{3}$ miles or 2·1 km) long. Clevedon in the West Country, one of the shortest piers, presented the most delicate appearance with cast-iron tracery-like arches. The pier became a natural focal point in resort towns where visitors could enjoy the maritime context for amusements and entertainment, as well as sea air invigorating walks away from claustral urban streets.

Hastings pier, opened in 1872 incorporated a pierhead pavilion for concerts and plays with a seating capacity of 2000. The Palace Pier at Brighton designed as an amusement and pleasure emporium with pavilion, dining rooms, smoking and reading rooms, provision for bathers, and small pleasure crafts, was completed in 1896. An oriental image was transferred from the Royal Pavilion (Brighton) to the Palace Pier by the prolific pier designer Eugenius Brick, and this idiom was adopted for many subsequent pier pavilions.

Today, few piers survive. Some as at Eastbourne have been regenerated by skilful maintenance and management to provide amusements, entertainment and deck chair relaxation. Some provide a useful means of taking brash and noisy entertainment away from the residents. Several piers are listed buildings, and even though extensive financial investment is required for maintenance, they continue to enjoy local loyalty and campaigning for continued use. Since 1945, the salubrity that generated an interest in seaside activities in Britain has been regenerated through the construction of leisure centres which include many types of water activities as well as orthodox swimming.

Rotherham Leisure Centre (Gillinson, Barnett and Partners, Architects)

1 entrance	6 main pool
2 squash courts	7 slides
3 multipurpose hall	8 beach
4 bar	9 sports hall
5 changing room	

pools are of irregular shapes with large areas of shallows, shelving up to a 'sitting out' beach with palm trees and sunshades. There is a three-lane water chute, inflated rubber rocks and a sand topping to the floor of the 'beach' provides a non-slip and sandy appearance. The dry floor areas have nylon carpet finish.

Bletchley Leisure Centre in the Midlands is located near an existing small town centre and the external appearance and covered corridor access is a contrast in character to the traditional buildings. The pool is housed in a translucent pyramid framed structure creating an oasis of tropical splendour within the indifferent English climate, reviving the aspirations of a 19th-century conservatory and 'Wintergarden'.

Similarly the Swindon Leisure Centre (Wiltshire), designed in 1970 to accommodate 3000 people, has the leisure pools under a fully glazed 45 m (147 ft) diameter dome. There is a non-rectangular pool with wave machine, a separate 'learners' pool, a separate bay with a multi-lane water slide and a diving pool set at a higher level and with underwater viewing windows. Apart from the pool area, flexibility is an important aspect in the basic planning of the centre, and a large flexible area is included for spectator sports (as wrestling), dances and pop concerts.

Crowtree, Sunderland (north-east England) provides an extensive leisure centre for family enjoyment with space for 3500 to 4500 people involved in the wide range of activities at any one time. The centre includes three leisure pools in a setting of sunshine, tropical planting and pipe music; water fun is provided by slides, cascades and

fountains. Modern leisure centres follow the tradition of the entertainment centres of the 19th century, with an appropriate emphasis on leisure activities and flexibility as opposed to the spectator promenading and ballroom functions of their predecessors. The scale of the buildings present the same problem of appearance as the modern hypermarkets. Where large community buildings are constructed in existing towns, there is a need for qualities of scale and accessibility that have been lost in the motorised American urban environment.

The design of multi-purpose leisure buildings present a range of problems concerned with flexible planning, lighting, heating, ventilation and noise. The ceiling heights must be related to the range of possible uses. There must be lighting not only for alternative uses, but for daytime and evening conditions. Multi-purpose buildings demand a wide band of heating and cooling conditions and allowance for intermittent use.

Planting may be included to enhance the interior ambience, but plants require localised humidity and special lighting is required for plant growth.

For some leisure pools, as the Saar Louis (West Germany), strict disciplines as to user hygiene has made it possible to replace chlorination with oxygenation providing a virtually odourless atmosphere.

Noise and acoustics present a major problem with the need for absorbents that can withstand high humidity and a chlorine atmosphere in pool areas, adequate sound-proofing between particular uses and suitable acoustic conditions in multi-use halls.

Swindon Leisure Centre (Gillinson Barnett and Partners, Architects)

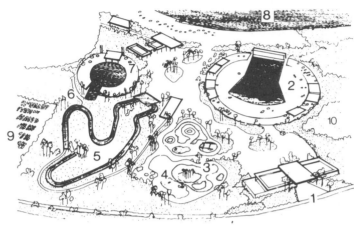

1	Main entrance	7 'Double Bubble' dive into a
2	'Ride the tide' wave pool		cushion of bubbles
3	'Squirt and splash'	8	Sailing boats, mini speed
4	'Spray'n play'		boats and paddle boats
5	'Zoom the flume' flume ride	9	parking
6	'Zip'n Dip' ride on cable trolley over	10	Kamitaze water slide
	the water, hanging from a grab rail		(location)

*Wet'n Wild, Florida: (above) diagrammatic layout;
(below) aerial view*

Water play

Water play represents the enjoyment of water activities apart from competitive sport. The obvious pleasure of slides, rides, splashing in breaking waves, surf, fountains, cascades, sprays, and chutes, have found expression in such devices as flume rides and wave machine constructions of water fun parks and leisure centres.

River Country, Walt Disney World, U.S.A.

River Country consists of a pool surrounded on two sides by rocks and trees, the third side consists of a sandy beach and the fourth side is open to the adjoining lake. The beach extends into a terrace area with cafe and changing rooms. The pool features a waterfall, slide, two interweaving flume rides, a multi-level flume ride (with water moving down through cascades and pools—participants ride on large inflated wheel tubes) and a cable ride that extends across the water.

The fibreglass channels of the flume rides weave and twist down through rocks and trees, and discharge into the pool. The movement of the water on the curves takes the ride up the sides of the channel. The water in the multi-level flume ride, consisting of simulated rock pools and cascades, swirls and circles so that skill is required to move from one level to another. Cascading water from above the course adds to the experience. The colours of the supporting structures, channels, platforms and walkways are mellow and subdued, and maintain the 'nature reserve' character of this section of the resort.

Wet 'n Wild, Florida, U.S.A.

Wet 'n Wild is a comprehensive water fun park with six principal activity areas. The park is located by a lake which provides for sailing, mini speedboats and paddleboats launched and landed on an extensive sandy beach. Two individual pools are surrounded

Jaya Jakarta: six lane slide (Biwater Treatment Co. Ltd.)

Jaya Jakarta: canal ride (Biwater Treatment Co. Ltd.)

by relaxation areas and the total park is landscaped with lawns and palm trees. One pool, partly fan-shaped provides waves and surf; another has both an overhead cable for trolleys on which visitors can ride over or drop into the water from a moving conveyor, and a bubble turbulent zone of water under a diving board that provides a cushioning effect to diving. Two extensive flume rides zigzag through landscaping to a discharge pool. There are two shallow pools (like the shallows at low tide), with sprays, pressure jets and play equipment and a third pool with a six-storey high, 300 ft waterslide.

Jaya Ancol Complex, Jakarta, Indonesia

In Indonesia, the Jaya Jakarta complex completed in 1974, consists of seven pools (flowing pool, diving pool, slide pool, canal ride, big pool, fountain pool and children's pool). The figure-of-eight flowing pool is over 300 m (984 ft) long, 8 m (26 ft) wide and 1·5 m (5 ft) deep and flows at a rate of 0·5 m/second, the flow being maintained by three booster stations around the perimeter. The pool is designed to accommodate 1500 people travelling on inflatable rafts.

The six-lane slide that discharges into the slide pool, is constructed of prefabricated glassfibre sections with steel supporting platforms. The slide is 37 m (88½ ft) long and 12 m (39 ft) at the highest point, and consists of four full-length and two half-length lanes. The canal ride is over 500 m (1640 ft) long and the speed of the water is maintained by booster stations. Pools on either side of the ride house tropical fish and marine life. Visitors move in gondolas along the canal through landscaped areas.

The wave pool at Jakarta, utilising a Biwave pneumatic wave machine (in which no moving parts are in contact with the water or the swimmers) produces waves approximately 1 m high at the deep end. The waves move a distance of 50 m (164 ft) to break on the shore beach at the shallow end of the pool.

The water park includes a Seaquarium and Aquarium with a large display pool for performances and four other tanks. The water treatment plant was designed and constructed by Biwater Group of Companies, who in collaboration with Imhof GMBH of West Germany, produce the Biwave-Imhof wave maker.

Wave machines and flume rides

The wave machine usually requires a combination of a rectangular and fan-shaped space, to discharge the waves in a satisfactory fashion on to the beach. At Rotherham Leisure Centre, the Biwave machine has been used in a free form pool with particular attention given to the design of the floor of the pool to

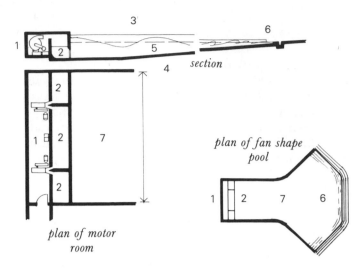

plan of motor room

Biwave wave machine, section and plan

1 motor room	5 static water line
2 forward chamber	6 'beach' end
3 top of wall	7 wave pool
4 8% slope	

give the waves direction. Normally, the Biwave wave machinery is accommodated in 200 mm concrete enclosed chambers with sealed access door to reduce fan noise. The water is purified and surface skimming takes place at the deep end of the pool. The machine is pneumatic and consists of fans forcing air in sequence into chambers at one end of the pool, producing either a multi-wave pattern or parallel wave forms. The key to interesting wave patterns is timing so that the wave is sustained and kept moving. This is done by electronic control by which the height and centres of wave patterns can be adjusted. The best application of Biwave requires a pool 35 m (115 ft) long to accommodate 700–900 mm (27–36 in) waves at 10–12 m (33–39 ft) centres. The pool should have a minimum depth at the deep end of 1·8 m (6 ft) and allowance must be made in the height of the sides of the pool for the maximum height of the wave at the deep end to zero at the beach end.

A flume ride consists of a sloping channel of descending water designed to provide a ride consisting of a solo journey with a final dive into a pool or in a 'boat' that plunges down into the spray of the run off trough.

Log flumes and hydro flumes are based on modular construction so that the units can be adapted to cost limits, siting and theme requirements. The components consist of lifts (for raising the boats), spillways, single and double down chutes, and loading stations. There are a variety of 'boat' designs and layouts. The compact log flume has an overall length of 607 ft, requires an area 100 ft × 300 ft (includes one lift and has a capacity of 960 persons/h).

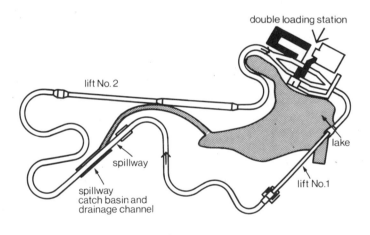

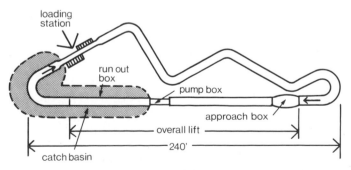

Flume ride: Basic layout consists of 600 ft journey with chute and lift. The water is contained within the fibreglass trough itself. Other layouts permit a longer ride with curves, spillway dips, lifts and chutes. (Arrow Development Company Inc. California, U.S.A.)

Dolphin pool, Marineworld, Florida

Aerial view Seaquarium, Miami, with peripheral monorail and geodesic dome to stadium (Photo: Press department, Miami Seaquarium, Florida)

Marine parks

Marineland, Florida, U.S.A.
Marineland, Florida, owned by Marineland Inc. was originally constructed in 1938 as an underwater motion picture studio. It is now a complete oceanside marine park. The organisation combines exhibition of marine animals, performances by whales and porpoises, and research facilities open to qualified investigators (provided by the Whitney Marine Research Laboratory). Marineland is a fully incorporated town (with mayor and council) with accommodation for education, visitors and tourists, a resort hotel, restaurant and marina.

The display and performance buildings consist of a large stadium for performances by both whales and porpoises, and a circular oceanarium for the permanent colony of porpoises. This can be viewed from two floors below water level and underwater corridors. A rectangular oceanarium provides a display of marine life and visitors can observe the ocean life through portholes and underwater passages. Marineland also includes Whitney Park showing a variety of marine animals.

Sea World, Florida, U.S.A.
The Sea World Marine Parks at Orlando Florida, San Diego and Aurora Ohio, are part of Harcourt Brace Jowanovich Inc., the American educational and publishing corporation.

The Sea World Marine Park in Florida covers about 50·5 ha (125 acres) and represents a 25 million dollar investment with 2 million dollars in landscape design. The entertainment concept consists of performing marine mammals in themed, scripted shows, and water ski shows. One admission price covers all shows, exhibits and parking and visitors select their own sequence of viewing shows.

The park consists of three stadia with pools for specific animal shows (penguin; whale and dolphin; seal and otter), and a large lagoon for water ski shows with both stadium seating and a floating stage.

There are also themed areas—a Japanese village and Hawaiian village, a fountain fantasy theatre, a sea aquarium, tide pool and a playground for children and comprehensive landscaping. The marine park lagoon has a 122 m (400 ft) sky tower which

Interior of sea aquarium, Seaworld

Fountain fantasy theatre, Seaworld. A display utilising water jets, projected film, lighting and sound

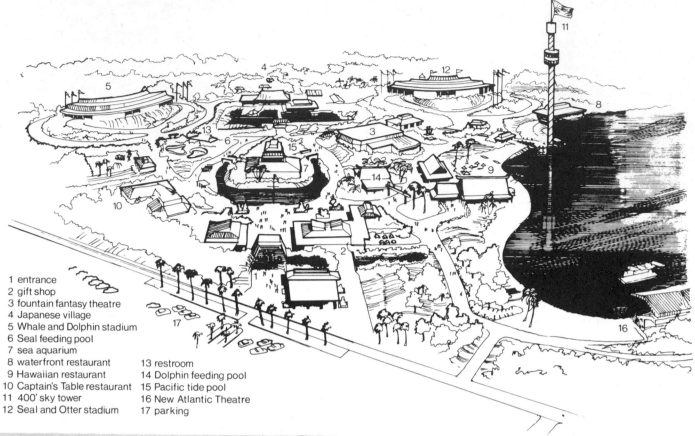

1 entrance
2 gift shop
3 fountain fantasy theatre
4 Japanese village
5 Whale and Dolphin stadium
6 Seal feeding pool
7 sea aquarium
8 waterfront restaurant
9 Hawaiian restaurant
10 Captain's Table restaurant
11 400' sky tower
12 Seal and Otter stadium
13 restroom
14 Dolphin feeding pool
15 Pacific tide pool
16 New Atlantic Theatre
17 parking

(*above*) *Layout of Seaworld*

(*centre*) *Performance pool and 'scenery', Dolphins at Seaworld*
(*Photo: Anthony Wylson*)

(*below*) *Themed transportation—Strollers, Seaworld*

serves as a landmark and as a viewing device for visitors to see over the whole park and surrounding countryside. There are four restaurants.

The stadium and pool sizes are 1-million gallon salt water performing pool with 3000 seats in an air-conditioned stadium for the killer whale show and dolphins and 61 850-gallon salt water seal and otter pool with an air-conditioned stadium with 3000 seats. Fibreglass is used in various aquaria where glass observation panels are included. Viewing panels are either plate or laminated tempered glass depending on the size of the pool or aquarium and the glass ranges in thickness from 15 mm to 50 mm ($\frac{3}{8}$ in to 2 in). The animal housing duplicates to the maximum extent possible, the natural habitats of the animals.

The Fountain Fantasy Theatre consists of water and a fountain synchronised to music, decorative lighting, projected slides and movies in a theatre atmosphere. It is a computer-controlled show and the seating provides for an audience of 900.

Japanese Garden, Seaworld: Pool with pearl diver display which includes observation panels below water line. (Photo: Anthony Wylson)

Sea Aquarium, Seaworld

The Sea Aquarium consists of a 150 000-gallon salt water aquarium, duplicating the life of a coral reef, with appropriate exotic fish life. This is constructed of reinforced concrete with a chlorinated rubber coating. In addition, there are wall and floor displays explaining the story of the sea and the ecological inter-relationships of its multitude of life forms. The Pacific Tide Pool provides an opportunity for visitors to see, touch and observe various seashore animals.

The majority of buildings are of steel frame construction with concrete block walls and sheet metal roofs. Tiered floors and the retaining walls to pools are of reinforced concrete.

The themed areas have sea associations. The Hawaiian village includes reconstruction of a 'trading post', 'outrigger canoes', waterfalls and includes a tropical garden with exotic bird life. The Japanese village provides an opportunity to show off Japanese traditional skills, Japanese style landscaping and pearl divers. The 62 m (400 ft) sky tower has a rotating and air-conditioned capsule with seating for sixty people.

Landscaping decisions have been made to allow for the free roaming animal population which, in respect to the bird population, is a particularly critical factor. Many of the birds breed and house themselves in planting selected expressly for those purposes. The expansive 16·8 ha (17 acres) lagoon is both part of the regional water system and provides land drainage within the park.

Overlooking the lagoon, there is a large 5000-seat stadium called the Atlantis Theatre. This provides viewing for water ski shows and with the combination of a 18 m × 15 m (60 ft × 50 ft) floating stage, it provides a theatre for stage entertainment. In addition to the stadium seating, there is space for overflow seating of 2000.

In 1977, Sea World in Florida drew 2·4 million visitors with a single day record of 21 161 visitors. Employment varies from 700 to 1000 persons depending upon the number of guests. Parking spaces are being increased from 2400 to 3400 and there are also nineteen bus-sized spaces for tour vehicles.

Landscaping at Seaworld for free roaming animal population and land drainage within park

Atlantis Theatre and floating stage, Seaworld.

Marineland, Los Angeles, animal pools (Photo: Anthony Wylson)

Hanna-Barbera Marineland, California, U.S.A.

The Hanna-Barbera Marineland, originally opened in 1954 and now a joint venture of the Taft Broadcasting Company and the Kroger Company, is situated on the Palos Verdes Peninsular, Los Angeles. The location provides panoramic views of the ocean, conveyed from the moment of entering Marineland, with views through the glass windbreaks of the entrance and from the sky tower adjacent. The change in ownership resulted in extensive re-landscaping with pools, tropical plants and a variety of trees including Italian cypress, coral, hibiscus, olive and palm. Courtyards within the park include touch tanks (where small tidal pool sea creatures can be picked up and closely examined), a sand pile, an amusement area for children, a cliff walk and picnic spots.

The variety of levels descending from the entrance to the rocky sea coast provides an interesting interplay of terraces and projecting structures. The highest terrace has the stadium with the most spectacular show, the killer whale. There are also stadia for performances by pilot whales, white-sided dolphins, bottle-nose dolphins and sea-lions. There are feeding pools and a pond for a variety of species of wildfowl. The stadia have light canopy roofs for protection against occasional showers and strong sun. Several pools were initially designed to be viewed from both above and through glass panels in the walls of the pools. The 'Passages beneath the Sea' aquarium, sponsored by the Encyclopaedia Britannica, displays rare sea life in thirty specially designed tanks.

Besides the main attractions, the park has a marine animal care centre with a clinic designed so that the public can view and ask questions regarding medical procedures. The immediate coast to the park includes Sea Lion Point, a rocky peninsular inhabited by a colony of wild sea-lions, providing an interesting point of contact with marine animals in their natural state.

Marineland, Los Angeles—Plan

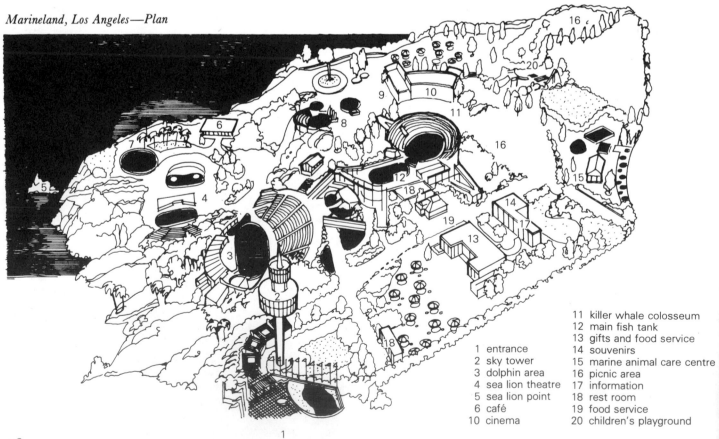

1 entrance
2 sky tower
3 dolphin area
4 sea lion theatre
5 sea lion point
6 café
10 cinema
11 killer whale colosseum
12 main fish tank
13 gifts and food service
14 souvenirs
15 marine animal care centre
16 picnic area
17 information
18 rest room
19 food service
20 children's playground

Marineland, Los Angeles
(above) general view

(right) animal pools (Photos: Anthony Wylson)

The terraces include a cafe, a seaside courtyard with a display of giant sea turtle, Japanese Koi fish and California Harbour Seals. Additional entertainment include larger-than-life Hanna-Barbera cartoon characters (Scooby Doo, Yogi Bear, Jabberjaw and Satchel), a roaming comedy band, macaws that perform on a mobile stage and a movie theatre. The initial signpost and information board arrangements are particularly clear. This is important for careful timing by visitors to synchronise the various performances within one visit. The park provides parking for 2600 cars and over the past few years had an average maximum of 12 000 visitors per day (1 million visitors per year).

6. Jeux d'eau et parcs marins—Résumé

L'eau a toujours joué un rôle important dans le domaine des loisirs, non seulement en tant que spectacle visuel, fontaines et cascades, ou pour créer une certaine ambiance, telles que les jetées avec attractions de nombreuses stations balnéaires d'Angleterre, mais aussi en tant que moyen de divertissement et de loisirs. Il existe des jardins d'eau avec fontaines, ruisselets, bassins, gorges, chutes d'eau, machines à faire les vagues et cascades, et les nouveaux centres de loisirs sont également équipés pour le sport. Les parcs marins de Californie et de Floride rapprochent l'intérêt scientifique et éducatif des possibilités de divertissement des animaux marins, tout cela dans un contexte de loirirs. Les exemples sont nombreux: Marineland et Seaworld en Floride, et Hanna-Barbara Marineland à Los Angeles.

6. Wasserspiele und Wasserparks—Zusammenfassung

Wasser hat von jeher eine bedeutende Rolle in der Freizeitsgestaltung gespielt, nicht nur durch seinen visuellen Einsatz in Form von Fontänen und Kaskaden oder um einen gewissen Hintergrund an der See in Form von Piers zu schaffen, sondern auch als Mittel zur Erholung und Entspannung. In Wassergärten werden Springbrunnen, Spritzer, Teiche, schwimmende Balken, Rutschen, Wellenmaschinen und Wasserfälle benutzt, und in den neuen Freizeitszentren gibt es Möglichkeiten zum Wassersport. Die Marineparks von Kalifornien und Florida vereinen wissenschaftliche und Bildungsinteressen mit dem Vergnügen durch Einsatz von Meerestieren zur Unterhaltung. Beispiele sind Marineland, Florida, USA, Seaworld, Florida, Hanna-Barbera Marineland, Los Angeles.

٦ ـ الألعاب المائية والحدائق البحرية ـ موجز

قامت المياه دائما بلعب دور مهم في وسائل الترفيه في وقت الفراغ ، ليس فقط باستعمالها كوسيلة مرئية من خلال النافورات والشلالات أو لخلق الجو المحيط مثل الأرصفة الممتدة في البحر في مصايف انجلترا ، بل وأيضا كوسيلة للمتعة ونشاطات الاستجمام . توجـد حدائق مائية تستخدم النافورات والبخاخات والبرك وركوب الزوارق على القنوات الصغيرة والانابيب المائية وآلات خلق الأمواج والشلالات . وتهيىء مراكز الاستجمام الجديدة التسهيلات لرياضات الاستجمام . تجمع الحدائق البحرية في كاليفورنيا وفلوريدا المتعة العلمية والتربوية مع قدرات الحيوانات المائية على الترفيه ، وكـل ذلك داخل نطاق بيئة الاستجمام . الأمثلة : مارينلاند في فلوريدا بالولايات المتحدة ، وسي وورلد في فلوريدا وهانا باربيرا مارينلاند في لوس انجلوس .

Chapter 7

Circuses

The modern circus has its origins in the skilled cavalry riding of the 18th century. The pleasure gardens of London gave an opportunity for trick riders to show their skills to an audience, and in 1768 Philip Astley, a former sergeant-major, established a circus routine. He discovered that, when riding in a circle, centrifugal force helped him keep his balance when he was standing on the horse's back.

A year later Astley found it an advantage to move his circus ring near to the Surrey end of Westminster Bridge and constructed a covered stand for spectators. The establishment was called the Royal Grove. The name 'circus' was first adopted for the 'Royal Circus', a rival enterprise started by Charles Hughes, one of Astley's horsemen. At the same time the traditional fairs were in a decline and showmen were looking for new outlets in which to provide their entertainment. They found that the performances of rope dancers, jugglers and acrobats were appreciated by the ringside audiences.

In London the circus idea generated from this situation. In France, Astley established a circus where the 13 m (42 ft) diameter ring was adapted to become a standard size. Further circuses were set up in European centres. Charles Hughes introduced the circus to Russia at the Royal Palace at St Petersburg, and another Englishman introduced the idea to America opening circuses in Philadelphia and New York. Hughes attempted to combine theatre and stage putting a stage on the side of the ring and, although there is a difference between the illusion of the stage and the actuality of circus, the stage and circus format grew in popularity.

By the end of the 18th century, circuses had spread throughout Europe and America and performances were given in both permanent and semi-permanent buildings. Several of the buildings were destroyed by fire, which was also the fate of many theatres of the day. Theatres, such as the Theatre Royal, Dublin would be adapted for horse track races, extending the stage into a circuit at the side of the stalls and at the base of the tiered seating. Permanent circus buildings were gradually compromised by the requirements of the theatrical spectacle and drama. The tiers of encircling seats were broken to accommodate a proscenium and stage, and equestrian dramas became popular.

In London, permanent circus buildings included Astley's amphitheatre, ultimately run by Sanger's and demolished in 1893; Olympia; Covent Garden, which staged regular circus acts in the 1880s and 1890s; the Westminster Aquarium; Crystal Palace, and Hengler's (now the London Palladium) off Oxford Street, the Holborn Amphitheatre and the London Hippodrome. By the early 19th century, travelling showmen were using 'tent' accommodation and the 'Big top' tent had been established in America by 1826.

During the early years, circuses were dominated by the horse and zoological acts gradually became popular. Menageries of wild animals were included as the display of the performing animals could be seen to provide additional revenue. The flying trapeze was invented in 1859 and acrobats became an important part of the circus routine. Technical developments of the mid-19th century improved circus training and management, and the image was further popularised by processions through the host town advertising the arrival of the circus. In Britain a decline in interest in the 1920s was arrested by the establishment of Bertram Mills International Circus at Olympia, and in the 1950s Tom Arnold's Circus achieved similar importance at Harringay.

In America, the circus developed on a different scale. The use of railroad transportation permitted large equipment and the enterprises grew in size through amalgamation. Not only were there tents holding 10 000 spectators, but the central 13 m (42 ft) ring would be surrounded by additional rings and stages so that two or more acts could take place at one time.

The Ringling Brothers, Barnum & Baileys 'Greatest Show on Earth' had one tent with three rings and five stages, all surrounded by a hippodrome track. The arrangement ruled out single acts and had to include spectacular processions and aerial ballet for effect.

Modern circus entertainment

Permanent buildings
In Europe, few purpose-built circuses have been constructed and even fewer remain. There were two circuses in Blackpool but only the Tower Circus remains.

The Tower Circus seats 1782 persons and is located at ground level within the space formed by the four columns of the tower structure. It is a simple circular arena with the entrances on opposite sides of the ring. The orchestra gallery is over one entrance and a small seating gallery over the second. There is a steeply raked seating at balcony level, and the four tower columns form major features within the circus space with arabesque pendentive-type ornamentation. A private box extends from one column, and the lighting-sound control console extends from another column. The auditorium space is compact, similar to theatre in-the-round, with stage machinery that can lower the arena floor to provide a circular pool. This is used to effect with performances incorporating lighting effects and fountains. Like the Tower Ballroom, the decor provides an opulent interior as a background to the

(right) Tower Blackpool: Pendentive, balcony seating, box and ringside seating

(below) Tower Blackpool: Circus ring (Photos: Anthony Wylson)

entertainment. Historic interiors that provide a context in which the entertainment ambience is part of the decor, require special lighting effects and stage lighting installations that integrate with the ceiling features.

The Circus in Copenhagen originally built in 1885 but reconstructed after a fire in 1914 and built as a multi-use arena continues to provide circus entertainment. In this case, although the building is circular, the ring is not centrally placed, but extends from a proscenium, which provides access for acts. Behind the proscenium, there is an extensive saddlewalk, preparation area, stage and a fly tower over.

The orchestra gallery is over the proscenium and there is a pool under the circus ring for use for aquatic displays.

Circus entertainment is not limited to the conventional ring. The New London Theatre, with an auditorium that can be arranged as an arena stage, has been used for circus and the animals were accommodated in caravans on an open building site nearby. Acts normally associated with the circus continue to find a place in the Revue Theatres of

Paris and Las Vegas, and the Hotel Casino Circus Circus provides continuous entertainment over the gaming areas.

'Circus World'

The 'Circus World' park Barnum City, Florida, presents circus entertainment in a wide context. Not only is the conventional show presented on a broad stage as opposed to a circus ring, but the components of circus entertainment are individually presented in a theme park.

The Ringling Bros and Barnum & Bailey Circus World started in 1973 with a preview centre and the 60-acre circus theme park was opened in 1976. The park has several performances of the individual shows within one day, and visitors select the order in which to see the entertainment. The features include a circus show in the 1500-seat Day Theatre; a

Benneweis Circus, Copenhagen: Exterior (Photo: Anthony Wylson)

Theatre of Illusions presenting a magic and illusion show; a Circus Cinema located in a historic railroad car originally used for transporting the Ringling Bros circus; an Imax production using a 68 ft by 91 ft screen; participation circus where visitors are invited to join in with the experts on the high wire, flying trapeze, tight rope and trampoline; 'Clown-a-Lot', a circus themed play area for children; roller coaster rides; a 'Circus World's Own Heritage' exhibition, and a menagerie. In addition there is the traditional carousel, gift shop, restaurants, a clown make-up parlour, and the in-park parades, elephant rides and ad-lib clowns.

Benneweis Circus, Copenhagen: Ring and 'proscenium' (Photo: Anthony Wylson)

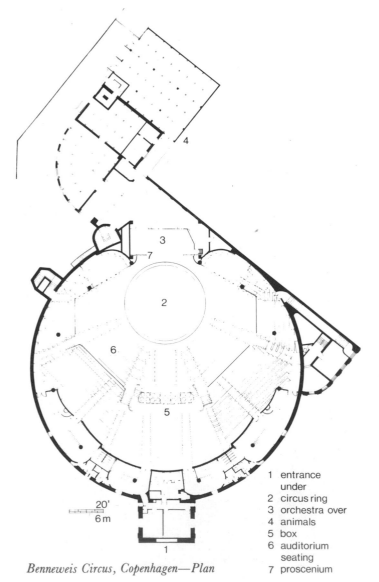

1 entrance under
2 circus ring
3 orchestra over
4 animals
5 box
6 auditorium seating
7 proscenium

Benneweis Circus, Copenhagen—Plan

Benneweis Circus, Copenhagen: Ring surround (Photo: Anthony Wylson)

The theme park is being extended to provide a further roller coaster with a 1067 m (3500 ft) run and a 29 m (95 ft) climb, a rehearsal ring and special theatre where visitors can see animals in training, trapeze artists at work and other production activities. The extended park will cover 33 ha (80 acres). The circus theme park opens every aspect of the circus to the visitor and provides a historic and technical record in exhibitions and cine performances.

Circus tradition

As entertainment, circus remains a spectacle with a display of skill, agility, strength, ingenuity and management of animals, and slapstick comedy as a release. The entertainment does not depend on language but has a direct appeal in the quality and glitter of the performance. Although acts associated with the circus continue to find a place in the Revue Theatres of Paris and Las Vegas there is a problem of schooling and training new talent.

In Britain the circus, like the cinema, has lost much of its family audience to television. Some circuses are able to gain some advantage by appearing on television, and have the advantage of being mobile so that they can move to the crowds. At the same time they gain no government financial support or subsidy. Traditional circus skills have been passed down through families but this is an unreliable way to gain continuity. Some countries

Circus World. Menagerie where children can feed, photograph and pamper the animals

have maintained prestige in circus entertainment by establishing circus schools to encourage young talent. Such a facility in Britain is being canvassed by several circus companies, and would provide a centre to attract and train enthusiasts. It could also provide circus entertainment with a point of contact to establish standards that will assist in both regaining the interest of the public and restoring circus as an accepted form of popular entertainment.

A British company with concern for circus revival is Gerry Cottle's. The company not only provides the accommodation for the annual Circus World Championships, but has also provided a 'flying

Circus World. Participation Circus in which visitors experience high wire, trapeze and trampoline

Circus' for three seasons in the Middle East and Iran. Gerry Cottle's Circus has traditional circus format with modern equipment. The transporters are modified large freight lorries, providing accommodation for the managers and performers, generators, offices, and transportation for animals and equipment. These vehicles form a protective circle for the big tent and an area on the opposite side from the public entrance, to prepare the acts before they move into the ring. The tent manufactured in

Italy is normally 57 m × 44 m (187 ft × 145 ft) and seating 3000 but can be extended to 70 m × 44 m (230 ft × 145 ft) to seat 6000. It is constructed of fireproof plastic supported by eight masts and thirty-eight quarter poles. Arena lighting is located on the masts and there is overhead lighting, spotlights and effects lighting. Heating is provided by hot air fan heaters. There is external display illumination suspended above the roof of the tent. It takes 5–6 hours to set up and 2 hours to dismantle it.

Gerry Cottle's Circus
(above) High wire performance and band platform at one end of 'Big Top'
(below) Lion cage performance set up as second ring (Photos: Anthony Wylson)

7. Les cirques—Résumé

Le cirque a connu un intérêt accru au cours des dernières décades et il est de tradition que ce spectacle attire toute la famille. Les quelques cirques permanents restants attirent plus particulièrement les touristes et le parc de Floride sur le thème du cirque, Circus World, offre sur le même emplacement, différents aspects du spectacle du cirque. Parmi d'autres établissements permanents, citons: le Tower Circus à Blackpool, Angleterre, le Cirque Bennewers `a Copenhague. Il exite, aujourd'hui, un très petit nombre de cirques ambulants, dont le Gerry Cattle.

7. Der Zirkus—Zusammenfassung

In den letzten Jahrzehnten ist das Interesse am Zirkus gestiegen, Jedoch beruht diese Familienunterhaltung auch weiterhin auf Tradition. Dauernd erstellte Zirkusgebäude sind eine Touristenattraktion, und der mit dem Thema 'Circus World' in Florida bestehende Park besitzt viele Aspekte der Zirkusunterhaltung auf einem großen Gelände. Beispiele sind der Tower Circus, Blackpool, England, Bennewers Circus, Kopenhagen, Dänemark, Circus World, Florida, USA. Heute gibt es nur noch einige wenige fahrende Zirkusunternehmen, ein Beispiel ist Gerry Cattle.

٧ ـ السيرك ـ موجز

لقد تزايد الاهتمام بالسيرك بدرجة كبيرة في الحقبة الماضية ، ولكن السيرك التقليدي مازال يزود الترفيه للعائلات . تعتبر مباني السيرك الباقية الان من المعالم التى تجتذب السياح ، وتنقل لنا حديقة «عالم السيرك» في فلوريدا كثيرا من نواحي السيرك الترفيهية في ساحة كبيرة واحدة. الأمثلة : سيرك البرج في بلاكبول بانجلترا ـ سيرك بنيورز في كوبنهاجن بالدانمرك ـ عالم السيرك في فلوريدا بالولايات المتحدة الأمريكية . ولم يبق اليوم غير عدد قليل من السيرك المتنقل مثل سيرك «جيري كاتلز» .

Chapter 8

Stage entertainment

The basis of stage entertainment consists of providing a performance before an audience and relating audience to performance and also relating audience to individual spectator. This requires both an analysis of the type of performance and its requirements (with all the services, access and ancillary accommodation necessary) and an analysis of the standards and amenities required by the audience, and then relating these in the most effective way.

It is only possible here to refer to the main issues of design and to building types that represent established categories of stage entertainment. However, as stage design represents a major part of leisure entertainment, these aspects are of particular importance.

Over the last hundred years the theatre has been mainly based on the proscenium 'frame' stage with an auditorium incorporating balcony and boxes. This reflected the stratas within society and separated actor from audience. Furthermore, in the case of opera and some musicals, where the conductor must be seen by both singers and musicians, the orchestra pit itself comes between audience and stage. The early attempts to omit the circle merely spread the audience farther from the stage.

Following the 1914–18 war, there were experiments in arena theatre (*theatre en rond*) to bring performer and audience closer. There was also a tendency to increase the stage width to provide additional performance space. This went so far as to having the audience on a circular raked platform that could be rotated to each set, allowing the play to proceed from scene to scene without intervals. The desire to achieve a close contact between audience and performers has led to new forms in stage layout, and electro-acoustic solutions for music to avoid the intrusion of an orchestra.

The main categories of stage entertainment range from the traditional cultural interests of grand opera, ballet, legitimate drama (repertoire and repertory), and orchestral concerts, to popular entertainment of vaudeville, revue musicals, dance and cabaret. Whereas, in the first case the acoustics and viewing standards enjoyed by the audience are critical to the appreciation of the performance and the seating is directed towards the stage, the other extreme gives greater importance to the general atmosphere, mood and overall impression of the performance. In the latter, the seating layout may also have to provide an opportunity both for socialising by the audience and the service of food and drinks into the auditorium. Space may be required in which the audience can dance, before or after the show.

Promoters and trends

The development of new theatres since 1945 has been particular to various countries. The reconstruction in West Germany following the 1939–45 war and the independence of city states has led to theatre building being largely a provincial matter and the town theatre has remained one of mixed activity and repertory. German safety regulations encourage the proscenium layout with orchestra pit and safety curtains.

In France, to reduce the monopoly of Paris, substantial theatres have been built in the Provinces such as the Maison de la Culture at Grenoble, Amiens and Rennes, each with two theatres of different formats. Furthermore, Paris is synonymous with cabaret and several restaurant theatres (night spots) as the Lido and the Jardin Champs-Élysées, have been developed utilising complex stage machinery and effects.

In the UK, non-profitmaking theatres have been built mainly outside London. Local authorities have provided accommodation for touring companies and repertory companies both by taking over failing commercial theatres and by building new ones. Purpose-built theatres have been incorporated in the university building programme. The popularity of variety and 'pop' music has been reflected in the development of supper clubs and theatre restaurants.

In America, the new theatres have appeared in large municipal complexes. Centres for the performing arts, and multi-purpose theatres have been constructed as part of colleges and universities. The stage entertainment side is also represented by the sophisticated resort hotel 'showrooms' for star performances and musical spectacular.

Design considerations

It cannot be denied that stage entertainment can thrive in unfavourable conditions as fringe theatre and, in the case of the successful Paris Crazy Horse Saloon, the stage ceiling is so low that an energetic 'cabriole' could be fatal. Nevertheless the type of production and design policy provide the basis to the performance/audience relationship. Each type has distinct space requirements and presentation standards. The maximum distance of audience from performer is critical, with different criteria where facial expression must be appreciated as opposed to the appreciation of operatic gestures or the pattern of dance movement.

There is the relationship of the primary function of the stage and seating area. A proscenium provides a definitive frame for the performance within the context of scenery and many theatres today are designed with an adjustable proscenium. However, the audience has not only been democratised to replace privileged social display in private boxes by audience display in tiered seating, but a closer relationship between audience and performer has questioned the value of a proscenium. This is evident in the open stage layout (where stage and audience are in one space) and to a lesser extent, by steps, ramps and aprons additional to the conventional stage.

Simultaneous settings or changes of scenery in view of the audience, but integrated with the performance, draw the audience into the mechanics of production. This is taken further in the case of the television studio audience who become not only an integral part of the production providing the response element necessary for comedy, but the audience is televised as part of the presentation.

The other trend is towards realism and spectacular effects that can be provided by electro-mechanical devices, audio and lighting equipment, projection equipment and modern techniques. These can

provide an authentic context for the performance within the proscenium frame.

In planning terms, there are many alternative arrangements for stage and audience. It may be appropriate to have the stage extending into the audience (a thrust or three-sided stage), the audience partly or completely encircling the stage (theatre in the round) or the performance areas partly or completely encircling the audience. Each is suitable to a particular form of production and has inherent advantages and disadvantages to performer and spectator.

An assessment must also be made of the context of the performance in terms of handling scenery by stage equipment, the rate of set changes and the space for the preparation and storage of scenery and 'props'. If an orchestra is involved, the location of the orchestra in relation to stage and audience must be determined. Audio and lighting equipment and the location of control consoles and projection rooms are also important to the basic layout.

Ancillary to the stage are the requirements of the performers (access, dressing rooms, changing rooms, toilets, showers, green room, equipment locker rooms and waiting spaces). The stage hands also require locker rooms and a first-aid room. The theatre management require an office. The scenery and properties require unloading areas, handling, fabrication and storage. There are costumes to be unloaded, handled, repaired and stored. There may be animals to house, to feed and to clean out.

The servicing of the stage area with mechanical devices to provide variety in the shape and levels of the stage, quick set changes and audio-sound equipment that extends into the auditorium, can involve extensive additional space above, behind and at the sides of the stage. Likewise, a flexible auditorium format or interchangeable auditorium/performance areas will require the mechanical or manual movement of floor levels, enclosing walls and ceiling panels. Electro-mechanical techniques have opened new possibilities in flexibility of the layout.

There are also important regulations on fire precautions and means of escape that relate to exit ways, separation of stage from auditorium, materials used in construction, finishes and fire appliances.

Extensive stage production costs will be reflected in the standard of accommodation and facilities for the audience, although there are situations where the stage performance is subsidised to provide an attraction to another commercial use (such as resort accommodation) or subsidised as a social amenity. The shape of the seating area and the auditorium will be governed by acoustic considerations, optimum reverberation factors, distance of audience from performers, sight lines, statutory requirements for public safety, type of seating or standing for the audience, ancillary services brought into the auditorium and flexibility of use.

Furthermore, for the spectator, from the moment of arrival on the pavement near the theatre his route to his seat in the auditorium must be clear and attractive. The pavement canopy (marquee), the lobby, foyer, waiting area, cloakrooms, lounge, bar, toilet accommodation, sale kiosk are significant.

Performance area

The stage area where the performance takes place must develop from the nature of the performance or range of performances anticipated. The producer and artist require the facilities so that they can arouse from the audience a maximum of appreciation. The format of proscenium, open stage, arena or the scope to adopt of any one of these is a basic decision.

The proscenium provides a limited, unified, fixed frame for the pictorial composition of the performers who work to a limited orientation towards the audience. The whole audience will enjoy a similar relationship of performers to scenery, but the extent to which the seating capacity can be extended is limited by sight-lines from the seats at the side. The conventional form suited to most drama and musical performances is the proscenium with orchestra pit convertible to an extended forestage or extended stalls.

The open stage, in which the audience is in the same space as the performers, places the performers in a close relationship with the audience but can create problems with scenery and exits. This format is particularly applicable to vaudeville and revue where direct relationship between performer and audience is important.

The arena, or theatre in the round, which seats the maximum audience in the minimum space also draws performer and audience into a close relationship. The form limits the use of scenery and the rake of seating must be steep to avoid the audience having the visibility of one performer obscured by another.

The extended stage in which the performance area extends around the audience in the form of side stages or multi-prosceniums can reduce changes of scenery by having all the sets fixed and moving the action from set to set. Revolving the audience area towards the action has been adopted. Again for the musical spectacular the use of an extended stage can provide a greater breadth of performance.

The multi-form stage, in which two or more forms can be accommodated in one auditorium, provides an interesting design problem. The application of electro-mechanical techniques to the movement of parts of the theatre makes physical alteration of stage and audience areas a quick process but expensive in capital costs. Thus in many recent projects there is a combination of two or more auditoria, one based on proscenium and one adaptable to the arena or open stage.

Ancillary requirements

The space required for the unloading, the preparation and the storage of scenery will depend upon the type of performance. A musical revue may continue for a long season and the stage equipment necessary for quick set changes may provide the necessary storage space. Thus only maintenance space and storage for replacements would be required.

A repertory company may require to construct scenery for regular changes in programmes whereas a repertoire theatre would require storage space for scenery relative to their repertoire of plays. The 'long run' West End theatre would require space only for the current show, whereas the experimental or workshop theatre would require the space for developing ideas.

The dressing room arrangement will also depend upon the type of performance. 'Star' performers will expect a high standard of accommodation with sitting room, dressing area with shower and toilet *en suite*. There would be further male and female dressing rooms with adequate space for costume trolleys. If an orchestra is involved, there will be a conductor's room, musicians' rooms and changing rooms. Serving these areas there would be showers, toilets, a musical instrument store, wardrobe room, costume store, repairs and laundry. The performance area may be reproduced in size in a rehearsal room which should be accessible from the scenery dock. The rehearsal room is most likely to be used for other purposes, and if it is used as an experimental theatre, it requires to be accessible from the public areas.

The movement of scenery to achieve quick changes of stage sets is a primary consideration. The alternatives include, lifting scenery above the stage, moving into spaces at the side of the stage, or into the voids below the stage. The first requires a fly tower of adequate height to raise scenery, manually or mechanically, by pulleys secured to a grid. In some cases the scenery is stored in two levels requiring additional height to the tower. Horizontal movement requires manhandling, rolling on wagons or trolleys or revolving the supporting platform. If the space under the stage is used, a lift is required. This can be

Scenery fly tower and grid, Churchill Theatre, Bromley (Aneurin John, Borough Architect) (Photo: Anthony Wylson)

worked in conjunction with additional basement space so that several wagons or trolleys can be stored and rolled on to the lift. Space must be allowed for unloading the stage set not required.

The rear of the stage is masked by a Cyclorama which can be hoisted or rolled if constructed of lightweight materials, or can be the solid construction of the rear wall. In the latter case, provision must be made to allow for circulation by actors and staff at the rear of the stage.

Variety in production can be provided by stage lifts, traps, revolves, discs and, in some cases, additional equipment within the auditorium. A trend in spectacular revues brings the performance into the auditorium with a *passerelle* (suspended bridge) extending across the auditorium, discs suspended from the ceiling, or mechanical devices to provide performance space within the side walls of the auditorium.

In the case of orchestral use of the stage, a stepped platform would be provided for musicians and chorus, and the layout should give an emphasis to the width as presented to the audience. The musicians require to hear each other, and such conditions can be achieved by an enclosure around three sides of the orchestra.

Scenery fly tower and gallery to grid. Churchill Theatre, Bromley (Photo: Anthony Wylson)

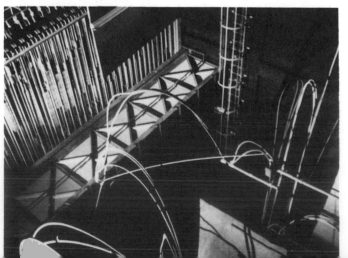

Safety curtain and fire precautions

As the scenery and 'props' constitute a significant fire hazard, the stage requires a safety curtain to prevent any spread of fire or the escape of fumes or smoke into the auditorium from the stage, for a period sufficient to enable all the members of the audience to leave. An additional precaution is provided through automatic opening vents in the ceiling of the tower or over the stage to draw out heat and smoke away from the audience.

A drencher system is also applied to the safety curtain to avoid it buckling under excessive heat. Automatic sprinklers would be required all over the stage and attention must also be given to escape routes from the stage, grid, flys and basement for actors and staff in case of fire. For the open stage, all scenery and properties must be non-combustible or of low flammability and there are additional restrictions regarding stage effects.

Orchestra

The location of the orchestra is traditionally between stage and audience in order that the conductor can direct both the orchestra and singers. This also locates the sound on the principal axis of the performance. If the pit extends too far under the stage, the use of this area for stage production is limited. The provision of a lift can permit alternative uses for the pit space such as an apron stage or extended floor to the auditorium. Furthermore, if the lift pit area is divided into several sections, there is greater flexibility in the alternative uses. The orchestra pit would accommodate, on average, twenty players although in the case of Grand Opera there could be a hundred musicians.

In the case of orchestras for musical revues, there are alternative locations to avoid a separation between audience and performance. In some of the musical spectacular shows of Las Vegas and Paris, the orchestra is located on a balcony at one side of the proscenium. With modern techniques of electronic control of sound and close-circuit television, the orchestra can be located away from the stage when the immediate inter-relation of orchestra, performers and conductor is not essential.

Television coverage

It may be necessary to consider the need for television coverage of the stage performance in addition to the theatre audience. TV technical equipment is bulky and requires manoeuvring space at stage level both across the front of the performance area and towards and away from the stage on a centre axis. The latter would require a narrow centralised platform extending into the seating area.

Although some filming can be covered by 'Zoom' cameras at the rear of the auditorium, a quality picture requires close position for the cameras. There could be an element of conflict between audience and cameras, but the intrusion can be reduced by careful planning conveying the significance to the theatre audience of the addition of a more extensive television audience.

The provision of an extended narrow thrust stage can provide a working platform for cameras. The layout at the Empire Television Theatre in Paris has extended wings and side galleries to provide a variety of camera positions.

Stage lighting and sound equipment

Stage lighting and sound equipment requires expert advice. In principle it must be possible for any part of the stage to be lit from several different angles. The main location of lighting is from overhead within stage and auditorium ceilings, from slots at the sides of the auditorium and stage, and less frequently from footlights. The overhead lighting will be supported on bars to project down to the performance area at approximately 45° and boom support from the side lighting positions. In the case of a television theatre the lighting grid is more elaborate and will extend over the stage and part of the auditorium.

The control of the performance will be by the stage manager at the side of the stage, and the control of lighting and sound will be from a control room at the rear of the auditorium. Provision should be made for follow spots suitably positioned to cover the stage area. In many theatres, a continuous gallery at the rear of the auditorium provides a flexible control and lighting facility. In some cases, but creating an obtrusive element, a console is located in a central position within the auditorium so that the controller can be aware of the conditions within the auditorium.

Seating area

The seating area for the audience will be considered with regard to viewing the performance. Viewing is most comfortable if the spectator is directed towards the performance. This can be achieved by curving the rows of seats or by a faceted layout.

The sightlines can be worked out graphically by computer or illustromat to achieve a clear view for each spectator taking an average seated eye level of 1.120 m. Particular attention should be given to the extent of the stage floor to be seen and the height of the proscenium opening in relation to the rearmost seats, if there is a balcony. In an auditorium where spectators stand to view the entertainment, an

Scenery descending to basement on stage lift. Churchill Theatre, Bromley (Photo: Anthony Wylson)

adequate rake can assist to allow for a diversity of eye levels.

The seating layout must not only provide satisfactory sightlines and comfortable condition for the spectator, but must comply with local authority regulations regarding the distance of a seat from gangways and exits, the space between rows and the materials used in the construction of seats and finishes. Space between seats, gangways and exitways must provide the required comprehensive, unobstructed and protected routes for escape in case of fire.

Whereas in Britain the width of rows is limited to a maximum distance to the aisle, the continental seating extends this principle and permits seating to extend between side aisles but with seatways increased proportionally. This has the effect of reducing the number of aisles but also reduces the number of rows. It locates the audience in the centre section of the auditorium with adequate legroom. Seats are best staggered and a centre aisle is to be avoided. The maximum gradient for an aisle without steps within British standards is 1:10, and the maximum slope of stepped seating is 35°.

The layout of the seating must also be relative to the stage format but will also take into account viewing angles if a proscenium is adopted. The size of the proscenium will be relative to the production. With drama and revue the average proscenium is

Stage lighting from ceiling of auditorium. Churchill Theatre Bromley (Photo: Anthony Wylson)

Crucible Theatre, Sheffield; entrance foyer (Photo: John Donat)

9–10·5 m (30–35 ft); for musical comedy the average is 12 m (40 ft); opera has an average of 18 m (92 ft) with a maximum of 24 m (79 ft). The section and enclosing surfaces will be profiled to permit good sightlines and also acoustic qualities necessary for the production. Whereas the ideal theatre will have provision for controlling reverberation, the acoustic properties of various uses (orchestra, soloist, performer or drama) will provide a wide range of design criteria. The surface finishes will be considered in the context of decor, maintenance, fire regulations and acoustic qualities.

Theatre-restaurant seating

The seating layout for the theatre restaurant or hotel showroom, supper club or night club, where food and drink is served prior to the performance, presents additional planning problems. If tables radiate from the stage, the audience have the problem of adjusting from sitting and facing at right angles to the stage, to positions orientated to the stage. If the tables are short, and there is adequate rake or stepping, the reshuffle can provide adequate sightlines. Swivel chairs can provide some assistance if the movement is silent. Booth seating consisting of half-circles of seating directed towards the stage provides a better compromise.

If tables are arranged radiating from the stage, the longer tables will be nearer the stage, with shorter tables or booth seating in a stepped layout towards the rear of the auditorium. This arrangement can provide a flat area in front of the stage which can also be used for dancing. A steep rake to the seating layout to provide a view of the dance pattern would be advantageous for musical cabaret. However, the musical spectacular may include a variety of levels on the stage to achieve effect and better visibility of the show for the audience.

Particular attention must be given to the service of drinks and food to the 'multi-level restaurant'. Usually time for clearing and serving drinks is limited.

The decor and lighting change from restaurant to theatre is visually important to achieve the 'evening out' or night club ambience and devices are used (such as change in lighting effects and adjustment in floor levels) to facilitate the change. Thus the interior design will both reflect the organisation of the evening and provide a sympathetic ambience for each activity. This is successfully done at the Paris Lido where the restaurant/ballroom character is physically transformed into a cabaret restaurant by lighting effects and adjustable floor levels.

Acoustics

The acoustic consideration of the auditorium must take into account the shape of the auditorium, the level of background noise, the reverberation time and the elimination of echo. The enclosing surfaces should avoid concave shapes and provide diffusion of sound. Deep balcony overhangs are to be avoided.

Extraneous noise must be kept out by the structure of the building and by sound locks formed by foyer and lobby. Particular attention should be given to avoid the transference of internal mechanical noise, vibration or noisy uses adjoining the auditorium.

Reverberation time is the length of time at which a sound dies within the auditorium and is affected by the absorption quality of surfaces within the auditorium. Generally the period of reverberation should be short for clarity of speech, longer for music and more extended for choral music. The acoustic conditions for these alternative uses are considerably different and an auditorium would require a major change in the acoustic qualities of the auditorium (as the acoustic laboratory of the Pompidou Centre in Paris), or electronic control of reverberation to achieve satisfactory audio conditions for multi-use.

Echo is caused by time lag between sound heard by a direct path and the same sound heard by a secondary reflected path. Avoidance of echo requires careful consideration of absorptive surfaces at the rear of the auditorium and the avoidance of surfaces that concentrate or converge sound patterns. A flutter echo heard as a metallic ringing sound (due to regular reflection between two paralleled surfaces) is likely to be created if the performance is between two parallel surfaces.

Furthermore, for orchestral music, the diffusion of sound by the profile of the ceiling is desirable, and a varied treatment of side walls can avoid distortion of the sound source. Early reflectors are important to give clarity and should be balanced with dispersive surfaces, these can assist actors in an up-stage position where the projection of the actor's voice is reduced by the proscenium. However, the plan and section of the auditorium have acoustic significance beyond the scope of this chapter, and expert advice should be sought at the early design stages.

Suggested optimum mid-frequency (500 hz) reverberation times for some auditoria (Sound Research Laboratories Limited, Sudbury, Suffolk, England)

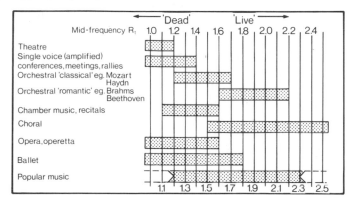

Recommended range of mid-frequency reverberation time values for different uses of medium size multi-purpose auditoria (Sound Research Laboratories Limited, Sudbury, Suffolk, England)

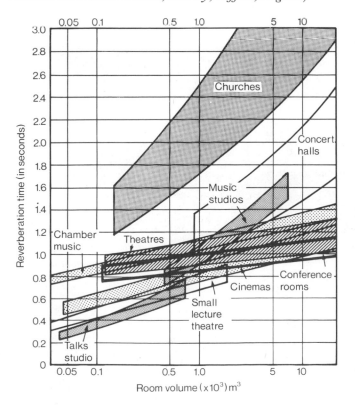

Front of house

The foyer is a particularly important area serving as a waiting space, meeting place and as a circulation area. It distributes audience from entrance foyer to auditorium. The foyer can also check extraneous noise. It may include or provide access to a bar, coffee bar, sales kiosk, exhibition space, restaurant, management, cloakroom and toilets. Many traditional English theatres combine the foyer space with the lobby and access to booking office windows. This can cause congestion and can destroy the exclusive theatre environment to the audience before and after the performance and during intervals.

Examples—drama/concerts

The examples that follow aim to represent the principal stage entertainment format used for popular entertainment.

Crucible Theatre, Sheffield; exterior

Crucible Theatre, Sheffield; thrust stage (Photos: John Donat)

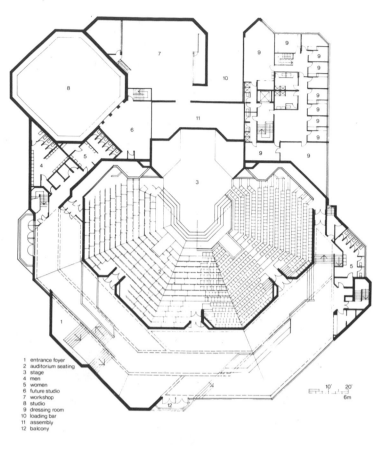

1 entrance foyer
2 auditorium seating
3 stage
4 men
5 women
6 future studio
7 workshop
8 studio
9 dressing room
10 loading bar
11 assembly
12 balcony

Crucible Theatre, Sheffield (above) Plan; (below) auditorium and thrust stage (Photo: John Donat)

Crucible Theatre, Sheffield (thrust stage)

The Crucible Theatre designed by Renton, Howard, Wood Associates with Theatre Projects Consultants Ltd, for theatre services and Tanya Moiseiwitsch stage consultant was completed in 1971.

The planning is based on a soundproof 36·5 m (120 ft) diameter octagon with a central thrust stage giving a maximum distance of 18 m (59 ft) from the centre of the stage to the rear seats. The seating rake is 21° to 28°. The stage level was dictated by the level of the unloading bay and workshop spaces. Stage lighting is mainly accommodated in a diagonally set 'egg box' catwalk complex over the stage and four concentric half octagon lighting catwalks directing lighting at 45°, 125°, 225° and 315° to the centre line of the stage. The thrust stage consists of 1·5 m × 1·8 m (5 ft × 6 ft) timber modules which can be lowered by 5·4 m (8 ft) increments or totally removed. Flying height is 8·8 m (29·3 ft), and scenic backing is based on five towers, built up in stages to a height of 6·7 m (22 ft) and triangular in plan with sides 2·1 m × 1·5 m × 1·5 m (7 ft × 5 ft × 5 ft).

The foyers are on two main floors with intermediate levels, wrapping around three sides of the octagon. The long entrance foyer provides access to box office, cloakroom, theatre shop, grill bar, lavatories, studio theatre and a staircase leading to the theatre foyer. The latter gives access to the rear of the auditorium and provides extensive views over Sheffield.

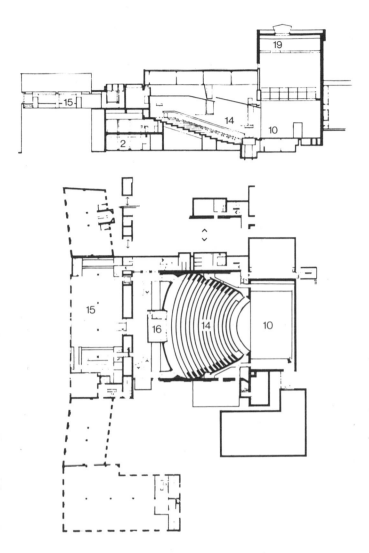

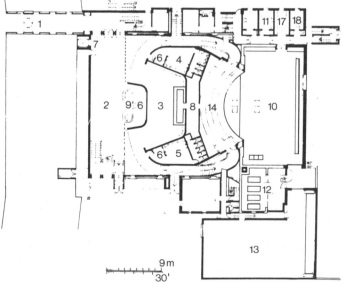

The Thorndike Theatre, Leatherhead, Surrey (repertory)
This was completed in 1969 and designed by Roderick Ham and Partners with Theatre Projects Ltd, as Theatre Consultants. The architects' brief was for a repertory theatre including a stage with fly tower and flying equipment, workshops and paint shops for making scenery, facilities for actors, administrative offices and foyers with coffee bar, licensed bar and exhibition space. A restaurant and a club bar were also to be included. The site is in the centre of Leatherhead with a narrow access through existing buildings to Church Street. The restaurant and club bar is located on the second floor of the existing Church Street buildings and is accessible from the street or from the theatre foyer.

The auditorium seats 526 (with space for six invalid chairs) with continental form seating from side aisle to side aisle, and row steps of 300 mm (12 in).

The forestage lift can be lowered to form an orchestra pit and the appearance of the proscenium is played down with no proscenium wall apparent from the auditorium. The stage has a fly tower and is equipped with a counter-weight flying system, and the control and projection room is situated at the back of the auditorium. Since completion, the rehearsal room has been developed for experimental theatre productions.

(top) Thorndike Theatre; section

(centre) Thorndike Theatre, Leatherhead: plan at restaurant level

(below left) Thorndike Theatre, Leatherhead: plan at ground floor level

(below right) Thorndike Theatre, auditorium (Photo: Rank Strand Electric)

1 entrance	6 coat	11 dressing rooms	16 projection room and
2 main foyer	7 lifts	12 boiler	lighting control
3 snack bar	8 store	13 workshop	17 property store
4 men	9 box office	14 auditorium seating	18 stage manager
5 women	10 stage	15 restaurant	19 fly gallery

Royal Exchange Theatre, Manchester: exterior view showing tubular structural frame supported on main columns of existing building (below left) theatre module within Royal Exchange trading hall; (below right) interior view showing central lighting and balcony seating

1 entrance lobby
2 former trading hall
3 auditorium
4 box office
5 café-bar
6 refreshments
7 scenery storage
8 seating units
9 workshops

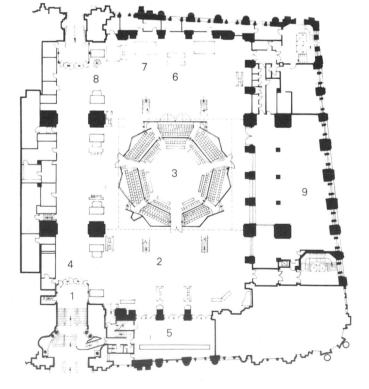

Royal Exchange Theatre, Manchester (theatre in the round)

This theatre was constructed utilising the disused cotton trading hall of the Royal Exchange Building, Manchester. The design team for the building was Levitt Bernstein Associates in collaboration with Richard Negri. Ove Arup and Partners were the structural engineers.

Structurally it was necessary to carry the weight of the theatre to four pillars to avoid additional loading on the existing floor, with the result that the auditorium comprises a framed module suspended within the existing hall.

The stage and seating layout is 'theatre in the round', based on a seven-sided figure and with seating for 740. There are six rows of seats on the ground floor and two rows on each of the balconies, with no seat farther than 9 m from the stage. Structurally, the roof of the module is supported on a steel framework extending to the existing columns of the hall, and the balconies are hung from this framework. The steel is unclad which imposes stringent fire requirements for the spaces around the module. The module is enclosed in glass and the hall can be used to provide lighting effects and for its acoustic properties. The reverberation time of the hall is 7–8 sec whereas the auditorium is nearer 1 sec.

The stage is approximately 8·2 m (26 ft) in diameter. Performers enter from the hall through the same seven doors that are used for both the audience and for scene changes. There is no fly tower and the clear height above the stage is 7·3 m (23 ft) with a further 2·5 m (7 ft) for the depth of the roof trusses.

Lighting and sound control is open to stage and audience and it is located with the stage manager on the second balcony.

Royal Exchange Theatre, Manchester: interior from second balcony

The Institute for Research and Co-ordination of Acoustic/Music at the Pompidou Centre, Paris

The Pompidou Centre has the distinct objective to unite cultural activities and to offer a global image of contemporary creativity to the visitor through the plastic arts, industrial design, music and books. The presentations are activated by public participation in creative experiences and in the ties which they create with the artists that are present.

The Institute aims to provide a collaboration between musicians and scientists with the aim of putting the resources of today's technology at the disposal of musical creation. The introduction of electronics and data processing into creative music has extensive implications. IRCAM aims to become a meeting place where composers, interpreters and researchers of different disciplines work together.

The building is below ground level adjacent to the Pompidou Centre. It covers 3000 m² and is 16 m deep at the lowest point. The building accommodates studios and research laboratories and an experimental hall 17 m×25 m high with space for 400 people. The hall has a three part mobile ceiling and prismatic wall and ceiling panels that can be adjusted to different acoustic conditions.

The ceiling panels can move vertically on columns close to the walls, and the columns can move horizontally with the ceiling panels, on floor tracks. The wall and ceiling panels give seven different acoustic conditions including reflection, dispersion, absorption sensitive to base frequency and absorption sensitive to high frequency. The electronic control can provide a vivid range of acoustic and reverberation conditions. Stage lighting is accommodated on *passerelles* immediately below the ceiling panels.

The programme of research into electronics and music started in 1975 with projects covering computer languages for musical programming, the filing and recording of sound, psycho-acoustical exploration of musical perception and the construction of a digital synthesiser which opens new inroads to the manipulation of sound in real time.

Pompidou Centre Paris: Acoustic Laboratory (BST Buhnen-und Studiotechnik GmbH)

1 mobile ceiling unit with adjustable panels
2 adjustable wall panels
3 passerelle with lighting

Eden Court Theatre, Inverness, Scotland (multi-use)
The riverside site adjoined a Bishop's palace to be
incorporated for use as offices, dressing rooms, green
room and exhibitions. A minimal distance to the
stage from dressing rooms governed the layout of the
new building on the site, and the relationship with
the existing palace and site boundaries determined
the hexagonal plan. The foyer spaces reduce on the
upper floors providing the interesting stepped pitched
roof form rising to the wedge shape mass of the
auditorium. The auditorium seats 830 in raked stalls
and 493 seats in three tiers of boxes that extend
around the auditorium from either side of the
proscenium opening. This provides a strong audience
awareness and promotes the three-way relationship
between actor, audience and individual spectator.
The stage projects in front of the proscenium, but the
safety curtain is on the line of the front of the stage
allowing sets well downstage. Plans exist to continue
the seating in the form of movable tiers behind the
acting area to create courtyard theatre form with
platform stage.

A reverberation time of 1·3 sec was adopted as a
compromise suited to multi-use. The stage is 24·3 m
wide×18 m deep (80 ft×60 ft) with a control
motorised section so that the stage can be moved
forward or back to form an orchestra pit for a
maximum of sixty musicians. There is a fly tower and
grid over the stage with counter-weight flying system.
There are also full cinema projection facilities. John
Wyckham Associates as theatre consultants,
co-ordinated the project, and the architects were Law
and Dunbar-Nasmith, with Ian MacIntosh as
specialist consultant.

1	entrance foyer	6	bar	11	wardrobe rooms
2	box office	7	auditorium seating	12	toilets
3	cloakroom	8	stage	13	foyer
4	restaurant	9	green room	14	dressing rooms
5	kitchen	10	public rooms	15	offices

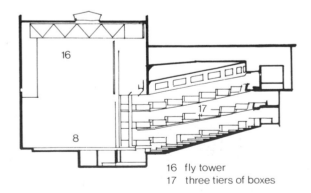

16 fly tower
17 three tiers of boxes

(above) section; (left) showing arrangements for opera/ballet,
drama and platform stage

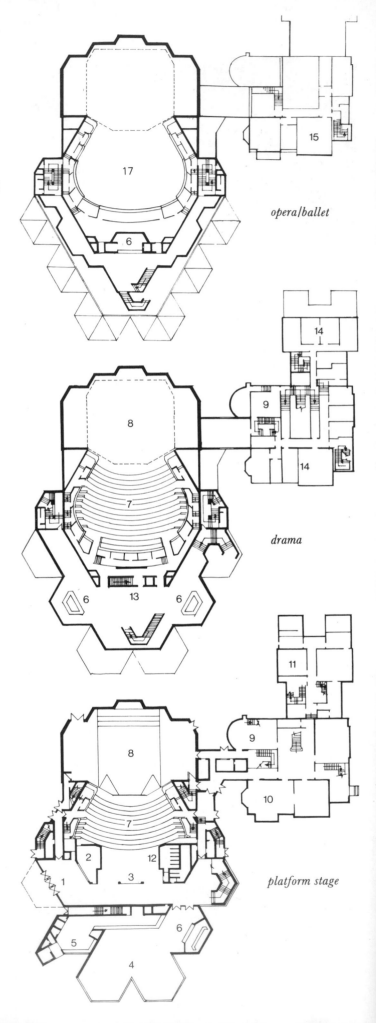

opera/ballet

drama

platform stage

Eden Court, Inverness: auditorium seating

Barbican Arts Centre London: plan and section of model (Photo: John Maltby)

Barbican Theatre, London (repertoire)

The Barbican Theatre is an integral part of the Barbican Arts Centre and the architects Chamberlin, Powell & Bon have developed a theatre concept by Peter Hall and John Bury. The auditorium with steeply raked seating and three narrow balconies seats a total of 1228, with a fourth balcony for lighting and students. The 'continental' type seating is based on a 1 ft 9 in width per seat and 3 ft 4 in overall row width. From a central position on the stage, no spectator is more than 20 m (65 ft) away, and there is a removable proscenium. The back three sides of the stage are surrounded by screens which can be lifted or used as part of the sets. The 14·6 m (48 ft) deep stage is divided into nine lifts which can be individually raised, lowered or raked. Above the stage is a two-level fly-tower, 110 ft to grid, to enable the maximum repertoire storage to take place. The scene-dock is directly behind the stage area, planned to store an eight-show repertoire and scenery is stored on large truck units. Quick-change dressing rooms are provided directly off the stage area. Large rehearsal rooms are located under the auditorium. Scenery and property work areas are below the stage and dressing rooms are located above the stage.

Cottisloe, National Theatre, London (studio theatre)

Peter Hall, the director of the National Theatre, started discussions in 1973 to turn a space 20 m × 17 m and 12·5 m high into a theatre to serve as an experimental studio, a showcase for visiting theatre groups and a conventional theatre where new work could be simply and quickly staged. The 'Courtyard' form with galleries designed by Iain Mackintosh of Theatre Projects Consultants Ltd, provides the required flexibility. The void under the central area allows adjustment to the floor pattern, providing either a stage at one end and stepped seating with two galleries on the sides and rear of the seating area, theatre in the round or open stage. Alternatively, the floor can be left clear of seating for actors and audience to intermingle during the performance, as adopted for a medieval passion play performed in a peripatetic style; recapturing the spirit of the Inn Yard Elizabethan drama. The Cottisloe can accommodate an audience of 400.

Cottesloe, National Theatre, London

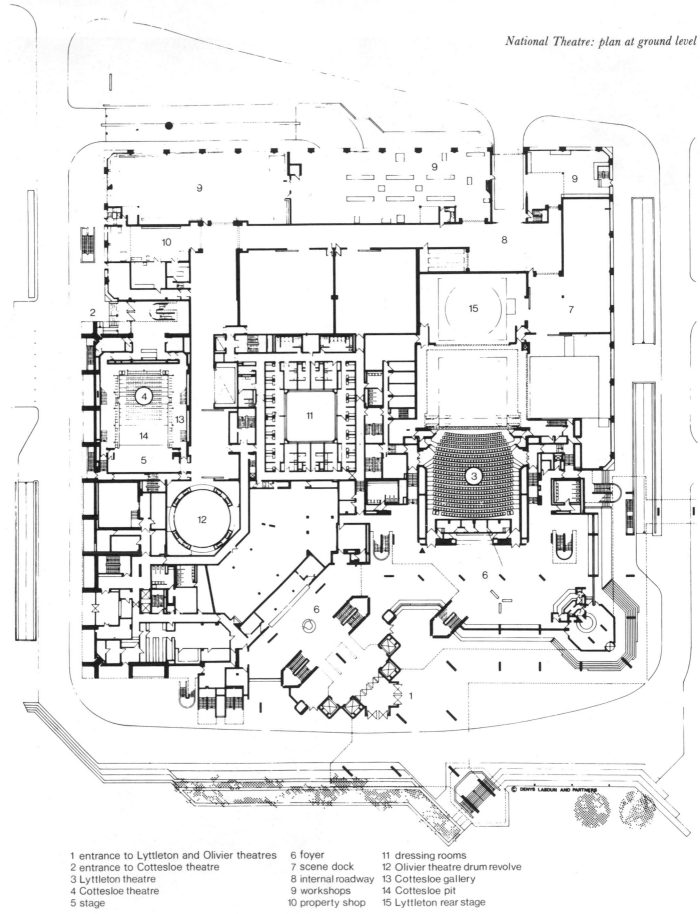

1 entrance to Lyttleton and Olivier theatres   6 foyer   11 dressing rooms
2 entrance to Cottesloe theatre   7 scene dock   12 Olivier theatre drum revolve
3 Lyttleton theatre   8 internal roadway   13 Cottesloe gallery
4 Cottesloe theatre   9 workshops   14 Cottesloe pit
5 stage   10 property shop   15 Lyttleton rear stage

The National Theatre, London

The National Theatre situated on the south bank adjacent to Waterloo Bridge, was designed by Denys Lasdun and Partners. It includes three theatres (completed in 1976/77): the Olivier theatre with a fan shaped auditorium, open stage and seating 1160 in two stepped tiers; the Lyttleton theatre with an adjustable proscenium arch and seating for 890 in two tiers; and the Cottesloe, a rectangular studio theatre with a galleried courtyard form with space for 400 people. There are extensive workshops, wardrobes, property shops and rehearsal rooms at the rear of the building. The foyers, corridors and river terraces, with panoramic views of the City of London, are designed as accessible spaces used for exhibitions, pre-performance live music, and include bars, bookstalls and restaurants.

Olivier, National Theatre, London (Photo Donald Mill for Denys Lasdun and Partners)

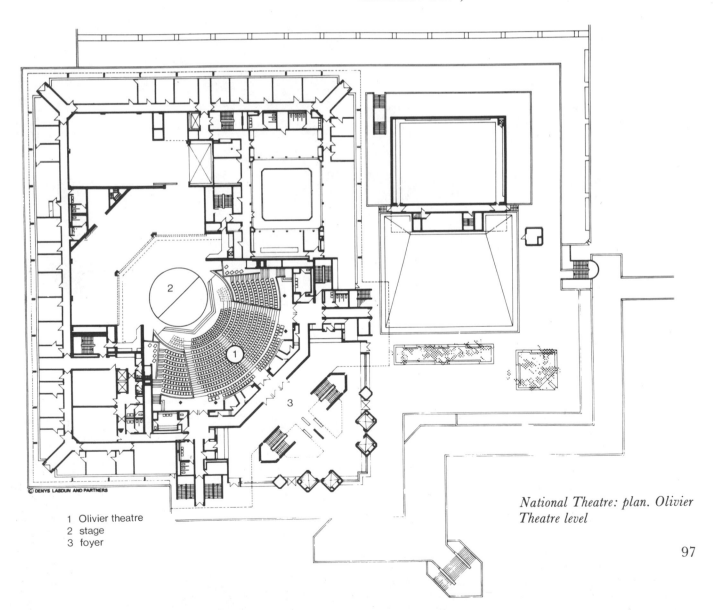

1 Olivier theatre
2 stage
3 foyer

National Theatre: plan. Olivier Theatre level

97

Stage entertainment

Television studio, B.B.C. Television Centre, White City London
(top) plan of seating and sets for t/v production with audience
(centre) view of seating for comedy drama
(bottom) view of sets and monitors   (Photos: Anthony Wylson)

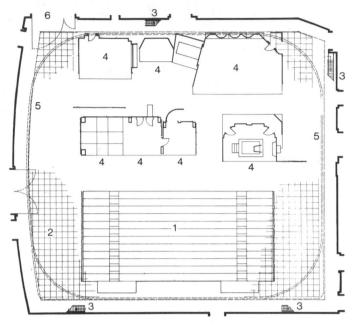

1 seating
2 lighting grid over
3 access stairs to gallery
4 sets
5 ceiling track
6 access for scenery

Television studio: production with audience (Thames Television)

New London Theatre: arrangement for television production with audience

L'Empire, Paris; interior of television theatre (Societe Francaise de Production et de Creation Audiovisuelles)

L'Empire, Avenue Wagram, Paris (television theatre)
The French audio-visual company, Societe Francais de Production et de Creation Audiovisuelles covers all aspects of film and television production. The Empire in the Avenue Wagram, Paris, which was formerly a theatre, has been converted into a multi-media centre with television theatre and film reviewing cinemas. The television theatre combines the stage layout of a conventional theatre with fly tower, fire curtain and forestage with provisions for television filming. This includes a variety of television camera positions, space for cameras to manoeuvre, and an extensive ceiling grid over the stage and part of the auditorium for television lighting.

The auditorium stalls and balcony can seat 600 people and the main control consoles are located immediately below the balcony. The control rooms form part of a wide gallery that also allows for follow spotlights and cameras. There are also side galleries extending from the balcony front to the forestage with staircases leading down to the stalls. This provides camera space and opportunities for artists to enter the theatre other than from the stage. The current stage set has a central section extending into the seating area which, with the wide forestage either side, provides a platform for cameras to manoeuvre. The lighting grids that extend over the audience are accessible from galleries that span the full width of the auditorium. The 'section' profile of the theatre includes a shallow rake for spectator seating.

The basic relationship between auditorium floor and stage provides a continuous level at the point where the extended forestage meets the raked auditorium floor. This provides easy movement for cameras. The current stage arrangement provides an interesting relationship between stage and seating appropriate to variety performance.

L'Empire, Paris; plan and section of television theatre. (Societe Francaise de Production et de Creation Audiovisuelles)

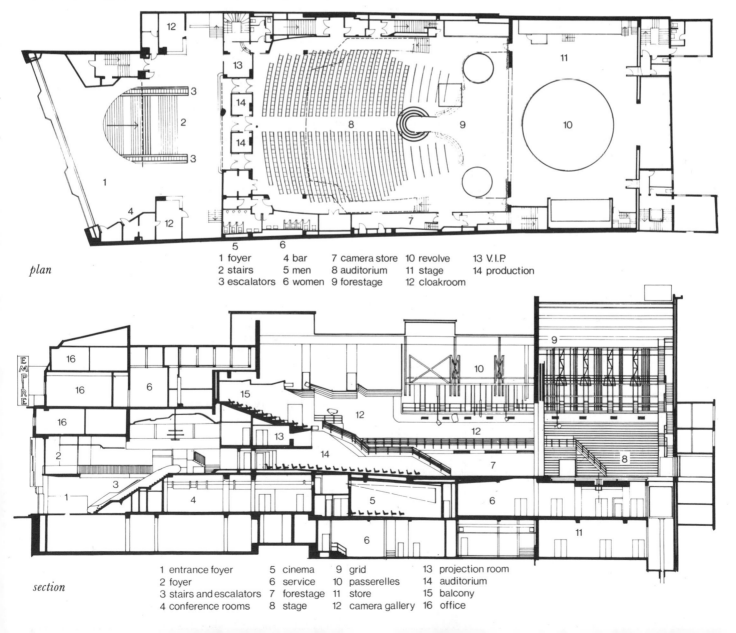

plan

1 foyer	4 bar	7 camera store	10 revolve	13 V.I.P.
2 stairs	5 men	8 auditorium	11 stage	14 production
3 escalators	6 women	9 forestage	12 cloakroom	

section

1 entrance foyer	5 cinema	9 grid	13 projection room
2 foyer	6 service	10 passerelles	14 auditorium
3 stairs and escalators	7 forestage	11 store	15 balcony
4 conference rooms	8 stage	12 camera gallery	16 office

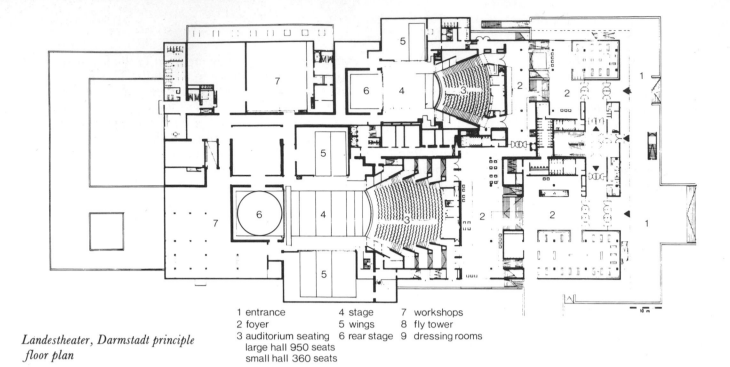

1 entrance	4 stage	7 workshops
2 foyer	5 wings	8 fly tower
3 auditorium seating	6 rear stage	9 dressing rooms
large hall 950 seats		
small hall 360 seats		

Landestheater, Darmstadt principle
floor plan

Landestheater, Darmstadt (two-theatre complex)

A two-theatre complex planned within a narrow rectangular site. The front section of the site accommodates an underground car park. Both auditoria are designed for opera and drama with the dressing rooms below the auditorium and at stage level, and both the Green-rooms and rest rooms are above the auditorium and have views across the city. In order to provide flexibility to the forestage area and a close unity between stage and audience, the proscenium frames to the auditoria are moved to the back of the stage and proscenium wings are moved into side recesses so that the stage can open to its full width of over 18 m (60 ft). The wings can be moved backwards or forwards so that the whole or part of the orchestra space can be incorporated in the stage. On either side of the front row of seats, the stage can be extended into the auditorium. These areas concerned can be entirely masked by panels or opened in segments or to their full breadth, the panels being rotatable and designed to take scenery on the reverse side. In both cases the stage is divided into five lifts with a revolve stage on a trolley stored at the back of the stage; and the orchestra pit/forestage area is provided with three lifts.

The architect was Rolf Prange and the stage technical consultant was Adolf Zotzmann.

Landestheater, Darmstadt: site plan

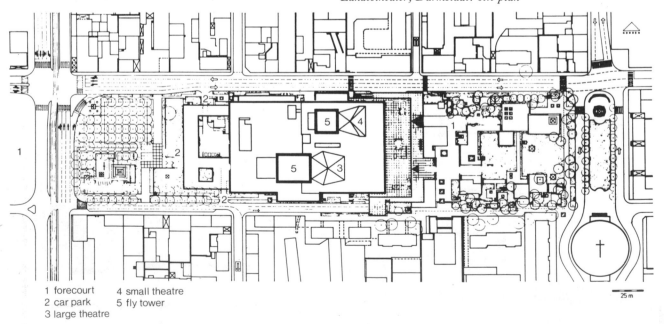

1 forecourt	4 small theatre
2 car park	5 fly tower
3 large theatre	

The Wessex Concert Hall, Poole Arts Centre, Dorset
The Poole Arts Centre combines theatre, cinema, studio theatre, gallery and arts/crafts studios, with bars, restaurant coffee shop and foyer. Also provided within the centre there are the administrative and rehearsing headquarters for two professional orchestras.

The concert auditorium, the Wessex Concert Hall, can be converted into a ballroom. The Wessex hall with seating for 1500 and provision for eight disabled people, is designed acoustically for orchestral performances. The orchestral platform has the capacity for a full symphony orchestra of 120 musicians and there is fixed seating at the rear of the platform for a choir. The floor of the hall is constructed on two sections; the top section has fixed seating, and the lower section with a flat maple strip floor. This floor can be raked for seating which can be winched away on seating trolleys into a storage area. The stalls provide seating for 1004 and the circle has 489 seats. For a flat floor arrangement, 600 people can be seated for a banquet.

Wessex Concert Hall
(top) auditorium for concert; (bottom) auditorium for dancing;
(Photos: Harris Morrall, Bournemouth)

Landmark Hotel Casino, Las Vegas: Revue 'showroom' with wide forestage and banquette seating

Examples—revue/theatre restaurants

Outside England the word 'Revue' describes a non-stop spectacular show with extravagant costumes, effects and scenery, with singers and dancers performing story lines as a vehicle for lavish audio-visual entertainment. This is true of the Paris shows evolving from the music hall tradition such as the Moulin Rouge, Folies Bergère, Casino de Paris and the Lido. Apart from the new Lido, the shows were in adapted, existing buildings. The Paris style revue has been established in many cities (Beirut, Barcelona, Las Vegas, Miami and Tokyo), promoting new buildings for stage entertainment, in which provision is made for extensive built-in mechanical equipment, a large scenery dock and extreme efficiency in change-overs. There is also food or drinks service to the audience. The heavy capital cost is set against long runs. In the UK, the supper-club night spot has also grown in popularity. They include a space for dancing and stage facilities for 'star' artists, cabaret and pop-groups as at the Fiesta, Sheffield and Cesar's Palace, Luton.

Cesar's Palace, Luton, England: interior (Photo: Anthony Wylson)

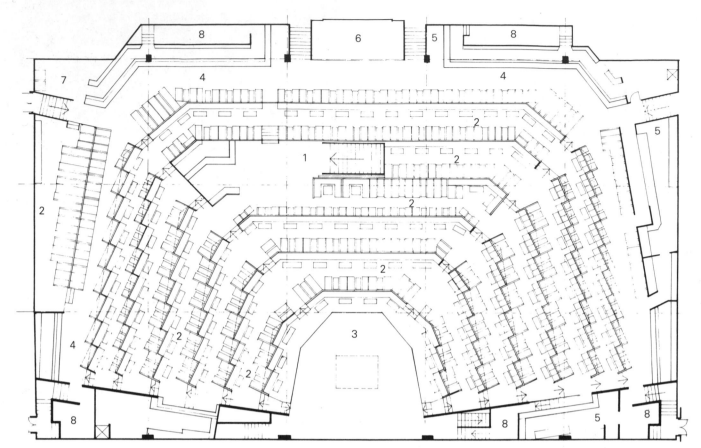

Fiesta, Sheffield: plan at auditorium level

1 stairs from entrance foyer
2 tables and seating
3 stage
4 bar
5 food service
6 console
7 kitchen service
8 store
9 entrance
10 box office
11 foyer

Fiesta, Sheffield: plan at entrance level

Fiesta Theatre Club, Sheffield

The club is part of a leisure complex situated in the centre of Sheffield. The development for Epic Northern Properties was designed by Jefferson, Sheard and Partners, and included shops and supermarket, car parking, a bowling alley and a ballroom. The Fiesta Theatre Club was designed by Booton and Farmer for Norton Entertainments Ltd, to use the space allocated for a bowling alley and convert it to a night club.

The layout is on two floors with the lower level and entrance approached via broad external stairs and courtyard areas. The entrance level has reception foyer, cloakroom, male and female toilets, kiosk, bar, separate disco-bar, staff facilities, administrative offices, dressing rooms for star performers and cast, band room, kitchen storage and mechanical services equipment.

A feature staircase leads up into the centre of the theatre and a private staircase leads from the dressing rooms to the stage. The auditorium and stage are within a rectangle. The thrust stage located in the centre of the long side is sprung polished maple to allow for dancing during intervals and is enclosed by a decorative curtain. An orchestra gallery is situated at the side of and at a slightly higher level than the stage which also overcomes the lack of backstage space. The lighting console is at the rear of the auditorium. The theatre has six bars situated within the enclosure to the auditorium, and the stepped seating, suitable for dining is based on tables for two, four, six and eight persons. The kitchen servery at one corner of the theatre has hoist service from the kitchen on the level below.

Fiesta, Sheffield: interior (Photo: Anthony Wylson)

Zeigfeld Room, MGM, Las Vegas

The huge MGM complex in Las Vegas has two theatres. One seating 1200 for dinner and drinks is for entertainment by top-line stars, and a revue theatre, the Zeigfeld Room, seating 850 for dinner or drinks. Michael Knight was the adviser on stage layout and mechanics. He was presented with the problem of accommodating five big production numbers, each set in a different style. It had to be possible to set any number in five minutes or strike in two. All scenery had to be designed with great

1 Ceiling drop	8 Rolling truck	15 Console
2 Disc	9 Silver Myler ceiling	16 Side masking
3 Revolve (16'diam. travels vertically ±20')	10 Cyclorama	17 Counter weights
4 tabs	11 Black masking	18 Seating and tables
5 Side waggon	12 Scene dock	19 Banquette seating
6 Lift (travel −20' to +24')	13 Grid	20 Entrance
7 Revolve (22'diam.)	14 Side stage	21 Access

MGM Grand, Las Vegas: Zeigfeld Room: plan and section of stage area and auditorium

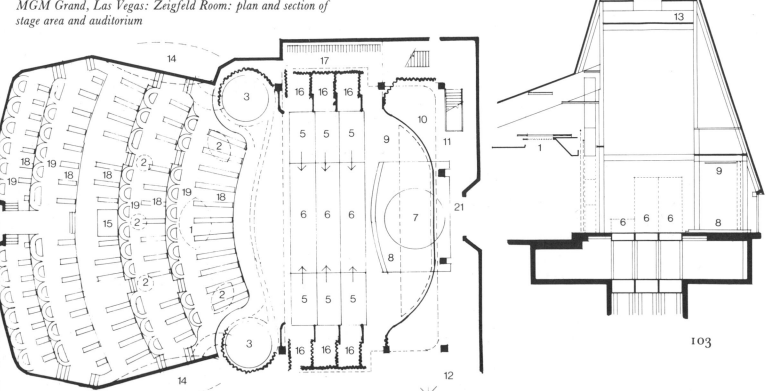

103

mobility and the stage set out with areas for setting and striking while the show was in progress. The design adopted a 21·6 m wide and 9·7 m high (72 ft×32 ft) proscenium with 4·8 m (16 ft) diameter side revolves making a total stage width of 31·6 m (104 ft). From these revolves there is access to side stages (3 m or 10 ft above the main stage level), 6 m or 20 ft along the sides of the showroom. These again can link to an extensive *passerelle*, which descends from the ceiling, making it possible with stage and side stages for the cast to do a complete circuit. The ceiling over the audience has three 1·5 m (5 ft) discs, two 3·3 m (11 ft) oval discs and a 4·8 m (16 ft) centre oval. Each disc can descend carrying cast and scenic elements and, with the *passerelle* and tracks for flying cast, the performance can be extended into the auditorium. The stage has a maximum depth of 20·7 m (68 ft) with flying space over. The extensive basement has three hydraulic lifts 8 m×3 m (36 ft×10 ft), and when the lifts are down the stage is filled by three rolling beams and three floor wagons from either side (the side floor levels being raised to normal floor level). There is also a large motorised truck 8 m×6 m (36 ft×20 ft) which can carry sets downstage. Off stage, there is a scenery dock 18 m×12 m (60 ft×40 ft) and 9 m (30 ft) high. The basement provides space for scenic storage and a dolphin tank.

The lighting control system is a 120 way Thorn Q—File 2000 and the control in three sections can take 5000 A each.

The orchestra is located in a large sound-proofed room in the basement, and every instrument has an individual microphone and the conductor watches TV monitors. There are tape decks for backing tracks and up to fourteen hand-held radio microphones can be used on stage. The sound console is situated in the middle of the auditorium, and the bank speakers are centrally positioned over the proscenium. The tiered seating in the auditorium is a combination of banquet and tables with chairs on a radial plan.

MGM Grand, Las Vegas: 1200 seat Celebrity Room (Photo: Las Vegas News Bureau)

Beirut

The Casino, Beirut was created by Charles Henchis and was rebuilt in 1967 representing the largest revue in Europe. Stage and theatre planning was by Michel Knight and Robert Bahl. The layout included lifts, floor wagons, treadmills on stage and both *passerelle* and ceiling devices in the auditorium space. The semi-circular *passerelle* with a similar component

Casino, Beirut: segment sphere descending from ceiling and opening

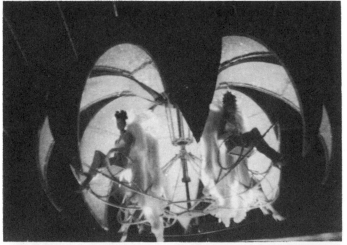

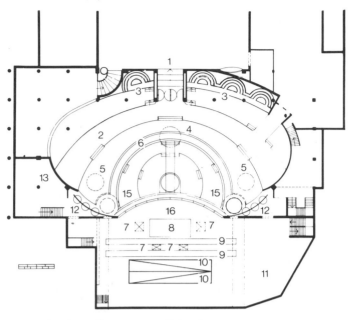

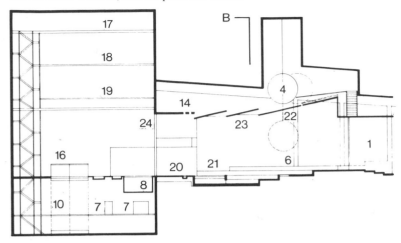

1 entrance foyer
2 auditorium with tables
3 booth seating
4 feature sphere over
5 discs over
6 glass top walk
7 trap
8 pool
9 treadmill
10 lift
11 stage machinery
12 revolving panels
13 band over
14 rain trap
15 glass top revolve
16 stage
17 fly floor
18 loading floor
19 grid
20 rain trough
21 glass floor
22 sliding panel
23 louvres
24 proscenium

extending through on the stage can provide a rotating circular deck (with glass top or artificial ice top) for dancers (or scenery), or the top can be removed to form a circular water channel (with fountains or steam).

The centre of the semi-circle is also linked with the stage, the combination dividing the auditorium floor into three areas. The ceiling has five tracks to carry dancers from the back of the auditorium to the front of the stage, and three devices to lower dancers over the audience. The largest device which is centred in the *passerelle*, consists of a 3 m (10 ft) sphere with segments that open to reveal a glamorous display.

Casino Revue Theatre, Beirut: general view of interior with disc features in auditorium

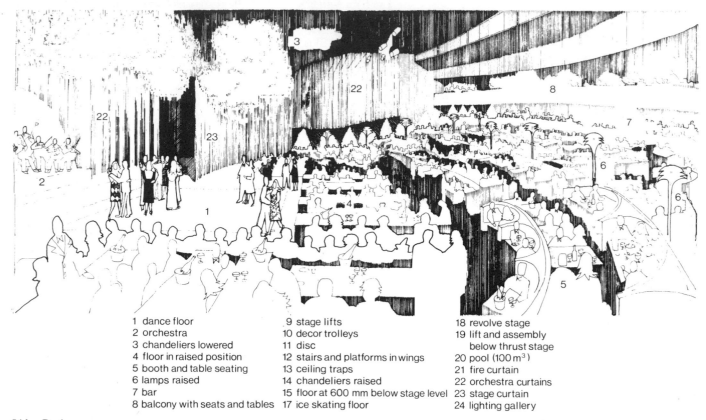

1 dance floor	9 stage lifts	18 revolve stage
2 orchestra	10 decor trolleys	19 lift and assembly
3 chandeliers lowered	11 disc	below thrust stage
4 floor in raised position	12 stairs and platforms in wings	20 pool (100 m³)
5 booth and table seating	13 ceiling traps	21 fire curtain
6 lamps raised	14 chandeliers raised	22 orchestra curtains
7 bar	15 floor at 600 mm below stage level	23 stage curtain
8 balcony with seats and tables	17 ice skating floor	24 lighting gallery

Lido, Paris:
arrangement for dinner dance

arrangement for revue

The Lido, Paris

The Lido cabaret started in the Champs-Élysées in 1946 and since 1977 the Lido show has been presented in a new Lido Normandie theatre restaurant formed through subdividing the Normandie Cinema in the Champs-Élysées. This is a unique luxury night spot in which the interior changes from the ambience of a dinner dance to the correct sightlines for a cabaret theatre. The theatre seats 1200 for dining in a mixture of free chairs and booth seating. The principal floor adjustment is the 'orchestra' area immediately in front of the thrust stage that remains at the same level as the stage for dinner dance (with dancing on the stage area) and descends to 610 mm below stage level for the cabaret show. At the same time, chandeliers and tall table lamps that form important elements within the large space, retract to allow clear sightlines for the stage show.

The stage consists of proscenium area and thrust stage. The latter consists of a large lift that permits the alternative platforms (dance floor, revolving stage, skating rink and swimming pool) to be brought to the performance level. The operation of removing a platform is done within the sight of the audience. There are four lifts to elevate stage sets stocked in the basement and in the upper wings. There is also a *passerelle* available for use across the stage and the current stage set includes wing platforms and stairs at either side. The principal finishes within the night club are leather, wood and velvet and the curtain consists of hanging cords of glittering blue nylon rope. The overall impression is one of luxury.

The orchestra is located in a side balcony and the sound is transferred to the audience with the aid of panoramic speakers over the auditorium area. The light effects control desk has 150 integral memory circuits for lighting, and there is interior circuit television to control the show and to provide security. The light gallery above the balcony extends the full width of the auditorium. The floor show extends into the auditorium with, for example, the arrival of a helicopter over the audience. The stage layout combining a wide forestage with a centre stage projecting into seating area brings the spectators and dancers into close proximity and provides for breadth of display.

The dinner dance arrangement with the chandeliers and lamps reducing the auditorium space to a more intimate scale, also reduces the apparent stage area to a small central space for the orchestra. The kitchens are below the auditorium. There is a long bar at the rear of the auditorium, and a balcony with additional tables and seating for dining.

8. Spectacles de scène—Résumé

La scène a toujours joué un rôle primordial dans le domaine du spectacle. Non seulement les formes de présentation sont diverses, mais il existe une grande variété de relations scène-public, depuis la scène conventionnelle jusqu'au genre théatre-studio. En outre, les exigences des techniques audio-visuelles, électro-mécaniques et d'enregistrement pour la télévision ont ouvert des voies nouvelles à la conception de la scène et de la salle. Les aspects de la plannification du spectacle de scène sont développés plus particulièrement car ils représentent une base essentielle de la conception du spectacle pour le spectateur. Parmi les exemples donnés figurent: la National Theatre de Londres, le Lido, le Palais des Congrès et le Centre Pompidou à Paris, Stardust à Las Vegas et Beyrouth.

8. Bühnenunterhaltung—Zusammenfassung

Die Bühnenunterhaltung hat von jeher eine wesentliche Rolle in der Freizeitgestaltung gespielt. Die Präsentation ist nicht nur unterschiedlich, von intimem Drama und klassischer Musik zu großer Oper und Musicals, sondern das Format der Zuhörerschaft von konventionell bis zu den flexiblen Studiotheatern ebenfalls. Ferner bieten die Bedingungen für Fernsehaufnahmen, audio-visuelle Verfahren und elektromechanische neue Planungslösungen für Bühne und Zuhörerraum. Die Planungsaspekte der Bühnenunterhaltung werden umrissen, da diese eine bedeutende Grundlage für die Form der Zuhörerunterhaltung darstellen. Beispiele sind das National Theatre, London, England, der Lido und Palais de Congres, Paris, das Pompidon-Centre in Paris, Stardust, Las Vegas und Beirut.

٨ ـ الترفيه المسرحي ـ موجز

كان للترفيه المسرحي دائما دوره الرئيسي في مجال الترفيه وقت الفراغ ، ليس فقط لوجود التنوع في أشكال التقديم من الدراما والموسيقى الكلاسيكية الى الأوبرا العظمى والاستعراضات الموسيقية ، ولكن أيضا لوجود التنوع في تصميم شكل « المنصة ـ الجمهور » من خشبة المسرح القديم الى مسرح الاستوديو المرن . بالاضافة الى ذلك فان احتياجات التسجيل التلفزيوني والوسائل الشمعية المرئية الفنية والالكترونيات تقدم الحلول الجديدة للتخطيط في تصميم المسرح والصالة . تم وضع الاطار لنواحي تخطيط الترفيه المسرحي حيث أنها تمثل الأساس المهم في الترفيه عن الجمهور. الأمثلة : المسرح القومي في لندن بانجلترا والليدو وباليه دوكونجريه في باريس بفرنسا ، ومركز بومبيدو في باريس ، وستاردست في لاس فيجاس وبيروت .

Chapter 9
Cinema entertainment

The cinema is essentially a 20th-century building form for popular entertainment, having its origins in the travelling fairs and music halls at the end of the 19th century. The Bioscope entertainment of the fairground in the 1890s developed to a considerable size but transportation of enclosures to provide this scale of accommodation presented a problem to the travelling showman. Music hall used cine films as intermittent entertainment. Thus the early permanent cinemas took their form from the music hall, with auditorium, proscenium and stage, orchestra pit, pavement paybox and entrance foyer. The legacy from the showground was the ornate Warbitzer organ.

As the demand for film entertainment grew, other existing buildings were adapted to cinema use. In 1907, the first purpose-built cinema was designed and the need for statutory standards for public safety were established in Britain through the Cinematographic Act of 1909. This defined standards regarding the enclosure of the projection rooms to separate the risk inherent in the inflammable film material from the audience, to regulate exitways and fire appliances. Similar building controls were adopted in America, although varying in detail from State to State.

The typical cinema building of this period was represented by the Globe Cinema at Putney in south London with its ornamental façade to the street, the classical interior decoration and simple exterior form to the auditorium.

In America, there was rapid growth in the number of cinemas and the competition affected the decorative surrounds to the screen. As the film industry gained confidence, cinema design developed in a competitive context. The luxurious, sophisticated and spacious buildings designed by Thomas Lamb brought an elegance, normally associated with live theatre, to popular cinema entertainment. Also in America, John Emberson developed a design

approach using fantasy and atmospheric interiors to reflect the romantic and exotic character of the epic films of the day.

The size of movie theatres increased. The Roxy, in New York, built in 1927 and designed by Walter Ahlschlager, had a seating capacity of 6000.

In England progress was affected by the 1914–18 war, but the momentum was revived in the 1920s. English designers were influenced by both the trends in America and the new rationale embodied in the 'modern architecture' movement developing in Europe. The result generally combined an efficient plan with embellished and sophisticated decor. Nevertheless, the 'atmospheric' school had its followers both in England and France.

The development of small cinemas in France produced buildings of particular interest. The small 'newsreel' or 'intelligentsia' cinema was compact and distinctive of these small cinemas in Europe, the Cineac in Amsterdam designed by Duika in 1934 takes its place amongst the best examples of the modern movement. In fact the new architectural philosophy promoted a new approach in design. With the German tradition of small opera house buildings that expressed the auditorium and generous foyers as articulated visual components, and also the recognition of the German designers of the specific 'night qualities' inherent in cinema design, new criteria became established. The Universum in Berlin by Eric Mendelsohn, with its horseshoe shaped auditorium and functional lines without contrived atmospherics, was an early example in which technical efficiency was a priority.

In 1928, the advent of the 'talkies' radically affected cinema design. Acoustic considerations, the size and the shape of the auditorium conflicted with the scale adopted for silent films. The technology of sound improved with the introduction of multi-cellular high-frequency horn loudspeakers in place of a rudimentary centrally positioned speaker

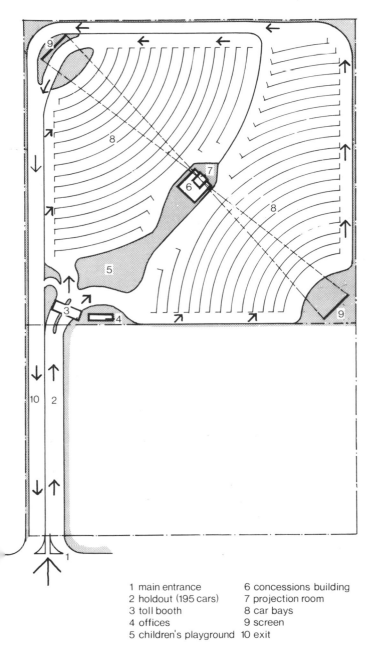

1 main entrance
2 holdout (195 cars)
3 toll booth
4 offices
5 children's playground

6 concessions building
7 projection room
8 car bays
9 screen
10 exit

Drive in Cinema at Flint, Michigan, U.S.A. (Architects: William Riseman Associates, Boston, Mass.)

that made up in volume what was lacking in quality.

The drive-in cinema, also started in the 1930s, consisted of a terraced fan-shaped area for parking cars with viewing from each car directed towards a large screen in the order of 30·4 m × 15 m (100 ft × 50 ft). Each parking space had a post speaker which was taken into the individual cars to provide the sound. Drive-in cinemas are associated with countries with a conducive climate, a high car population, and road systems that permit an outflow of many cars at one time. Existing drive-in cinemas hold up to 2000 cars with an average size designed for 500 to 1000 cars.

Generally the basic components within the cinema consisting of auditorium seating, screen, projection room, entrance foyer, ancillary accommodation, staff rooms, space for mechanical services and external display have remained similar through the developing stages. Projection techniques have mainly favoured direct projection, but rear projection and complicated mirror systems have been used to overcome problems of layout and headroom.

Auditoria

Auditoria have developed in two basic patterns; the single floor or stadium and the multi-level, using balconies and/or mezzanines. The steel frame building with an impressive elevation to the street and an utilitarian light clad massive roof form behind, became a simple formula for many structures as cinema became the 'high street' club for popular entertainment.

Recent technology

Subsequent to 1945, the cinema industry was stimulated by competition from television and other popular interests to find effective methods of attracting audiences. The element of romantic escapism carried less weight in a society able to grasp better standards of living and exciting opportunities for travel and holidays. The 1939–45 war had stimulated technological developments in cinematography in photographic emulsions, colour systems, and lenses for cameras. These provided the means to develop larger screen size without reducing picture quality. In 1952, Cinerama was introduced using three synchronised projectors each directed towards one-third section of a wide screen to give in total a very large picture. Stereophonic sound was relayed through five speakers.

The result was an impressive audio-visual experience. In 1953, Cinemascope was introduced using an auxiliary anamorphic lens assembled in front of the normal projector, permitting screen widths of double the previous size. Such innovations on existing cinemas favoured a reduction in height of the screen in relation to the increased width (particularly in the case of an auditorium with a balcony), and a single projector rather than three. Cinemascope, Todd AO System, D.150 System and Imax established further patterns for wide-screen projection that aim to achieve a greater visual impact, spatial sound and realism.

Projection equipment

Expo fairs since the 1960s have used cinema projection for conveying trade or cultural information in a dynamic, attractive and entertaining way. This has resulted in a diversity of experimental projection, arrangements including multi-screen projection, 360° screen hemispherical projection surfaces and mixtures of cine film, stills and auditorium effects to achieve a rich audio-visual experience. (These were referred to in Chapter 5.)

The Disney theme parks use 360° projection and this was also used in the short-lived Circlorama in London. 360° projection has a circular auditorium with a perimeter screen providing a continuous picture that encircles the audience.

Circarama, used in Disneyland and Walt Disney World can continually replay one film to a continuous flow of tourist visitors, but the lack of commercial films for 360° projection denies a wider use of this format.

A more recent development for popular entertainment is the multi-screen presentation with images projected by cine-camera and slide projector as used in both the 'New York Experience' and the 'London Experience'. This arrangement can provide an imaginative means to communicate information by using moving pictures, superimposed stills, stereophonic sound, auditorium and other effects, to create an audio-visual experience that extends from the screen to the whole auditorium.

For the future, holography represents a particularly interesting development. A hologram is the reconstruction of an object or scene as a 'complete' three-dimensional image (definition from the introduction to the Light Fantastic 2 exhibition by Holoco Ltd). It is possible to make holograms of living subjects and moving objects 'frozen' in three dimensions. It is also possible to show white light reflection holograms. This method brings the technique nearer the non-laser-owning public, and is being used for the development of full colour holography.

The hologram development generated by the discovery of laser (light amplification by stimulated emission of radiation) has a basis for holographic movies in the multiple frame pulsed holographic film produced in Moscow and the Benton hologram developed by the Polaroid Corporation. In both cases the application is limited by a restricted viewing angle. The spherical theatre designed by Anton Furst (of Holoco Ltd) and Anthony Hunt Associates, structural engineers, is an indication of an auditorium for holographic entertainment in future years.

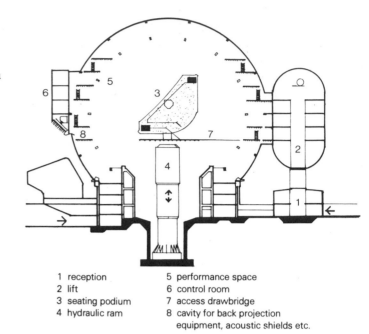

1 reception
2 lift
3 seating podium
4 hydraulic ram
5 performance space
6 control room
7 access drawbridge
8 cavity for back projection equipment, acoustic shields etc.

Auditorium for Holographic entertainment of the future

Ancillary spaces

Apart from the basic accommodation of cinemas, the ancillary spaces have varied from era to era. At its height of popularity the cinema commanded a priority role for family entertainment and was securely established in every high street. The cinema would include a cafe, restaurant and ballroom. A licensed bar is a normal feature in the specialist cinemas aimed at adult audiences. The space for mechanical services has increased as comfort standards relating to heating and ventilation have increased. Interior lighting and exterior display developed to provide imaginative effects and bold street illuminations. In some cases the external illuminations provide the principal identity of the cinema, as in the case of Studio 1 and 2, Oxford Street, London.

In recent years, commercial pressure on the cinema industry has caused a significant reduction in the number and size of cinemas. Promoters have subdivided existing cinemas so that several small auditoria under the same management can provide a diversity of film entertainment with the added flexibility of auditorium size. Automation in the projection room is reducing the need for technical staff in any one cinema, and Cinemation used by Rank has the complete programme, auditorium lighting sequence, interval music and curtain control, monitored electronically.

The public support for the cinema that transformed cinema entertainment from an intermittent music hall performance to the universal family entertainment of super-cinemas, has been dissipated by television, greater social mobility and freedom, and higher standards of living. Thus there have been few new cinemas in Europe in recent years, and where new cinemas have been constructed, these are a secondary element to a commercial redevelopment. Nevertheless, the criteria for design to achieve technical conditions necessary for the highly developed cinematographic equipment available, is exacting. At its best, the anticipation of high standards of comfort by the public and local authorities' regulations to maintain safety, the cinema can still provide a sense of occasion.

Planning

As with any spectator auditorium, the location of a commercial cinema must take into account parking and access for patrons, street advertising, exitways from the building, and control of noise. There must be sufficient space within the structure to allow for the projection beam, and satisfactory viewing conditions for patrons.

A cinema layout consists of four basic components; the auditorium with seating facing the screen; a projection room with projection equipment and lighting and sound controls; adjoining public spaces as entrance foyer, ticket office, kiosk, cloakroom, lavatory accommodation, bar, etc.; and management, office and staff facilities, storage and engineering spaces.

The maximum distance of seating from the screen is recommended as five times the width of the screen for matt white non-directional screens, three times the width of the screen for 35 mm projection and 2·5 times for 70 mm projection (Philips recommend a maximum distance of twice the width of the screen). The overall length of rear seating should be not more than three times the width of the screen for mat white non-directional screen, two times for 35 mm projection and 2·5 to 3 times for 70 mm projection (Philips recommend 1·7 times the width of the screen). The position and overall length of the front row of seating and distance from the screen will be determined by the minimum viewing angles (horizontally and vertically).

The rake of the auditorium floor should not exceed 1:10 with ramped aisles, and 35° for a stepped auditorium. Clear headroom must be provided under the projection beam.

The point of entry will be governed by the location of foyer. Access at the rear of the auditorium is less likely to create a disturbance to the audience if entry is permitted during the performance. In some cases a central 'vomitory' is used and this is particularly relevant to cinemas where the foyer is on the same level or below the front of the stalls.

The height:width proportion of the screen will depend on the projection format. The standard ratio is 1:1·375. The screen is usually stretched on a tubular frame with black masking overlapping the sides to define the picture. In most cinemas, the masking is adjustable to accommodate various aspect ratios.

Generally, the screen is protected by a decorative curtain when not in use. To provide interest during intervals, the curtain will have decorative lighting located at floor and ceiling level or projected from the projection room. In some cases, the screen has been left without curtains and decorative lighting is projected on to the screen during intervals. In the last decade there has been a trend to extend the curtain treatment along the side walls to achieve an expansive effect and to provide a simple wall finish that can mask acoustic materials and services.

The projection box forms the operational core of the cinema containing projection and sound equipment and control consoles for screen curtains, masking, interval music, decorative lighting and auditorium conditions. The process has become more automated over the years with non re-wind film carriers for one projector providing, with Cinemation, scope for the automation of a complete programme.

The accommodation of cinemas into development projects means that it is sometimes necessary for the access area to convey the public some distance from the point of entry from the street. If the auditorium is at basement or first floor level, the foyer will incorporate staircase, escalator or lift. At the same time where there are several auditoria in one cinema, the foyer must provide clear direction from the ticket office to the auditorium concerned.

The entrance foyer of the 'High Street' (or provincial) cinema differs from that of the theatre in that the ticket kiosk may be providing for both advance booking and seats for a programme immediately available. Allowance should be made for queueing without obstructing the exit of the audience of the preceding programme. In the UK, the ticket office requires a classification board to advertise the category of films being shown and a statement of seat prices. The sales kiosk (confectionery, ices, etc.) is an important component in the foyer and needs to be positioned between the entrance from street and the entrance into the auditorium. In the 'West End' cinema (such as in Central London), the foyer waiting space would include cloakroom, waiting space, possibly exhibition space and a bar. The kiosk requires a stock room and, where refreshment is provided in the auditorium, a refrigerator room and dry store should be accessible to auditorium staff.

Lavatories for patrons should be related to the

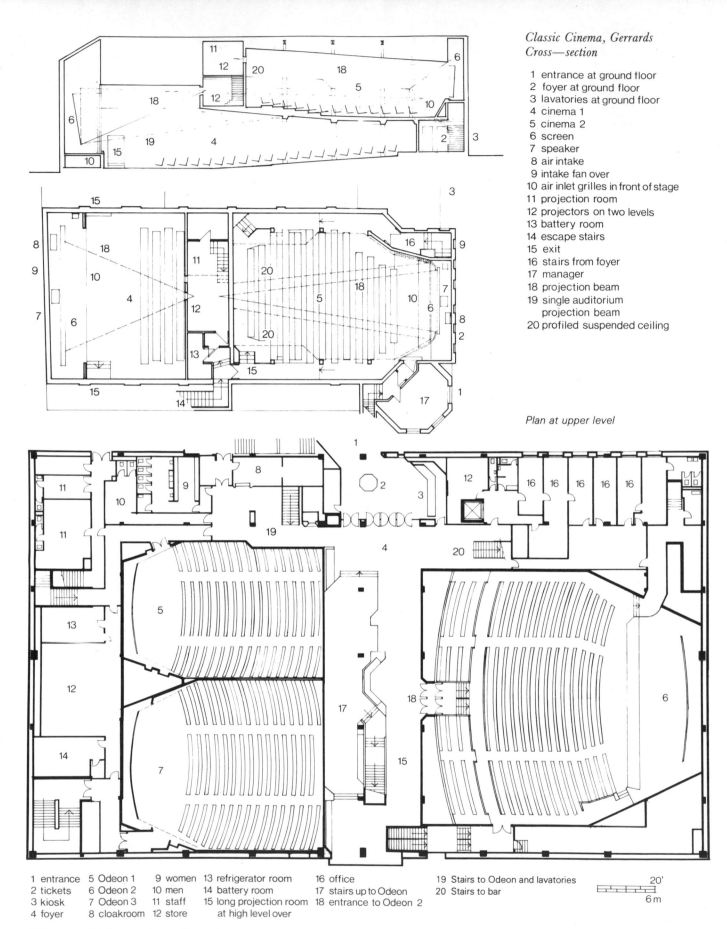

1 entrance at ground floor
2 foyer at ground floor
3 lavatories at ground floor
4 cinema 1
5 cinema 2
6 screen
7 speaker
8 air intake
9 intake fan over
10 air inlet grilles in front of stage
11 projection room
12 projectors on two levels
13 battery room
14 escape stairs
15 exit
16 stairs from foyer
17 manager
18 projection beam
19 single auditorium
   projection beam
20 profiled suspended ceiling

Plan at upper level

1 entrance	5 Odeon 1	9 women	13 refrigerator room	16 office	19 Stairs to Odeon and lavatories
2 tickets	6 Odeon 2	10 men	14 battery room	17 stairs up to Odeon	20 Stairs to bar
3 kiosk	7 Odeon 3	11 staff	15 long projection room	18 entrance to Odeon 2	
4 foyer	8 cloakroom	12 store	at high level over		

20'
6 m

Kingwest, Brighton—cinema floor plan

Kingwest Leisure Centre: projection room

main circulation routes, either with access from the rear of the auditorium (which means that the public do not leave the auditorium once admitted to a programme) or from the foyer.

The fire requirements for cinema are referred to in Chapter 12, but in multi-use buildings particular attention should be given to the availability of exitways when the cinema is in operation. The external display will include a company 'image', a canopy and readograph giving film titles. There could also be wall display panels for posters, etc.

The accompanying illustrations show a range of cinemas in popular use. These include a small auditorium in a hotel complex; larger auditoria constructed as part of office development schemes; and a cinema that has dealt with the problem of noise and access to first floor level; one of the rare

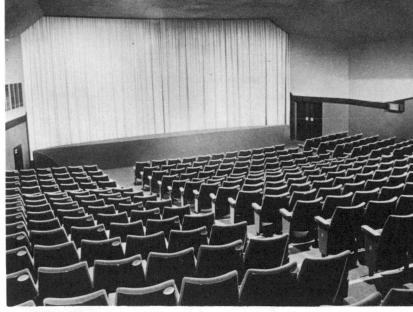

Kingwest Leisure Centre: screen with decorative lighting

independent cinema buildings built since the 1950s and a 'twinning' exercise that has been applied to many of the older cinemas. The Kingwest at Brighton and the Classic Cinema, Gerrards Cross adopt a centralised projection suite serving several auditoria and the 'London Experience' is the EMI special effects cinema in Leicester Square, London.

Kingwest Leisure Centre: (above) ticket office (below) cinema foyer; (top right) auditorium with rear access looking towards rear wall; (bottom right) auditorium with central access.

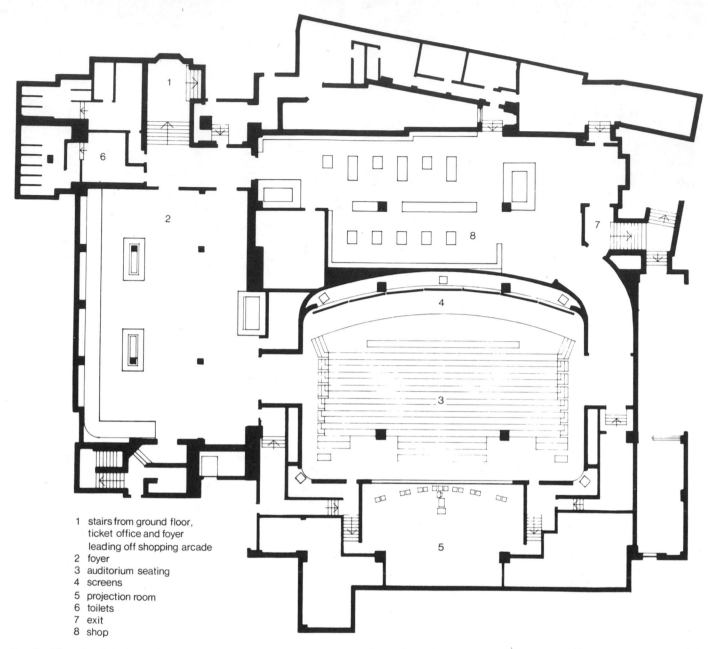

1 stairs from ground floor,
  ticket office and foyer
  leading off shopping arcade
2 foyer
3 auditorium seating
4 screens
5 projection room
6 toilets
7 exit
8 shop

London Experience, Leicester Square, London: Plan of auditorium
(basement level)

(below) multi-screen and auditorium effects

(below) Slide projectors and cine-projector
(Photos: Miller & Harris, London)

Scala Cinema, Birmingham, showing wall curtains to mask acoustic treatment and to provide continuity with screen curtains. Air inlet grilles are immediately below screen on ramped floor (Photo: John Whybrow Ltd.)

(below, right) Scala Cinema, Birmingham. Foyer (Photo: John Whybrow Ltd.)

(below) plan and section

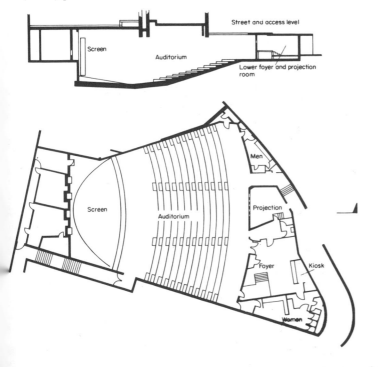

Scala Cinema, Birmingham. Architects James A. Roberts and Associates (Wylson and Waterston, Consultants to Compton Cinemas). A stadium type auditorium at basement level constructed as part of a commercial redevelopment. The entrance is at ground floor level with an extensive canopy projecting over the pavement and giving the cinema identity from the long office building above. The ticket office and foyer is as a shop unit, with a staircase leading down to the cinema foyer. The auditorium seating 604 has four gangways and a screen for 70 mm projection. The original projection room layout was arranged for Todd AO with five sets of speakers behind the screen and 24 ambient speakers recessed in the ceiling.

Odeon, Elephant & Castle, London. Architects Erno Goldfinger and Associates. The Odeon at Elephant & Castle is a rare example in which an independent cinema has been built as part of a redevelopment scheme. The entrance foyer, under the slope of the auditorium, is visually open to the wide pavement and provides for ticket office and sales kiosk. The lavatory accommodation is positioned between auditorium and foyer providing sound insulation from heavy traffic noise. The auditorium seats 1040 and consists of a stadium layout with central access. The screen was designed as an independent structure within the auditorium and was originally without masking. The exterior form and principal structure beams to the roof express the cinema functions.

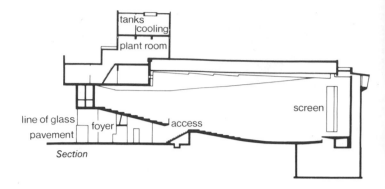

Section

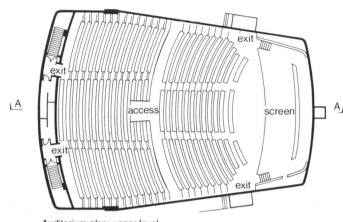

Auditorium plan: upper level

Odeon, Elephant & Castle, London (Architect: Erno Goldfinger) (above) Interior showing free-standing screen (Photo: Sam Lambert, London); (right) Section and plans; (below) exterior view; (below, right) model of roof structure that accommodates projection beam.

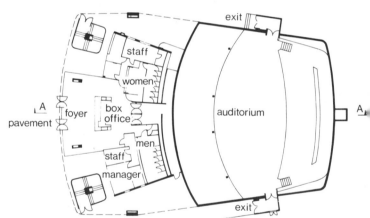

Plan at pavement level

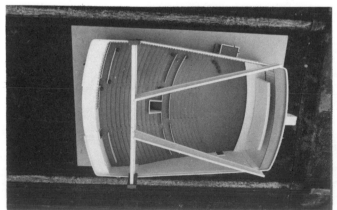

Minema, 45, Knightsbridge, is a small cinema within the structure of the Berkeley Hotel, Wilton Street, London and with access from Knightsbridge. It is used both as a commercial cinema and for private film hire, seminars, lectures, company meetings, auctions, and executive conferences. It has fixed seating for 68 in a simple rectangular raked auditorium with a compact projection room at the rear. The screen size is 3·6 m × 2 m (12 ft × 6 ft 9 in) and the rear seats are 14 m (46 ft) from the screen.

Minema, Berkeley Hotel, Wilton Street, Interior views (Photos: Anthony Wylson)

9. Le cinéma—Résumé

L'industrie du cinéma a connu son record de popularité et, aujourd'hui, prend place dans le vaste panorama des spectacles populaires. Les techniques se sont perfectionnées pour impressionner encore davantage le public, tandis que la planification a été influencée par un patronage plus réduit. Seules quelques techniques d'audio-visuel, utilisées dans les expositions, ont été adoptées pour une utilisation commerciale plus élargie. Des exemples comme 'London Experience' à Leicester Square, Londres, et les cinémas pour automobilistes, allient les images de film et les effets dans la salle pour donner au spectateur une expérience audio-visuelle complète.

9. Kinounterhaltung—Zusammenfassung

Die Kinoindustrie hat ihren Höhepunkt in der Beliebtheit hinter sich. Heute hat sie ihren Platz in einem weit gespannten Panorama beliebter Unterhaltung gefunden. Es haben sich Verfahren entwickelt, die die Erfahrungen des Publikums verbessern, und die geringeren Besuchsziffern haben sich auf die Kinoplanung ausgewirkt. Für den allgemeinen gewerblichen gewerblichen Gebrauch wurden nur einige audio-visuelle Verfahren übernommen, die auf Ausstellungen eingesetzt werden. Bei Beispielen wie 'London Experience' werden Dias under Zuhörerraumeffekte miteinander verbunden, um ein total audio-visuelles Geschehen hervorzurufen. Beispiele sind die London Experience, Leicester Square, London, England und Freiluftkinos.

٩ ـ الترفيه السينمائي ـ موجز

لقد عاصرت السينما وصناعتها ذروة الشعبية ولكنها اليوم تأخـذ مكانها في الاطار الواسع لوسائل الترفيه المفضلة . لقد تطورت الوسائل التقنية لزيادة متعة الجمهور وتأثر تخطيط دور السينمـا نتيجة النقص في عدد روادها . عدد قليل فقط من الوسائل التقنية السمعية المرئية هو الذي استخدم للاستعمالات التجارية العامة . مثلا : « لندن اكسبيريانس » الذي يتضمن صور أفلام السينمـا الساكنة ومؤثرات الصالة لتقديم التجربة السمعية المرئية الشاملة . الأمثلة : « لندن اكسبيريانس » في ليستر سكوير بلندن انجلترا ، وأيضاً دور السينما « درايف ثن » .

Chapter 10

Discos and dancing

Social dancing in Europe and America is expressed historically on aristocratic court balls and plebeian country dances. By the 18th century, the spacious houses of the nobility became the centres of social activity, while the assembly rooms at holiday and health resorts were used frequently for balls. The waltz began to find favour in the second half of the 18th century and presented a significant change in dancing manners.

By the turn of the century, the appeal of the waltz began to fade, and new dances of the early 1900s emanated from America together with ragtime music. From a variety of new forms such as the 'bunny hug' and 'turkey trot', emerged the foxtrot, quickstep, slow waltz and tango with the couples dancing both close and moving as one.

The 1920s saw changes in the social life of London. The great houses could not be maintained and were pulled down. There were fewer private balls, and dinner-dances in hotels became fashionable with night club dancing as an after theatre activity. The small dance floors restricted serious ballroom dancing and the scene of orthodox ballroom dancing was transferred from high society to the spacious suburban dance halls and to ordinary people who enjoyed the sense of occasion that the ballroom dancing provided. Formal dancing gave an opportunity for socialising in an acceptable context, providing a structure to social behaviour at a time of social change.

The first Palais de Danse was opened in London in 1919 reflecting a post-war revival of spirit, and the form was followed throughout the country. These dance halls set out to provide low cost admittance, good bands and spacious floors to enable working people to take up dancing. At the same time, the dance floors used by high society decreased in size, reducing the dancing itself to a shuffle.

With the increase in popularity of Dixieland jazz in the 1920s, the Charleston had a short-lived intense popularity. In the 1930s, Cuban dance rhythms became popular in the form of the rhumba and congo. Also group dances as the 'Lambeth Walk' in England and the 'big apple' in America enjoyed a passing popularity.

In 1929, the 'Jitterbug' crossed the Atlantic to England having found vigorous popularity in America. This started a sequence of dance forms including jive, rock 'n roll and the twist, increasing both the dynamic content of social dancing and the opportunity for individual interpretation. At the same time, with a growing strength in professional teaching of dancing, schools were established to promote competition dancing. An official Board of Ballroom Dancing formed in 1929 established the rules for the numerous competitions held each year, and in 1950 the International Council of Ballroom Dancing was founded and eventually the four standard dances (waltz, fox trot, tango and quick step) with Viennese waltz and Latin American dances became the basis of the competitions.

For the young in recent decades, the reaction to orthodox ballroom dancing identified in the discotheque venues, became a powerful force. A sequence of popular dance forms followed rock 'n roll, as the cha-cha and the twist. This promoted a move towards social dancing in which partners were physically separate. In fact not only was there no apparent need for a partner, but there became no need to learn any particular steps. It became just dancing 'your own thing', and being part of a group at the same time. Disco dancing has become less exclusive to young people, but the dance pattern suggests that outside the ballroom, contemporary social dancing is not only an opportunity for individual display to the partner or the group, but also the self-expression of free form dancing. Thus, there are the two forms of social dancing to be accommodated; orthodox or competitive ballroom dancing requiring space for regular dance patterns, and disco non-progressive dancing that can be accommodated in a more limited space with special lighting effects. In both cases ancillary space is usually required for spectators and seating for socialising.

Ballrooms

The ballrooms of the Alhambra and Tower (see Chapter 2) built for the visitors to Blackpool conveyed an elegance rarely created for social dancing today. The Tower ballroom can accommodate 2500 dancing and 4000 spectators in a large space with a dance floor approximately 30 m × 18 m (100 ft × 60 ft), two tiers of galleries at the sides, and a large stepped balcony at one end with fixed seating. The floor is sprung and the orchestra and organ console is set on a proscenium framed stage.

The modern ballroom as part of a hotel complex, is more often a large multi-purpose space, suitable for banquets, exhibitions and conventions as well as dancing. The typical layout is a large rectangular space, with removable partitions for subdivision, a generous foyer the length of one long side, the kitchen servery extending the full length of the opposite long side, a stage at one end (or a demountable stage in a more central position) and a furniture store immediately accessible.

Lighting must be arranged with dimmers, spotlights and chandeliers to provide an appropriate ambience for each use. In planning the total hotel the noise factor is significant. The design of the floor is of particular importance, as a sprung floor is required for dancing and a fully supported floor is suitable for the alternative uses.

The ballrooms of the major hotels, such as the Hilton, vary in size from 40 m × 20 m (131 ft × 65½ ft) (at Tel-Aviv) to 67 m × 25 m (220 ft × 82 ft) and divisible into nine separate spaces (at San Francisco). In London the ballroom at the Royal Garden Hotel, Kensington is approximately 40 m × 30 m and the Hunter Hotel in Grimsby has a space 14 m (50 ft) square. The longer spans required by a ballroom in a hotel complex can either be accommodated in the podium and slab principle (in which the public rooms are within an extensive podium block and separate from the structural short spans of the bedroom accommodation 'slab'), or in a courtyard plan where the large spans are achieved under the courtyard with short spans of the accommodation on the periphery. Both the Atrium Hotel, Brunswick and the Hilton, San Francisco which are courtyard plans, adopt the latter, with the ballroom located under the courtyard. One ballroom of the Royal Garden Hotel

adopts the former principle, with a second ballroom space projecting beside the main entrance as a distinct form.

Some leisure centres include dance-hall spaces that convey the ballroom character, with galleries and staircases for promenading, relaxing and viewing. This is evident in the Rank Organisation Kingwest Centre at Brighton. Furthermore, several social clubs with dancing provide two dance areas of different character suggesting that an alternative to the conventional discotheque ambience is needed. This form is evident in the British EMI Romeo and Juliet clubs.

Ballroom examples

London Hilton, Park Lane, London. Within the Hotel the function rooms consists of a Grand Ballroom, 24·4 m × 38·4 m (126 ft × 80 ft) divisible into three sections, a foyer, a Crystal Palace Suite (divisible into three sections 24·2 m × 7·7 m (79·5 ft × 25·5 ft) and four smaller rooms. The Grand Ballroom has a banquet, reception, and an auditorium capacity of 1000 for each use. The dividing screens fold back into recesses and one divider is formed by a double partition to provide maximum sound control. The ballroom has substantial chandeliers and decorated feature wall panels. The foyer extends the full length of one side of the ballroom and can be opened up into the ballroom space.

Hilton Hotel, London. Ballroom banquet and dancing (Photos: Iain Irskine, London S.W.1)

Kingswest Leisure Centre was opened in 1965, consisting of three cinemas, a ballroom, a cabaret restaurant and a discotheque. The ballroom has a floor space of 8000 square feet and 4400 square feet at balcony level, providing space for 600–650 for a banquet or dinner/dance and 2000 for straight dances. With the central stage, the floor can be arranged for auditorium or conference seating of 800 and 150 in the balcony. The three cinemas are on the upper floor levels, with access by escalator, the Jenkinsons Cabaret Bar with restaurant is at ground level, and the discotheque is at basement level.

Kingwest Leisure Centre, Brighton

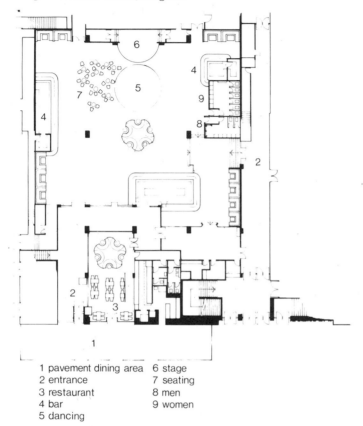

1 pavement dining area 6 stage
2 entrance 7 seating
3 restaurant 8 men
4 bar 9 women
5 dancing

Ground plan: plan of Jenkinson's Cabaret Bar

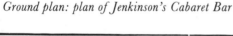

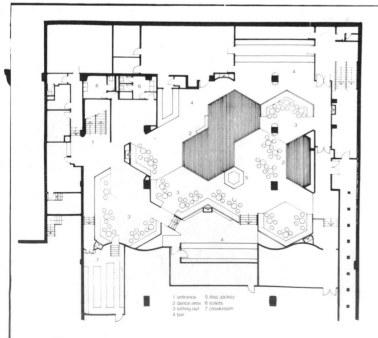

1 entrance 5 disc jockey
2 dance area 6 toilets
3 sitting out 7 cloakroom
4 bar

Basement plan of discotheque

1 entrance 7 dancing at lower level
2 sitting out 8 offices
3 bar 9 servery
4 function room 10 men
5 committee room 11 women
6 staff

Ballroom—gallery level

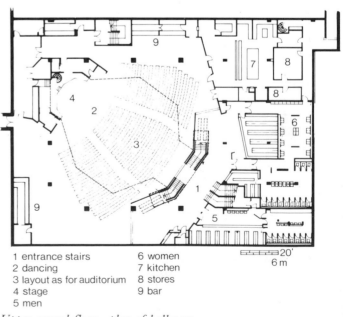

1 entrance stairs 6 women
2 dancing 7 kitchen
3 layout as for auditorium 8 stores
4 stage 9 bar
5 men

Upper ground floor—plan of ballroom

Kingwest Lesiure Centre, Brighton. (The Rank Organisation)
(above) Ballroom (left) Stairs to balcony from dance level; (right)
Stage and dance area. (Centre left) Cabaret and ballroom. (Below)
Discotheque (left) dance area and DJ console; (right) seating area
(Photos: Anthony Wylson)

The Queen's Room, on the liner Q.E.2. This ballrom was
designed by Michel Inchbald, FSIA. The almost
rectangular space has been given an appearance of a
greater length by mirrors, and 2·7 m (9 ft) low ceiling
is decorated with perforations for recessed lighting,
and the structural columns are given a trumpet form
expanding into the surface of the ceiling, both
features to give the effect of greater height to the
ballroom.

The end walls have sculptured wood block
treatment with inset mirrors. The shape of the
columns has been reflected in the design of the chairs
and tables.

The Queen's Room, Q.E.2 (Photo: I.P. Studios, London S.W.1)

The Palace Suite, Royal Garden Hotel, London, is situated on the lower ground floor, consists of a long space approximately 28·5 m × 16·1 m (94 ft × 53 ft) divisible into two spaces by a sound proof partition. A kitchen servery extends the full length of one long side and a reception room (foyer) extends the full length of the opposite side. The reception foyer can also be subdivided. A recessed area provides for a stage which can be curtained off. The stage can be extended with an apron. The lighting over the main ballroom area is recessed into ceiling wells. There is a press gallery also the length of one long side. The majority of the floor area is constructed as a dance floor. The capacity for dining is 450 (at separate tables) and 420 for dinner/dance, 600 for banquet, 1000 for cocktail gatherings, 900 for auditorium seating, and 1500 for receptions. The reception area (foyer) is served by a bar at one end and the concourse entrance has alternative access from the hotel foyer or independent access from the entrance drive. The concourse also gives access to lavatory and cloakroom accommodation.

(right) Royal Garden Hotel, Kensington: Ballroom Plan

(below right) Berkeley Hotel, London: Ballroom. (Interior designer; Michael Inchbald FSIA) (Photo: McMaster Christie Studios Ltd.)

(below) Royal Garden Hotel, Kensington: Ballroom (Photo: Conderoy & Moss Ltd.)

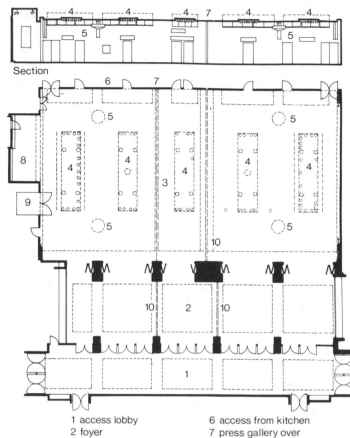

Section

1 access lobby
2 foyer
3 ballroom
4 recess in ceiling for lighting
5 chandelier
6 access from kitchen
7 press gallery over
8 stage
9 lift
10 dividing partition

Discotheques

Originally the main feature of the discotheque, a product of the swinging 1960s, pop culture, monied youth, mass-produced unbreakable records, and stereophonic amplified music, was the provision of dancing facilities to popular recorded music. New discotheques are operated in conjunction with a bar, restaurant or cabaret and have live music as part of the evening. The commercial aim of the 'disco' is to increase the attraction of the revenue earning function, and to provide a socialising ambience in which visitors can relax and indulge in group identification.

The scale of premises range from the adapted small hall or pub to the popular venues with space for 1000, such as the E.M.I. 'Romeo and Juliet' venues in Britain. The appearance ranges from simple decor to the up-market sophisticated night spot interior. Likewise the atmospheres can range from violent noise and strobe lighting to a sophisticated and quieter ambience.

The breakaway from the conventional 'ballroom' or 'palais' was caused by the emergence of young people with purchasing power and with a capacity to create a unifying cultural image.

Young people became an economic force generating a market for their own music, records and patronising venues in which to enjoy their own dance style. The early discotheques consisted of strobe filled cellars with psychedelic lighting. The format developed as the original participants matured. The current variety of discotheques, with strong or sophisticated decor, nostalgic 1920s or space-age themes, imaginative and varied lighting appeal to a wider audience. Some establishments include generous space for the spectator element with a protected more intimate atmosphere for socialising away from the dancing. There are also live groups, intermittent cabaret and 'gogo', licensed bars, snacks or restaurants adjoining.

Planning

The initial assessment concerning the design would include a definition of the location; admission policy; music policy; pricing policy; and compatibility with the adjoining facilities. The location or siting should allow easy access, clear visibility for the front of the house and avoidance of conflict with adjoining premises.

The admission policy is important in identifying the group that is to be accommodated, who will feel at ease and will enjoy the exclusiveness of that particular group. Such target groups would be defined as teenagers, the twenty to twenty-four year olds; particular social groups; twenty-five-plus age group; the mixed groups of a tourist resort; the captive audience of a cruise; the membership of a club and so forth.

Likewise the music policy must be decided on the same basis but also taking into account the important role of the disc jockey. As the 'master of ceremonies' he controls both mood and music. The location of the console in relation to the dance floor is important. It may be necessary to allow for live music and/or intermittent cabaret entertainment, which would entail a stage with suitable lighting, curtains and access from dressing rooms.

The basic circulation pattern is from the car park, entrance, foyer, cloaks, bar or restaurant to dance area with space for watching or quiet relaxation. The basic planning will take account of 'fire compartment' regulations, means of escape and exit in case of fire, and standards of fire protection that relate to equipment, finishes, location of fixtures and emergency lighting.

The important factor is the customer's enjoyment. In the celebrity 'disco', the reception area may be generous with space for demonstrative greetings and farewells. The atmosphere of the main space must convey intimacy, warmth, collective separateness, a sense of occasion and a sense of excitement. The layout—furnishings and decor—form the basic structure, whereas the adjustable elements such as lighting and sound, provide the mood. There should be space for spectators and also an area not dominated by the music. An important element in the planning and seating is to give the patrons an opportunity to be within their own group and also to meet other people. The casual meeting is important in this respect. Movement from level to level, staircases, contrived restricted circulation, group seating, can all generate a socialising atmosphere. Whereas a vigorous display of apparently unlimited energy or communion between dancer and music

D.J. console desk by Juliana's group of Companies

may be the nature of the young persons 'disco', the sense of occasion, elegance, warmth and relaxed behaviour is the character of the discotheque for older people.

The dance floor is the visual focus and the centre of activity. Controlled lighting can redirect interest to other features, such as bar, a cabaret, or live band when the 'disco' is not in use. Alternatively an empty dance floor can be disguised by mobile projected patterns, screens, curtains or a physical change of the area.

In the larger discotheques catering for significant numbers, where people are arriving and leaving at the same time, principal circulation patterns are important. It is advisable to avoid 'dead end' circulation as, for example, a cloakroom in which, after leaving their coats, people have to return through other waiting people. The movement around

Le Perroquet, Berkeley Hotel, London: Restaurant and discotheque

Josephines; Dance area and Bar

a bar is important to sales. It is essential to have a section free for service, in particular when drinks are served in limited interval time. The length of the bar, area for standing to drink, area for seating and the actual type of seating are all related to the overall character of the design. If there is a waitress, food or drinks service, the circulation pattern to and from the kitchen and bar is important.

The technical equipment for sound and lighting is continuously being improved. Lighting of discos is characterised by the rotating mirrored sphere and pulsating strobe lighting. Within the dance area, the control of lighting and sound which combine to create mood will be carried out by the disc jockey. The lighting—spots, floods, colour filtered, etc.—can be synchronised with the sound so that by frequency banding, light becomes an analogue of the music. The quality of the lighting, the freshnett wash effect, ultra-violet light (that makes some clothing appear luminescent), chaser lights, violent lighting; all combine to give an audio-visual experience.

The sound equipment may consist of two disc tables, space for storing discs, and a control panel. The quality of cassettes is improving, and where there is vibration or movement (as in the case of passenger ships) cassettes may be preferable. The number of speakers will depend on the size of the dance area and the available finances. The order of stereophonic speakers, and the space necessary for their accommodation in the ceiling or against a wall should be identified. The quieter areas, sitting and bar, may have a separate sound distribution at a reduced noise level controlled either by the disc jockey or at a separate control point. As the key person, the disc jockey must always be visible and in a position where he or she can see all areas used for dancing.

Discotheque examples

Le Peroquet, Wilton Street, London
Le Peroquet, designed by Michel Inchbald, FSIA, is part of the Berkeley Hotel, Wilton Street, London, and was designed as a daytime bar and buttery that becomes a dine and disco at night. Le Peroquet is on three levels with entrance at street level, bar at intermediate level, and both restaurant and discotheque at the lowest level. Cascading water at each level terminates in a water feature as a backdrop to the dance floor. The stepped ceiling structure and ventilation ducting is masked by a false ceiling of stalactite hexahedrons with a central mirrored fissure as a feature in the ceiling. The changes in level are protected by open devices—a water barrier, a window box and fixed swivel chairs.

Josephine's Night Club, Sheffield

The Club for 400 people consists of a discotheque, two bars, a wine bar and a restaurant, with sophisticated decor for over-twenty age group. The club is at first floor level with access from a paved piazza (part of a new office development) with an entrance vestibule containing ticket office, cloakroom counter and toilets. The decor includes stainless steel (for which Sheffield is famous) in contrast to the rich wine coloured velvet and felt interiors.

The layout includes differing floor levels and lowered ceilings over the sitting alcoves. The restaurant is set at a high level at one end of the club, and it is separated from the main area by a curving screen of tubular stainless steel tubes in front of a caroline draped, metallic threaded curtain lit from concealed lighting above. The bars have dark rosewood plastic laminate tops with an upholstered bar rail in black vinyl, with concealed lighting below illuminating Dralon-upholstered bar front panels.

Fixed seating is upholstered in Dralon with deep buttoned backs in semi-circular alcoves with fixed, pleated Dralon curtaining backgrounds. Loose seating consists of upholstered low circular stools and high bar stools. Loose tables are circular with brushed aluminium laminate faced tops.

Cabaret facilities are provided by a small raised stage with electrically operated curtains, and a concealed remote controlled film screen for back projection. Lighting in four colours is recessed and dimmer controlled or switched to sound impulse.

The stereo sound system, decorative lighting and effects lighting is controlled from a console with the disc jockey's console adjoining the dance floor. Mirrored panels are set in the ceiling over the console to provide a view of the controls and lights used by the disc jockey. The dance floor is illuminated by eleven suspended cartwheel lighting features with ceiling mounted spotlights to give general lighting.

The interior design consultants were Shepherd, Fowler and Robinson of Sheffield.

Josephine's, Sheffield: Plan

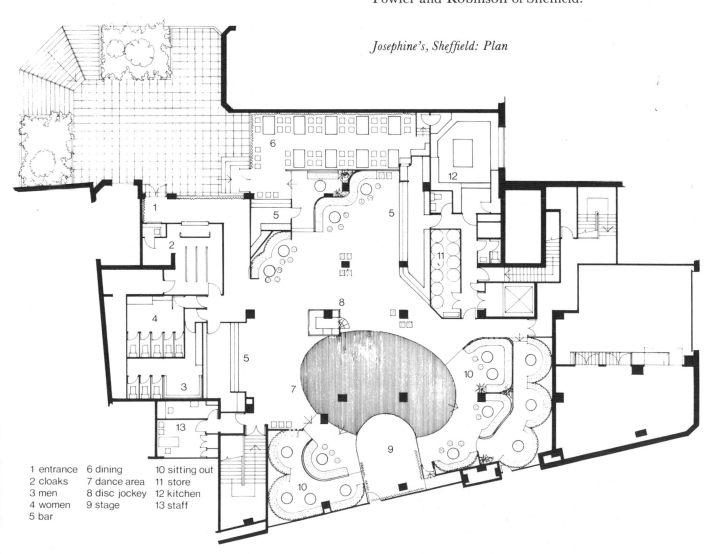

1 entrance	6 dining	10 sitting out
2 cloaks	7 dance area	11 store
3 men	8 disc jockey	12 kitchen
4 women	9 stage	13 staff
5 bar		

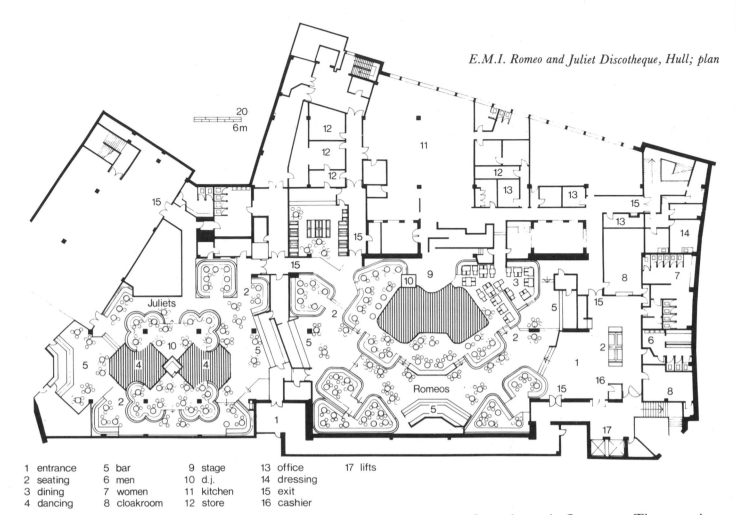

1 entrance	5 bar	9 stage	13 office	17 lifts
2 seating	6 men	10 d.j.	14 dressing
3 dining	7 women	11 kitchen	15 exit
4 dancing	8 cloakroom	12 store	16 cashier

E.M.I. 'Romeo and Juliet', Hull, Yorkshire

The layout consists of two dance areas providing the opportunity to have the choice of different mood or type of music within the same venue. The main dance area, 'Romeo's' has a multi-level floor providing views of the stage (with live band and disco console), and with sitting areas providing both a position close to the dancing, and more remote, quieter, and banquette enclosed seating.

The area is served by three bars and a restaurant area positioned close to the stage. There is a wine bar area set apart from the main floor area. The stage is sometimes used for cabaret.

The second discotheque, Juliet's, which is also used as a room for private functions, has a central console between two dance areas. It has two bars and banquet seating provides enclosed spaces.

This disco is situated on a third floor above a supermarket. Access is by two lifts which also provide a means of controlling the rate of movement through the reception and ticket area. The entrance foyer provides a waiting area and access to cloakroom, lavatories and a place to deposit handbags.

E.M.I. Romeo and Juliet Discotheque, Hull: (left) bar; (right) stage and dancing area (Photos: Anthony Wylson)

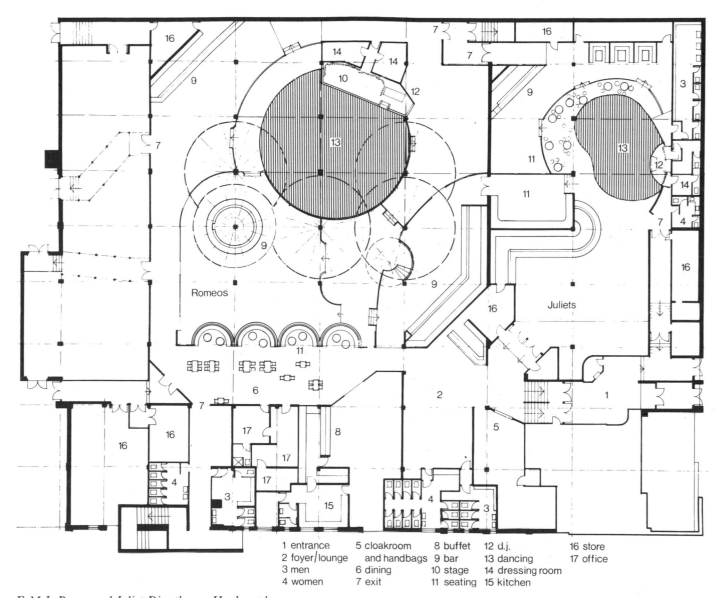

1 entrance	5 cloakroom	8 buffet	12 d.j.	16 store
2 foyer/lounge	and handbags	9 bar	13 dancing	17 office
3 men	6 dining	10 stage	14 dressing room	
4 women	7 exit	11 seating	15 kitchen	

E.M.I. Romeo and Juliet Discotheque, Hanley: plan

(below) E.M.I. Romeo and Juliet Discotheque, Hanley: Stage and dance floor

EMI 'Romeo and Juliet', Hanley, East Midlands
The principle of two discotheque areas forms the basis of the layout at Hanley. It is a ground floor location, adjoining a cinema.

A circular bar forms a feature in the 'Romeo' area, with floor and ceiling layouts reflecting the interlocking circle idea. A restaurant area overlooks the dance and stage area, and there is a separate dining area partially enclosed. 'Juliet's' is a themed area with Victorian decor and sitting areas created by decorated stalls with bench seating on three sides of each table. It has independent access from the street for private functions. The box office operates from the entrance foyer with a foyer lounge served by a bar providing access to both discotheques, cloakroom and lavatories.

22, Park Lane, London

The discotheque within the London Hilton in Park Lane is on the first floor planned with access both from within the 'patio' lounge of the hotel, and with direct access from the street. It was anticipated that guests would be from a wide age range, cosmopolitan, sophisticated, well to do and familiar with discotheque trends, and this influenced the selection of lighting and sound equipment and the choice of a 30's theme. The layout of the discotheque consists of an entrance area, with cloakroom and lavatory facilities, and the main disco with bar, seating and dance area. The entrance space is separated from the disco by a stainless steel vertical mullioned screen. The bar front is decorated with white neon lights, and the sitting areas have recessed wall features decorated with quadriglazer panels. The seating is on two levels permitting views of the dance area.

The disco installation and design was by Bacchus International Discotheque Services. The hexagonal dance area is illuminated by a recessed hexagon of lighting in the ceiling. This includes a central mirror mosaic ball, 500W coloured floods, swivel pinspots, strobes fitted with coloured gells, downlights, spotlights, clear strobes, scanner pinspots, bubble machines and a continuous line of pinspot downlights on the periphery to the hexagon. The dance floor is also illuminated with inlaid chaser floor lights. An infinity panel behind the console consists of two main light patterns formed by 400 6V lamps and four blue neon rectangles with surrounding lamps, chaser controlled. The decorative lighting is synchronised to the disc music.

London Hilton, 22 Park Lane. Plan of discotheque

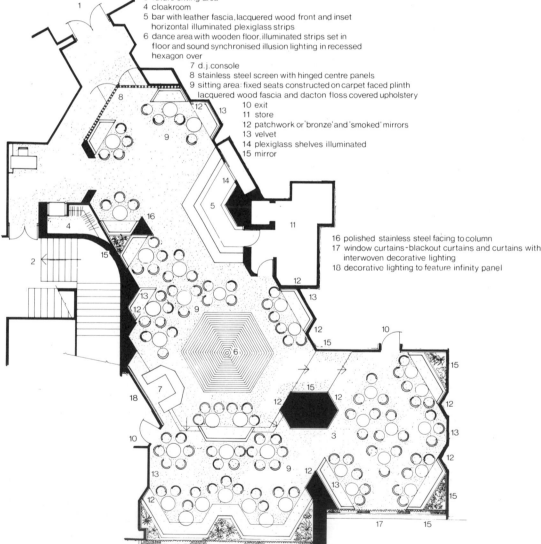

1 entrance from 'patio' lounge (and hotel)
2 entrance from street
3 future sitting area
4 cloakroom
5 bar with leather fascia, lacquered wood front and inset horizontal illuminated plexiglass strips
6 dance area with wooden floor, illuminated strips set in floor and sound synchronised illusion lighting in recessed hexagon over
7 d.j.console
8 stainless steel screen with hinged centre panels
9 sitting area: fixed seats constructed on carpet faced plinth lacquered wood fascia and dacton floss covered upholstery
10 exit
11 store
12 patchwork or 'bronze' and 'smoked' mirrors
13 velvet
14 plexiglass shelves illuminated
15 mirror
16 polished stainless steel facing to column
17 window curtains - blackout curtains and curtains with interwoven decorative lighting
18 decorative lighting to feature infinity panel

22 Park Lane. Illuminated dance floor and infinity panel (Photo: Sound Stills Ltd.)

The console consists of record storage for 500 singles and 100 LP's, two turntables, tape deck, microphone, headset, stereophonic mixer (with stand-by), switch panel, 12-zone dimmers, to control sound and light effects, pulse processor; chaser controller and strobe controller.

The interior design by Inge Bech (Hilton International) in conjunction with Tony Lucas has taken into account the location within a luxury hotel, and the implications of existing dance facilities within the top floor restaurant. The pricing policy and decor are geared to both hotel visitors and non-residents and provides space for 114 people (and 156 people with the proposed additional seating area).

22 Park Lane. View of dance area and bars

10. Discothèques et dancings—Résumé

La danse a toujours occupé une grande place dans le divertissement populaire. La salle de bal traditionnelle, dérivée des cours royales, a connu sa popularité au temps du 'palais de la danse' et de la salle de bal des grands hôtels. La danse elle-même est devenue une activité aux exigences particulières et soumise à des concours. Au cours des dernières décades, l'expression traditionnelle s'est relâchée dans les discothèques où se retrouvaient les jeunes mais qui regroupent maintenant toutes les générations de danseurs, dans une ambiance détendue bien différente de celle des anciennes salles de bal. Les discothèques se trouvent maintenant partout: les Discothèques EMI en Angleterre, à l'Hôtel Hilton de Londres, et sur le Q2, la Queen Room.

10. Diskos und Tanzen—Zusammenfassung

Tanz hat schon immer eine Rolle in der gesellschaftlichen Unterhaltung gespielt. Die Ballsaaltradition, die ihren Ursprung an den Höfen hatte, wurde durch die 'Palais de Danse' und Hotelballsäle auch dem Volk zugänglich gemacht. Gesellschaftstanz wurde zu einer anspruchsvollen Wettbewerbstätigkeit entwickelt. In den letzten Jahrzehnten fand der weniger formelle Tanz seinen Ausdruck in Diskotheken, die hauptsächlich von der Jugend besucht werden. Diskotheken sind heute einer breiteren Altersgruppe zugänglich und unterscheiden sich vom traditionellen Ballsaal in Form und Stimmung. Beispiele sind die EMI-Diskotheken in England, das Hilton Hotel, London, England, der Queen Room auf dem Kreuzer Queen Elizabeth II.

١٠ ـ الديسكوتيك وصالات الرقص ـ موجز

حقق الرقص دائما دوره في الترفيه الاجتماعي فقد أصبح رقص الصالة التقليدي المستمد من حياة القصور الملكية محبوباً لدى الجمهور في « باليه دو دانس » وفي صالات الرقص في الفنادق ، وأصبح رقص الصالة الصحيح من نشاطات المنافسة وبراعة الأداء . في الحقبات الأخيرة وجدت أنواع الرقص الأقل رسمية مجالها في الديسكوتيك التي بدأت كمجال لرودها الشباب . وقد أصبحت الديسكوتيك الآن ملجأ لمجموعة أوسع من الأعمار ولكنها تختلف في التصميم والجو عن صالات الرقص التقليدية . أمثلة : ديسكوتيك ثي ام آى في انجلترا فندق هيلتون لندن بانجلترا ـ صالة الملكة في عابرة المحيطات الفاخرة « الملكة اليزابيث الثانية » .

Chapter 11

Casinos and gambling

Gaming and dice have ancient origins. There are records of prehistoric dice carved from the ankle bone of sheep. Ancient Chinese and Egyptian civilisations indulged in gambling with forms of draughts, chess, dice and dominoes. The earliest cards had a religious significance.

Throughout the centuries the inclination towards gambling has frequently led to conflict with authority. Since the middle of the 17th century there have been numerous statutes to control gambling, intended to prevent unproductive diversion of workers' time. Even so by the 18th century, gambling in Europe amongst all classes of society had reached alarming proportions. In the mid-18th century London was acquiring fame as a centre of gambling with clubs such as White's and Brook's at their peak of popularity. Later Crockford established his club in St James where stakes as high as £200 000 were played and lost in a single session of card playing. In the 19th and 20th centuries, anti-gambling laws were based on a 'moral judgement'.

In America, gambling had been established in the 17th century and followed the pioneer trail westward in the context of the wild west saloon. In the early 19th century, gambling activities developed along the Mississippi River with the growth of the paddleboat traffic. Thousands of gamblers were plying their trade on the journey from New Orleans to Louisville.

With the decline of the steamboat, saloons were established in the riverside towns. Gambling drifted westward to Chicago and Nevada. However, anti-gambling legislation in America followed the pattern of English law. A game played for stakes was lawful if skill predominated, unlawful if chance ruled. The status of particular games rested with the Courts, and each State has its own individual interpretation.

Europe's oldest gambling casino in Baden Baden, started 200 years ago and, initially famous as a health resort, has become the most fashionable casino in Germany. Public gambling became illegal in France in 1857, but following the success of Monte Carlo, pressure was exerted to change the law. In 1907, baccarat and chemin de fer were legalised and in 1933 roulette casinos were established in Le Touquet, Biarritz, Nice, Deauville and Cannes. Monte Carlo has become one of Europe's most luxurious holiday resorts with a social life centred on the Place du Casino and the picturesque gardens overlooking the International Sporting Club.

Gambling in both Europe and Nevada, USA has become a leading industry, not only stimulated by the lure of easy money, the excitement and social context, but it has also become recognised as a lucrative source of government revenue.

In the UK, many companies operating casinos have wider interests in the leisure, entertainment and hotel industries. For some companies there has been additional diversification in recent years.

The Ladbroke Group, which has both London and provincial casinos, began at the turn of this century as bookmakers. It is now a substantial public company covering leisure and service industries including luxury hotels, holiday villages, the Lucky Seven Social (bingo) clubs, restaurants, pubs, lottery management and hi-fi shops as well as owning racecourses and greyhound stadia.

The Playboy Organisation, established in America in 1953, has enjoyed a popular image through its decorative magazine and 'bunny' profile. Playboy Clubs, the first of which was established in Chicago in 1960, have been created in eight American cities and there are two Playboy resort hotels.

However, since 1966 and on the initiative of Victor Lownes, Vice President of Playboy Enterprises Inc., the Playboy Organisation has been active in the casino business in Britain. The Organisation first took premises in Park Lane (in a building designed by Walter Gropius) and in 1972 extended the London activities to include the elegant Clermont

Club in Berkeley Square. In the subsequent two years, casino clubs were established in Portsmouth and Manchester. With gambling permitted in the State of New Jersey, the Playboy Organisation have plans to construct a Las Vegas style hotel casino in Atlantic City.

Legislation

In the UK, prior to 1960, a Royal Commission was set up (stimulated by the maze of inconsistencies in the law on gambling), to examine the whole spectrum of gaming activities in the light of present-day needs. The recommendations resulted in the 1960 Act which made most forms of gambling in Great Britain legal, but the Act was insufficient to control casino gaming and organised crime gradually infiltrated the business.

Tighter legislation was introduced in the 1968 Gaming Act which concentrated on gaming activities and, for the first time, a carefully conceived system of controls was created. The 'Gaming Board for Great Britain' was set up with the duty of keeping under review the extent, character and location of all gaming facilities in licensed clubs. It regulates the conduct and rules of the games played and determines precisely, the advantages that can be permitted to the house.

The Act permits gaming to take place only in a licensed gaming club. Applications are carefully considered and generally a town must have a population of over 125 000 to justify a licence. Not only are the numbers of casino licences strictly controlled, but also the location within a town where they may be sited. The 1000 casinos in existence prior to the Act have been reduced to 124. In the casinos, every employee must be licensed and participants must become a member of a club forty-eight hours before gambling in that club. The hours and facilities are strictly controlled.

No advertising of clubs is permitted within the United Kingdom and each gaming club is only permitted two 'fruit' machines. No cabaret acts, live music or dancing is permitted within the casino club, and circulation between casino bar and restaurant is strictly controlled. There should be no distraction of the punter and the behaviour of the croupier is also strictly controlled. Dinner jacket pockets are sewn up, and in one club, the croupier must clap his hands to draw attention of the supervisor before taking a handkerchief from his trouser pocket.

Since 1961, in Great Britain, the finances directed towards gambling have increased. In 1970–71 £180 million was spent on horse and greyhound racing,

£126 million on the pools, and over £660 million on bingo and gaming, this making a total of nearly £2000 million spent on gambling. This compares with approximately £500 million per annum spent in Las Vegas on all things besides gaming and £300 million per annum spent on gaming in 1974.

Gaming activities

The gambling activities that have promoted specialised accommodation are low risk family gaming as bingo, housey-housey or keno; the casino, where gamblers can risk their money against a common gambler (called a banker or the house); and gambling on contestants as horse and dog racing, Jai Alai, boxing and other competitive games.

Popular gaming

Bingo from the 18th-century Italian 'lotto' and originating in ancient China, also known as housey-housey and as keno in America; the controller of the game calls out numbers from a container and the player crosses them off when they coincide with the numbers on the printed card he buys. As it is a sitting down game, accommodation is provided either in stadium layout or as lines of benches or seats and tables, with a clear view of the controller, and by controller of the participants.

Bingo clubs started in the UK in 1961 and have become a major leisure entertainment and socially congenial activity. With the decline in cinema entertainment, bingo has been adapted to cinema premises and clubs play an important part in the community life. In the UK 6 million people belong to bingo clubs and there is an average of 450 000 attendances at bingo clubs each day. Bingo—as gambling—is in the pools and lotteries league, where it is not immediately possible to choose one's losses. The stakes are small and the profitability to the company is independent of the principal bingo game. The company makes its profits from admission to secondary games (prize bingo or mechanised bingo), bar, restaurant and entertainments. The average spent on admission, books and entertainment per session is just over £1.00 per person.

Bingo is controlled by the British Gaming Board and a company wishing to start a club must apply for a Certificate of Consent. The local authority issues a licence and thereby controls the standard of the building, means of escape and general running of the gambling. The layout of a bingo club consists basically of an entrance area, auditorium and management accommodation.

The entrance area will include foyers, cloakrooms,

sales kiosk with stock room, bookselling counter served by a book store, and a cashier's office and window. The entrance hall will display information of times of sessions, licensing matters and club activities. The sales kiosk, as a cinema kiosk, would be in the order of 3 m × 2 m (10 ft × 6 ft 8 in) and designed to comply with local regulations and statutory hygiene standards. It would include an ice cream freezer, cigarette dispenser, small handbasin and it should be possible to close it off with a roller shutter when the kiosk is not attended. The adjoining stock room should have easy access from the street for deliveries.

The bookselling counter will have several sales positions (each 900 mm or 3 ft wide) depending upon the size of the club. The counter and space behind would be enclosed and served by a bookstore and with direct access to the cash office. The cash office will have a security designed cashier's window for dispensing change and winnings.

The conventional bingo auditorium (as established by the Rank Organisation and Ladbrokes) has fixed seats and tables in a stepped layout so that all

participants can hear the caller and participants can see both the caller's rostrum and information indicator panels. The participant must also be visible by the caller or attendants. The layout of fixed tables and seating must comply with licensing regulations and provide the required exitways. The auditorium will also have a security close-circuit television arrangement and a scrutineer's checking camera.

The caller's rostrum would consist of a raised area approximately 2·5 m × 2 m (8 ft × 6 ft 8 in) where the caller can present and control the game. The rostrum would have spotlight illumination, microphone, bingo blower and television camera. Sound equipment and electrical equipment for controlling the indicator boards and close-circuit television can be located under the rostrum. There would be a scrutineer's point adjacent to the caller's rostrum to enable claims to be checked and processed. This would consist of a 1 m × 2 m (3 ft 4 in × 6 ft 8 in) recess in the wall 1 m above the floor, to house the close-circuit television

Bingo Social club, South London—plan

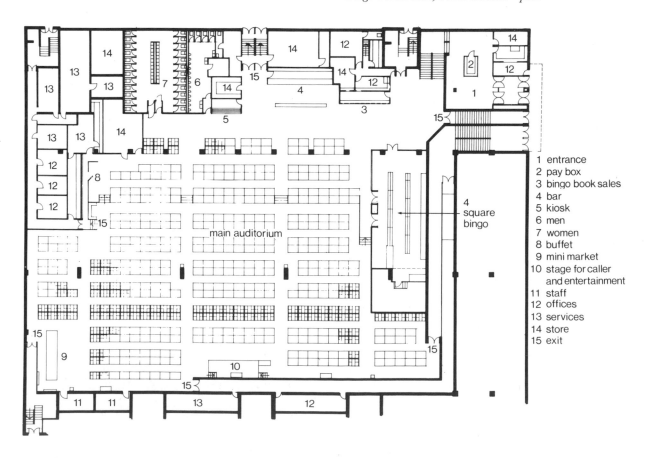

1 entrance
2 pay box
3 bingo book sales
4 bar
5 kiosk
6 men
7 women
8 buffet
9 mini market
10 stage for caller and entertainment
11 staff
12 offices
13 services
14 store
15 exit

checking camera and electronic dial board to communicate to the information panel. In addition to the caller's rostrum, there could be an entertainment rostrum for solo or musical entertainment with the appropriate stage equipment. The information and indicator panels show to the members numbers called, books sold, cash prize split and game prize split. The panels would be approximately 3 m × 2 m (10 ft × 6 ft 8 in).

Areas ancillary to the main auditorium could include prize bingo and mechanised bingo. Prize bingo requires illuminated showcases and a deep freeze display cabinet to display prizes, normally located adjacent to the main auditorium. There would be a prize bingo blower and playing console unit. Mechanised bingo consists of rows of machines in a space separate from the main auditorium and the prize money is directly related to the number of people playing.

Also accessible from, or opening into, the auditorium (depending upon licensing regulations) there would be a licensed bar (served by a bottle store), a buffet consisting of a sales counter for hot and cold food (served by normal kitchen, food preparation and storage facilities), cafeteria or restaurant. The club would also require members cloakroom and lavatory accommodation, administrative offices and staff facilities.

The social club entrance is at ground floor level, with a staircase leading up to the entrance foyer. On entering the main playing area from the foyer, ticket sales and toilets are in close proximity. The main bingo area can seat 1220 and consists of fixed tables

and hinged seats arranged in stalls. The seating is orientated towards a large stage and there are licensed bars, buffet bar and toilet accommodation in the spaces surrounding the auditorium. There is parti bingo in the corner of the auditorium farthest from the stage.

In Las Vegas, keno is played in keno parlours and restaurant lounges. A ticket is numbered one to eighty. A player marks the numbers he chooses from one to fifteen. A machine chooses twenty balls at random out of eighty. The numbers are announced and are simultaneously flashed on an electronic display board identical in layout to the keno tickets. Of the many gaming activities in Nevada casinos, keno is the most relaxed and the accommodation is designed accordingly.

Another form of popular gambling is the 'slot' machine, a coin operated gambling device also referred to as fruit machines or 'one armed bandits'. The majority consist of three vertical slots through which three reels rotate. Each reel has twenty to twenty-five pictorial symbols. When a coin is inserted and the handle pulled, the reels rotate and when they come to rest a line of symbols shows up on the slots. There are 8000 to 15 000 combinations of which twelve lines will pay out. There are also electronic slot machines, but the 'one armed bandit' has retained its popularity. In Las Vegas, where these machines appear in solid ranks covering acres of floor space, there are in the order of 100 000 machines, with 930 in one hotel-casino. There are also a few special variations as the Super 8 with eight reels rotating.

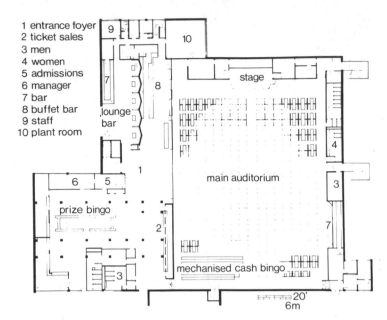

1 entrance foyer
2 ticket sales
3 men
4 women
5 admissions
6 manager
7 bar
8 buffet bar
9 staff
10 plant room

Bingo Social club, Luton—plan

Lucky 7 Prize Bingo, Luton (Photo: Anthony Wylson)

Bingo Club, Luton (Photo: Anthony Wylson)

Casinos

The casino activities fall into two categories—card-based games, such as chemin de fer, baccarat, punto bancho and blackjack, and dice games such as craps and roulette.

Chemin de fer is a game in which ordinary cards are dispensed from a wooden 'shoe' or dealing box. The 'Banker' puts his stakes in the centre of the table, and the players and banker play cards in competition. The table for nine players is approximately 2·6 m × 1·37 m.

Baccarat and punto bancho, in which twelve to fifteen people can participate, is played on a table divided into two and is similar to chemin de fer, except that the bank always stays with the house. To win, the players' cards must beat the bank. Punto bancho tables for ten players are approximately 3 m × 1·5 m and, for fourteen players, 3·5 m × 1·75 m. Baccarat tables are slightly smaller, although dual-purpose tables are also available. Players sit and spectators stand behind the players.

Blackjack, in which six or seven players seated, can take part, is the American version of the English game 'pontoon' and the French game 'vingt et un'. The tables are semi-circular or a faceted semi-circle with seating for players on the curved side and the croupier on the straight side. A small blackjack table would measure 1·6 m × 1 m although normally a table 2 m × 1 m would be required for seven players.

Craps, in which the players bet against the house using dice on a table, and in which a number of players can participate. The table is the largest and heaviest item in a casino, measuring 3·6 m × 1·5 m. Players stand with stickman central one side and chippers central on the opposite side.

Roulette is a sit-down game which consists basically of spinning a ball against a turning wheel, the ball comes to rest in a number. The roulette wheel requires precision in its manufacturing, and the tables are either American style or French style in layout. The American style table has players on a long and short side and the tables are overall 2·5 m × 1·6 m with large tables at 2·0 m × 1·6 m. The French style table has players on two long sides and the short side, and measure 3·3 m × 1·8 m. Players are seated and chipper and croupier work side by side from the extended section of the table.

Statutory requirements impose strict control on means of escape and relationship of spaces for gambling and other club activities. Correct lighting is important. Where pendant lights are used, the large tables require two fittings with shades to avoid glare. To allow flexibility in layout, some casinos use downlights recessed into a demountable ceiling system. However, the pendant light, with the concentrated illumination on and identification of individual tables conveys the traditional character of the casino.

A typical layout of a small casino in Britain would group roulette and blackjack tables to form a 'pit' with a 'pit boss' centrally placed and croupiers and chippers working within the pit. The players are outside the pit and gaps between tables would have a barrier rope. In addition, there would be a craps table, with chippers enclosed by a rope barrier, a baccarat table, and several poker tables. The gaming area would require a cashier's counter and inspectors must be positioned amongst the gaming tables to supervise.

London casinos

The character of Mayfair casino life brings an elegance and respect for decor that is sympathetic to conserving historic buildings of this quality. However, the table layouts, with the additional suspended lighting, is obviously dissimilar to the original function of the rooms. The chandeliers and wall panels require to be seen unobstructed by large furniture. This draws attention to the underlying design problem of adapting interesting historic buildings to new uses with funds sufficient to finance expensive maintenance. Nevertheless, there is a sophisticated social ambience that is consistent with the 18th-century creation.

One Mayfair club building was originally designed by William Kent in 1742 for an aristocratic hostess of the day, to provide an impressive setting for entertainment. The house includes an ornate staircase space (with high-level gallery and domelight) and elegant rooms at first floor level. The building was partly remodelled by Henry Holland for the second owner (the Earl of Clermont), and apart from the addition of a conservatory style dining room, the building has remained relatively unchanged since the 18th century. The principal rooms, intended originally for social functions, convey an elegance of decor and scale with chandeliers, decorative ceilings, fireplaces and door surrounds. As a casino, rooms on the first floor are used as gaming rooms with the ground floor providing space for entrance hall, cloakroom, bar and restaurant.

Another West End casino consists of a long narrow building with entrances and vertical circulation at one end. The long gaming rooms have tables in a line down the centre with members circulating on one side and croupiers and inspectors on the other. To comply with the licensing rules restricting the proximity of entertainment to gaming, the club has two entrances. One leads to a ground floor restaurant

Historic building utilised as casino club (Photos: Anthony Wylson)

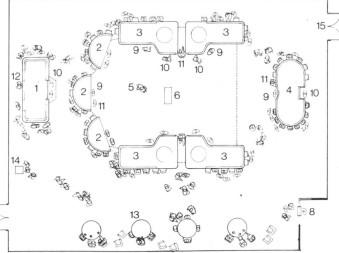

1 craps 12' or 14' x 5	8 cashier
2 blackjack 5'4" to 7'0" x 3'7"	9 dealer
3 roulette 8'6" to 10'10" x	10 chipper
5'2" to 6'0"	11 inspector
4 baccaret 9'6" to 11'3" x	12 stickman
4'6" to 5'4"	13 relaxation
5 pit boss	14 slots
6 bureau	15 exit
7 entrance	

(above) Hypothetical casino layout

West End casino (Photo: Anthony Wylson)

West End casino club showing layout in long floor plan (Photo: Anthony Wylson)

with small area for cabaret, and to a basement cabaret and discotheque. The principal entrance gives access to four floors (above ground) of which three are casino floors and one provides for bar and restaurant. The individual gaming floors are varied in character. At one level there is a shallow vaulted ceiling over the gaming tables and dining area. Other floors have acoustic tile suspended ceilings with recessed lighting which allows flexibility of layout. Apart from illuminated picture panels on the walls, the lighting and interest is concentrated on the tables. The total gaming facilities of the Playboy Club consists of one punto bancho, fifteen blackjack, eleven

roulette tables and one craps table in a total working area of approximately 4500 sq. feet.

Two Provincial casinos

A casino in the south of England, previously a tea room, provides a club on one level. The interior design was by Granville-Dixon Design Ltd. The layout includes slight variations in floor level to provide interest to the open plan. The wall finishes incorporate textures and dark colours and a 'Bunny' head motif is used in the carpet design throughout the entrance area and bar. The entrance space, with sales area and reception, has a curved panelled wall consisting of strips of antique mirror and strips of mahogany. The 'Playmate Bar' is suitably decorated with an illuminated glamorous display and the restaurant seating has a flexible table arrangement to allow two, four or six persons per table. Table

South Coast casino—plan (Interior designed by Granville-Dixon Interiors Ltd.)

1 reception	4 bar	7 cashier	10 black jack
2 men	5 store	8 dining	11 roulette
3 women	6 staff	9 punto banco	

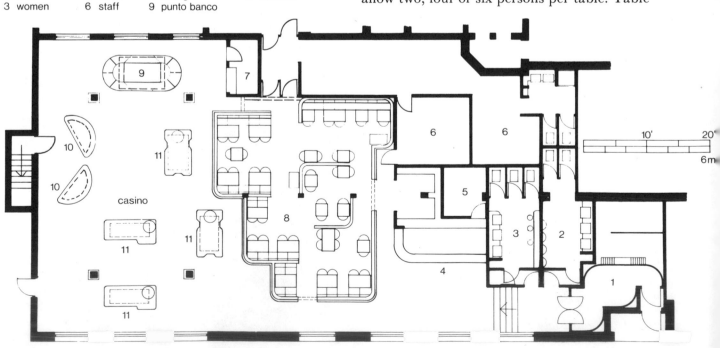

lighting is by hooded light fittings and the restaurant carpet has a diamond pattern.

In the casino area, the green baize colour is predominant and the wall finishes combine a green fabric interspersed with silver and antique green mirrors in a diamond pattern. The lighting to the casino area consists of downlighters directly over the tables to give a flexible system of ceiling lighting. Throughout the club the colours of costumes worn by the staff are related to the interior design scheme.

The latest addition to the club provides a discotheque and cabaret room with buffet and bar.

A club in Bedfordshire combines casino, restaurant and cabaret restaurant at ground floor level (described with theatre-restaurants), with a first floor bingo social club. The restaurant and casino entrances are adjoining, and the casino consists of an open plan with an interesting use of two levels. This provides a pleasant spatial character, whereby a visitor is able to look across the gaming tables as a spectator, each game being identified by individual suspended lighting. The gaming facilities include eleven tables and a sitting out area. The layout creates both a relaxed atmosphere with characteristic decorative lighting, in which individual games operate simultaneously.

Casino on several levels (Photo: Anthony Wylson)

11. Kasinos und Glücksspiele—Zusammenfassung

In den letzten Jahrzehnten haben sich unter strenger staatlicher Kontrolle und als Steuerquellen in Europa und in Nevada, USA Kasinos entwickelt, die Bestandteil der Unterhaltung wurden. In Großbritannien wurde die Kasinozahl durch Kontrolle beschränkt. Einige historische Gebäude wurden in elegante Kasinos verwandelt, und es entstanden neue Spielclubs. Unbenutzte Kinos fanden neuen Einsatz als Bingo-Clubs und bieten bescheidene Glücksspiele für die unteren Schichten. In Las Vegas fallen die Hotelkasinos in eine gesonderte Gruppe und bieten Glücksspiel und alles umfassende Anlagen für die Feriengestaltung.

11. Le jeu et les casinos—Résumé

Au cours des dernières décades, de nouveaux casinos se sont créés en Europe et dans le Nevada, aux Etats-Unis, sous contrôle statutaire rigoureux et en tant que source de revenu possible, pour faire maintenant partie du monde des loisirs. Dans le Royaume-Uni, le contrôle particulièrement strict, a limité le nombre des casinos. Des salles de jeux ont été aménagées dans le cadre élégant de demeures historiques, et de nouveaux clubs se sont ouverts. Les clubs civiques de loto (bingo) ont occupé la place laissée libre par les cinémas abandonnés et fournissent maintenant une certaine forme de jeu à la foule populaire de leurs adhérents. A Las Vegas, les salles de jeu dans les hôtels sont à une échelle tout à fait àpart, car elles font partie d'une chaîne complète de loisirs offerts au touriste.

١١ ـ الكازينات والمقامرة ـ موجز

في الحقبات الأخيرة ونتيجة لتشريعات الرقابة الصارمة وكمورد لعائد الضرائب ، نمت الكازينات في أوروبا وفي نيفادا بالولايات المتحدة لتصبح جزءا من ميدان الترفيه ، بينما حددت القيود في المملكة المتحدة عدد الكازينات . وقد جرى تطوير بعض المباني التاريخية لتزويد جو فاخر للمقامرة كما انشئت النوادي الجديدة . وقد أتاحت نوادي البينجو الاجتماعية استخدام دور السينما الزائدة عن الحاجة في شكل جديد يهيئ المقامرة البسيطة لعدد كبير من اعضائها . أما في لاس فيجاس فان نسبة كازينات الفنادق تقع في فئة خاصة بها حيث أنها تهدف الى تزويد جميع خدمات العطلات الى جانب المقامرة .

Chapter 12

Public safety: fire hazard

Security and public safety is an important element in the design of entertainment buildings. In most countries, a classification system serves as a basis to statutory safety requirements. However, the fire risk of various types of buildings must be assessed from the aspect of personal safety, safety of the structure and security of contents. The designer can assess the number and mobility of the occupants and derive a comprehensive means of escape within the relevant Codes of Practice or Regulations. Places of entertainment have a high density of occupation, with people who are not always familiar with the premises and with the possible slow reaction of the young and elderly.

The extent of potential damage to a building depends upon the amount, nature and distribution of the combustible material within it. The fire hazard can be reduced by:

1. Careful consideration to site layout and planning.
2. Adequate protected means of escape.
3. Consideration of surface spread of flame by materials and finishes.
4. Fire protection to the structure.
5. Compartmentation and separation.
6. Fire fighting equipment and access for fire appliances.
7. Ventilation to disperse smoke and hot gases.

The following information relates to UK safety regulations but the USA and other countries have similar requirements.

Site location

Entertainment accommodation may consist of either an independent building, or a secondary use within a large building, or it may be part of a leisure park with buildings of different character in a campus.

The designer will be concerned that the means of escape to safety is comprehensive, unambiguous, unobstructed, secure and available when the building is in use. The surrounding structure must be secure against the effect of fire and that any hazard arising from adjoining spaces must be taken into account. The place of safety is defined as a place where the occupant will be free of all ultimate danger from fire and it is normally a public street or an open space with safe access to a public street. Access is required for fire appliances and the correct fire standards must be included in the building as a whole.

The fire risk arising from individual buildings within a leisure park will be assessed. The access for fire appliances, the system of exit routes and the fire hazard of one building in relation to another will be given particular consideration. Adequate space between buildings can reduce fire radiation hazard from fire in one building to another.

The accessibility required for fire appliances and extent of hard standing in relation to the building varies with the height and volume of the building. Standards range from one side access for a building with floors no higher than 9 m and less than $7100\,m^3$ (where the appliances must be able to reach within 45 m of any part of the building) to full access from all sides for buildings with a volume of over $85\,000\,m^3$. The GLC (Greater London Council) standards are also graded. In high-rise buildings the installation of rising mains for fire fighting is required. For buildings of 18 m to 61 m (60 ft to 200 ft) high, there should be a dry main.

The spread of fire between buildings can be due to airborne debris, convected hot gases, fire spreading across from adjoining roofs and radiation across an open or enclosed space. These aspects are covered in the Building Regulations as far as separate properties are concerned, but basic site planning must also give consideration to the risk between building and parts of buildings within the same ownership. The risk of radiation transferring fire can be reduced by providing an imperforate barrier between the building and adjacent combustible material; by providing sufficient space to dissipate the heat, or by regulating the size, location and number of fire-resisting wall openings in relation to the distance from the potential fire hazard. The relationship of wall openings must also be designed to reduce the spread of fire from storey to storey.

In planning fairs, circuses and tented entertainment, the HMSO publication 'Safety at Fairs' provides general recommendations. A plan showing entrance and exits should be available on site and the layout should be agreed with the chief fire officer. The recommendations include details of access for fire appliances and space between vehicles, rides and devices to achieve clear exitways.

Means of escape

Well-planned circulation within the building is fundamental to means of escape from fire, failure of electrical supply and bomb scares, etc. The number and design of exit routes and escape stairs are carefully regulated by local authority, fire officers or mandatory standards.

The rate at which people move and the number of people to be evacuated controls the number and sizes of exits. Generally the travel distance to an exit route should not be more than 15 m (49 ft) in one direction and 30 m (98 ft) in more than one direction (except basements). Travel distances are related to occupancy and an average time of $2\frac{1}{2}$ minutes (based on a travel speed of 13·7 m (40 ft) per min) is the recommended time for evacuation for a closely seated audience. Usually, there must be more than one direction for escape and travel distances of 18 m (59 ft) and 15 m (49 ft) (normal seating and Continental seating respectively) from seat to exit.

Widths of exitways are based on a unit width assumed to discharge forty persons per minute, and the aggregate of units must relate to the number of people to be evacuated. Where there is a large number of people (as in an assembly room), it is necessary to provide sufficient number of exits to reduce overcrowding at exits and to avoid possible panic.

Generally, alternative exits (clearly indicated) should be located on diagonally opposite sides of the space concerned. Where there are two means of escape (one of which may be the main entrance), each should be designed to accommodate the full occupant capacity of the area concerned. With more than two means of escape, full occupant capacity should be shared between all escape routes less one. Escape route gangways for assembly rooms with provision of a closely seated audience should have a minimum width of 1·1 m and the fire risk is reduced to a minimum through strict control of materials in fittings and finishes. The escape routes are specifically arranged in relation to seatways, aisles, crossovers, exits, exitways and stairs to provide a comprehensive adequately illuminated route from each seat to a place of safety. Escape routes should be as unambiguous and direct as possible. Regulations control the construction of doors and their frames, glazed panels in the doors and the formation of lobbies. Glazed screens in exit routes can transmit heat radiation and additional width is required depending on the area and thickness of glass concerned (sheet glass to glass brick).

The escape staircases must be protected from heat and smoke and it must not be possible for the staircase well to provide a path for fire to pass from one floor to another. The escape stair enclosure must not include anything that would constitute a fire risk. Stores, cupboards or service enclosures should not open directly on to the enclosure. In most cases, toilets are considered a negligible risk. Stairs should never diminish in width in the direction of escape.

In the case of high buildings over 18 m (60 ft) it is necessary to designate some staircases for fire fighting and in such cases a high fire safety standard would be required with spacious lobbies in which fire fighters can work. Special conditions apply to staircases extending from floor levels above ground level to basement level and it is recommended that there should be separate egress for buildings with a single staircase.

Escape stairs must remain free from smoke and hot gases. This can be achieved by smoke lobbies and ventilators or windows provided at high level.

In assembly buildings generally, the British standard for treads is 280 mm (11 in) and 150 mm (6 in) for risers with 180 mm (7 in) for risers in the Building Regulations. There should be not less than three risers and not more than sixteen risers in one flight and not more than two flights without a change of direction. Staircases over 1 m (3 ft 3 in) wide should have handrails both sides and over 2·1 m (7 ft) escape staircases should have a central handrail. There are also similar recommended standards for tented accommodation.

Separate escape stairs should discharge to the open air independently of one another. Ramps are permitted in an escape route if provided with a nonslip finish and are constructed in an unbroken flight or uniform pitch not exceeding 1:12. Ramps should be provided with handrails and balustrades as for stairs. Attention should be given to the movement of the handicapped or disabled, and the correct standard of safety lighting to be applied.

In final escape exits through halls or corridors, the occupants should have the same degree of protection as the escape route and the space should not contain furniture or fittings which would constitute a fire risk or diminish the width of the exit route. The final exit door should be clearly visible from the foot of the stairs. Final exits should be located away from access to basements or other fire hazards. The doors should open outwards with a total width (excluding revolving doors) not less than the minimum required for the exit route. The exit door should be capable of being opened from the inside at any time the building is occupied, without the use of a key. Where there are extensive numbers of people the exit door should open when pressure is applied to it or a safety lock. There should be level going for an adequate distance either side of the exit door.

Escape routes discharging on to a roof deck or podium (if this has an adequate fire resistance), should have a clearly defined escape route with guard rail where necessary. Such routes should be fully protected from any fire risk in adjacent accommodation or from within the building.

For escape routes in a town centre complex incorporating 'mall' access a guide to means of escape is provided in the HMSO Publication 'Fire Precautions in Town Centre Redevelopment'. It should be possible to proceed from the occupancy with alternative routes, except where the route in question leads away from and not parallel with the frontage of the occupancy from which escape is being made. Occupancies located at 'dead ends' should always have alternative means of escape. The guide covers location and size of exit routes from a 'mall'.

In the case of fairs and tented entertainment, any tent, booth or enclosure requires adequate exits and the recommendations of 'Guide to Safety in Fairs' do not come up to the standards for permanent building. Where fifteen or more people are accommodated, two exits are required and sufficient exits to ensure that everyone can leave safely in 2 minutes or less. This would be calculated on the basis that eighty persons can pass through an opening 1·1 m wide in 1 minute. Where the structure holds fifty or more occupants, gangways 1·1 m wide are recommended with a maximum distance of 6·5 m from any seat to a gangway and a maximum travel distance by any person of 30 m to a place of safety. For pneumatic structures, travel distance to an exit should be minimal and rigid frames are necessary to support exits.

The maximum number of people admitted to any booth, tent or enclosure should be based on thirty-six persons per 10 m² for a standing audience and twenty-four persons per 10 m² for a closely seated audience (the areas including gangways and passages). Exit routes should be clearly indicated, illuminated as necessary and with effective emergency lighting fed from a different source from the normal lighting.

Fire spread

Combustible materials can be instrumental to the rate at which a flame spreads over the surface. Materials are classified from low (Class 0) to rapid flame spread (Class 4) by peremptory testing.

In leisure buildings not only the structures but also the combustible nature of wall linings, fabrics (curtains, seat covers, floor coverings) are controlled. For stage entertainment, where there is no fire curtain between stage and auditorium, all materials used on the stage must be rendered not readily combustible.

The increasing application of plastics for roofing finishes and insulation requires particular consideration. The use of translucent plastics for roofing which can have a high flame spread, toxic gas and smoke risk is controlled by Building Regulations.

Protection of the structure

The size of the structure whether single or multi-occupancy must provide structural stability for a period considered necessary to fight the fire and to evacuate the building. Above two storeys, any element that supports or carries another for which resistance is required should have the same fire resistance. Where there is a multi-use, the predominant occupancy must usually prevail for the basis of classification.

Structural materials behave in different ways under fire. A high standard of resistance is achieved by applying protective coverings and in the case of multi-occupancy structures, integral protection is recommended rather than hollow casings. The latter are also vulnerable to damage at working level. Attention should be given to the fire resistance of cladding and glazed panels. The method of fixing panels must maintain the fire standard. There is the possibility of gaps resulting from filling material disintegrating under heat of fire conditions. The structural hazard resulting from the expansion of panels due to high temperature and progressive collapse due to failure of one floor with its contents, overloading another floor.

Compartmentation and separation

The principle of compartmentation is the separation or division of occupancies into fire compartments of appropriate fire resistance with a limitation of 7000 m³ for assembly buildings. Within a multi-use building there are areas of high fire risk (such as storage, garage areas, unloading bays, waste disposal areas, central heating equipment, fuel storage, electrical plant rooms, production areas, display areas and areas with a complex decor) that require separation. A large building would be divided into fire compartments, each compartment being constructed and designed 'fire tight' relative to the use.

The enclosure walls, floors and ceilings must be consistent to maintain fire standards including doors, shutters, borrowed lights and glazed screens. Particular attention must be given to services passing through walls to avoid the passage of fire smoke, hot gases or toxic fumes. Ducts and shafts should have fusible-link-controlled dampers on the line of the compartment enclosure and combustible service pipes extending from one compartment to another can create a risk of spread through walls and should be installed and protected to Building Regulation requirements.

In the case of theatres, a fire resisting separation is created between the high-risk stage area, backstage accommodation and the auditorium. Usually in the event of fire, a fireproof safety curtain separates auditorium from stage to reduce the risk to the public. The auditorium extract ventilation system is reversed to provide a pressure to the safety curtain. This is aimed to counteract buckling through the build-up of pressure on the stage side. The stage would also have vents at high level to dissipate smoke and hot gases.

Fire fighting equipment and assistance to fire brigade

Fire-fighting equipment covers the installation of detectors and alarms, automatic fire extinguishing equipment, the provision of first-aid fire-fighting appliances, the provision of fire and explosion suppressants (where appropriate) and the provision of facilities to assist the fire brigade. Some equipment is mandatory, but other equipment will be needed to conform with insurance or local authorities' requirements. Many items will be a matter of recommendation and good practice. The selection of equipment must provide an appropriate system of defence against fire, taking into account occupancy and construction. Having assessed the building requirements for defence systems, it will be necessary to discuss with the fire authority and the fire insurance surveyor, in order to consider the economics of installation and in order to identify areas of particular risk.

Automatic detection requires quick response by fire fighting.

For the large multi-occupancy building, a two-stage alarm system provides an evacuation signal for the affected section of the premises, while at the same time an alert is sounded in the adjoining sections. If evacuation is required from the latter, a second stage alarm is given. This arrangement is particularly relevant where main escape routes from occupancies are directed on to covered malls or walkways. In addition, a public address system would be installed in buildings with extensive 'common' areas to instruct occupants in buildings.

For buildings in the 'assembly' category, all places, whether for public or private use, for recreational or social activities, will require an alarm system to comply with the proposed Section II, Part E of the Building Regulations, although some authorities would not recommend audible alarms in public areas. Detectors can be grouped to divide the building into zones, and to aid discovery of the fire by an indicator board that shows its location. This indicator board should be near the point of entry for the fire brigade.

Warning devices must normally be audible against background noise levels throughout the building in which they are installed. Where audible alarms are not considered desirable (e.g. where the public is in a confined space) the alarm may be given at an attended central point and warning passed by telephone, light signal or public address system to other parts of the premises. The warning system may also be connected to the fire brigade centre and other defence systems.

Automatic fire extinction systems should be chosen to ensure that they are suitable to the risk involved. The automatic sprinkler system is an efficient way of coping with the early stages of fire and will keep down the fire until the fire brigade arrives. The system should provide complete cover within a single fire compartment. Coupled with an alarm system, the sprinkler system can act as both extinguisher and detector. Automatic water sprays and drencher systems are used to cool window openings and other vulnerable surfaces exposed to the risk of severe radiant heat. Hand-operated drenches are used to reduce the likelihood of buckling by theatre stage fire curtains.

There is also first-aid fire extinguishing equipment to be sited in conspicuous and accessible positions;

they should be located near the escape facilities so that a safe retreat is possible. The hose reel and the fire brigade facility for their hydraulic hose reel should be provided for all entertainment buildings in the 'assembly' category.

Foam inlets are necessary in buildings where the heating installation is oil-fired, where oil storage tanks, oil-burning equipment, internal combustion engines or oil-filled electrical equipment are situated in basements, and where access is difficult for fighting purposes. The inlet should be located on an external wall and protected from undue heat or smoke.

To assist the fire brigade and to permit speed of action in buildings with extensive accommodation below ground level, plans showing critical information on gas, electrical and ventilation control points and fire equipment locations should readily be available for the fire officer. Additions to Part E of the Building Regulations may also include a requirement for fire lifts for buildings with storeys above 18 m above ground level.

In tented accommodation a layout plan should be available to the fire officer and each device, vehicle and caravan should be provided with first-aid fire-fighting equipment suitable for the risk involved as recommended in 'Guide to Safety at Fairs'.

Ventilation

Few people are actually burnt to death. The majority are overcome by smoke and hot gases often removed from the area directly involved in the fire, and it is therefore necessary to get smoke away from escape routes in the best possible way. In respect to basement areas it has been normal to provide pavement lights, knock-out panels or smoke shafts to allow firemen to ventilate smoke logged basements. It is now recommended that additional provision is made for air entry at low level in the basement.

Mechanical ventilation can complicate the smoke hazard in buildings and this risk should be reduced by separating systems provided for high-risk areas, staircases and lobbies, and separating ventilation plant rooms with carefully located air intake positions. Ducts passing through escape staircases or lobbies should have fire-resistant casing. Covering to trunking or linings should be generally non-combustible for basements. The ventilation system should have a control point accessible to the fire brigade and a smoke detector device should be incorporated to shut down or prevent recirculation of smoke contaminated air. Ventilation systems can be used to create a positive pressure as in the case of escape routes and theatres where air movement is directed away from the path of escape.

Legislation

Statutory control of safety in public buildings is implemented through licensing acts conferring authority to local authorities to uphold standards and regulations controlling building design and construction standards.

In the UK, the 1964 Licensing Act conveys power to the relevant fire authority to object to the renewal of licences of buildings for public entertainment, restaurants and clubs because of the fire risk. The Gaming Act 1968 entitles a fire authority to object to the granting or renewal of a licence by the Betting and Gaming Licensing Committee if the means of escape is unsatisfactory. The 1947 Fire Services Act conveys a duty to the fire authority to advise fire prevention measures if requested, and the 1936 Public Health Act gives power to local authority to advise, specify or ask for means of escape to be provided. The Fire Precautions Act 1971 institutes fire certificates for most buildings used by the public and confers authority to implement the necessary standards. The provisions relate to buildings as occupied and used as distinct from new buildings under construction.

In England and Wales (with the exception of Inner London) the Building Regulations include detail requirements for structural fire precautions (Part E). The recommended Section 11, Part E has been prepared and includes 'Means of Escape and Assistance to the Fire Service'. The addition will cover the number, size, form, location and lighting of escape routes, the construction of escape stairs and enclosures, emergency lighting, access for fire-fighting, provision of fire hydrants, fire lifts, foam inlets, smoke ventilation in areas below ground, hydraulic hose reels and classification of purpose groups (with particular reference to places of assembly). The implementation of Section 11 would standardise basic data such as 'occupant load factors' for building types and minimum provision for escape. Attention should also be given to the Chronically Sick and Disabled Persons Act 1971.

Scotland has separate Building Regulations conferred by the Building (Scotland) Act 1959 which includes 'Means of Escape and Assistance to the Fire Service'.

Building standards in Inner London are controlled by the GLC Constructional By-laws and Codes of Practice. Building standards in public buildings in the London area are enforced by the District Surveyor to each area.

Specific requirements for entertainment buildings are imposed by the Cinematograph Acts 1909 and 1952, the Cinematograph (Safety) Regulations 1955,

1958, 1965 and 1976 and for the GLC area, the GLC Technical Regulations 'Places of Public Entertainment'. There is also the Public Health Act 1936 Section 59 (giving powers to District Councils to enforce means of escape), the Fire Services Act 1947 (providing a duty to fire authorities to give advice on request as to fire prevention measures), the Private Places of Entertainment (Licensing) Act 1967, the GLC (General Power) Act 1966, the Theatres Act 1968 and the Sunday Theatre Act 1972. Codes of Practice relating to the Offices Fire Precautions Act 1971 Codes of Practice, issued by the British Standards Institution and the GLC Code of Practice 'Means of Escape in Case of Fire' are also relevant. There are also study papers and technical recommendations published by the Fire Research Organisation, the Fire Protection Association, HMSO, National Building Studies and Building Bulletins and HMSO Fire Research Notes, that refer to the general aspects of fire precaution and the particular requirements of public buildings.

12. Öffentliche Sicherheit: Brandschutz—Zusammenfassung

Die Sicherheit der Öffentlichkeit in Unterhaltungsstätten gegen Panik, Rauch, Brand oder bauliche Gefahren, verursacht durch Brand, gehen zu Lasten des Besitzers, Konstrukteurs oder der Städtischen Behörde. Ort, Fluchtmittel und Unterteilung sind Grundlage für die Planung. Bei der Detailkonstruktion haben Material—und Ausstattungswahl, Schutz von Konstruktionen und Belüftung zum Absaugen von Rauch und Dämpfen alle Bedeutung, ferner die Wahl von Brandlöschgeräten und die Vorschrift, Daß Brandlöschgeräte stets zugänglich sein müssen. Für öffentliche Gebäude gelten die allgemeinen Normen Für die Gebäudeausführung und die Vorschriften für bestimmte Veranstaltungen.

12. Sécurité publique = risques d'incendie—Résumé

La sécurité publique contre les risques d'incendie, d'émanation de fumées entraînant la panique, le danger d'effondrement de la structure elle-même en cas d'incendie, sur les lieux de loisirs, est la responsabilité du propriétaire, du concepteur et de la municipalité. L'implantation, les moyens d'évacuation et la compartimentation sont à considérer dès le début du projet. Au stade de l'étude détaillée, le choix des matériaux, la protection de la structure, la ventilation et l'évacuation des fumées, tous ont de l'importance, y compris la sélection des moyens de lutte contre l'incendie et la nécessité de préserver l'accès à ces équipements. Les édifices publics sont soumis à la fois aux normes générales de construction et à la législation relative aux activités particulières.

١٢ ـ سلامة الجمهور : أخطار الحريق ـ موجز

ان تأمين سلامة الجمهور في أماكن الترفيه من أخطار الفزع والدخان والنار أو أخطار المباني الناتجة عن الحريق هو مسؤولية المالك والمصمم والسلطة المحلية . وتقرير الموقع ووسائل النجاة والتقسيم هي الأمور الأساسية للتخطيط . واختيار المواد والتشطيبات ووقاية المبنى ، والتهوية لاخراج الدخان كلها لها أهميتها في التصميم التفصيلي الى جانب اختيار معدات اطفاء الحريق والحاجة الى وجود وسيلة الوصول الى أدوات مكافحة الحريق . ان المباني العامة تخضع لقياسات انشاء المباني العمومية وللتشريعات الخاصة بالنشاطات المعينة .

Chapter 13

Trends and comment

Chapter 1 outlined the qualities that have a leisure entertainment complement and which form a basis to leisure activities. In an age of scientific technology, novelty continues to provide scope for imagination. The fairs (both traditional and International Expositions) have served to launch many new forms of entertainment, and the contemporary 'fantasy retreat', the theme park, utilises this experience. Health continues to provide a justification for leisure activities. The non-competitive sport, water fun and the 'activity' resort not only give pleasure for most age groups, but satisfy a growing interest in keeping physically fit and well.

Dominance, self-respect, challenge, freedom, achievement and status are all important self-fulfilling activities. Without opportunities to satisfy these in leisure, the human spirit would be frustrated by the restrictions of the urban and industrialised work environment. It is a measure of the quality of life the extent to which an individual civilised potential can be realised.

Comfort, affection, security and involvement are subjective qualities that underlie the structure of personal relationships and development. They can be conveyed in both the spectatorial context and as individual experience in social entertainment.

Generally, entertainment as art provides a popular context in which both familiar and evocative experiences can be relived and new intellectual and emotional aspects can be explored. Fun, in simple terms, at its most effective, is seen as an uninhibited flow of energy through the individual, concentrating human faculties to a pleasurable and totally absorbing activity. The designer creates an environment in which this can be fulfilled.

Sociologists have identified the changing structure which is occurring in the balance of work/leisure. The politicians have yet to accommodate the implications into the various political philosophies that aim to identify national aspirations. There will be a need for policies that can embrace an increase in non-productive leisure time without destroying the motivation of work and industrial innovation. Furthermore, both the politician and planner concerned with the environment, are faced with the problem of resolving leisure needs within the existing urban fabric to restore a humane environment without destroying the continuity of existing communities

For individuals, there must always be freedom of choice implicit in entertainment. Improved standards of education create an expectation within the general quality of life that cannot always be satisfied by the relatively undemanding nature of routine industrial work. Leisure activities must provide the diversity of intellectual, emotional and physical needs of man, with the additional status given to leisure pursuits to give them credence as a context for self-fulfilment.

There must be a meaningful relationship between work and leisure. Not only is entertainment used to motivate learning, but leisure can be constructive and complimentary to work. (The firemen playing netball to keep fit between demands on expertise is an example.) Service industries that are non-productive in the conventional sense, but nevertheless provide for the well-being and diversity of interests in society will gain in importance.

Play as means of exploration and development of faculties, apart from orthodox sport and skills and utilitarian objectives, is important to both child and adult. As creative experience play can humanise urban living, ratify conventions and bring a new force to creative design.

The move from professionalism towards the involvement of the layman is an important aspect touching on many aspects of community life, affecting experiential or creative participation in the activities concerned. This is reflected in extensive 'do it yourself' involving particular considerations by the designers of the components which can easily be assembled by the layman.

Urban life must incorporate leisure and relaxation for all age groups without creating conflicts. The public look towards government to be instrumental to the improvement of conditions where aspects that have no natural cohesion.

Some entertainment skills such as the circus, require status and encouragement within the accepted cultural scene for a period or regeneration. However, in the UK there has been a continuous retraction. A British circus centre and school (having contact with existing centres of physical education) could give substance to this entertainment form. Circus represents a tradition of mobile entertainment, unique skills and animal care.

Health conservation is important and this is encouraged in the new leisure centres. Health clubs and some national companies are also setting-up gymnasia for their staff (office work in particular combines sedentary occupation with stress). There is a need for the monitoring of individual fitness within the leisure context so that health activities are relevant to age and occupation. This is advocated by experts such as Alistair Murray of City Gym, London, also responsible for the House of Commons gymnasium.

The Greek ideal of a broad-based social ethos that recognised social and personal fulfilment in work and leisure activities would appear to be relevant to the future. The wealth of a nation should not be assessed purely in material accounting terms but in the quality of life available to individuals. Without destroying enterprise and innovation to sustain industrial and commercial activities, the quality of life measured in opportunities for individual self-realisation and fulfilment should also be registered. (Apart from income *per capita*, there should be an indication of opportunities available to individuals for personal achievement.) This represents the broad function of leisure entertainment, as 'work' opportunities become generally less demanding through technological development.

Context for entertainment

It would require an extensive volume to cover the many aspects of design for leisure entertainment. In the categories selected for the previous chapters, interesting aspects such as puppet theatres, waxworks, exhibitions, carnivals, open-air shows and street entertainment regretfully have been omitted.

Nevertheless, there are basic forms on which entertainment has developed. From the aspect of the

Intermingle of performer and audience. Child being made up by clown at Circus World, Florida

person entertained, the spectator role and the participatory role are the main contexts for entertainment. At the same time structures for entertainment range from building as a means (represented by the studio space to be adapted to a particular activity) to buildings as the media to entertainment (for example, themed decor conveying a specific ambience).

Spectatorial entertainment such as theatres, concert halls, cinemas, circus and dolphinariums are continually regenerated by the demands of creative material, technology and the aspirations of the public. Basically an audience is being presented with an audio-visual performance.

An audience for entertainment is not always seated in an auditorium. The conveyance of spectators through the 'experience' is relevant both to the adventure areas of a theme park and to sight-seeing tourists. The transportation of spectators present the problems of embarking and disembarking, conditions of viewing from the vehicle, the selection of the style of transport (consistent with the experience) and facilities (such as additional entertainment) during the journey. The design of both the vehicle and the 'adventure' or tour, forms a comprehensive event equivalent to a staged performance.

New London Theatre showing alternative seating/stage arrangements achieved with revolve stage and seating component

The participatory aspect of entertainment has effected the traditional stage presentation drawing actor and audience, and spectator and audience into a closer and more dynamic relationship, to the point where they intermingle in a peripatetic performance. Furthermore, where skills are displayed, the opportunity is provided for audience participation as in circuses where members of the audience are invited into the ring.

South Bank, London. Temporary light roof structure over outdoor stage

Participatory entertainment has also expanded in response to a more enlightened, less convention restricted public, with the basic necessity for creative participation by children in an adventure playground, the individualistic expressions in disco dancing and the leisure sport and leisure skill activities provided in community and resort centres.

Design as means

With the need for adaptability, most buildings for leisure entertainment aim to resolve the advantages of maximum flexibility (to suit a wide range of users), the need to identify basic components that for comfort or security require to be fixed and permanent, and the restraints of financial viability. A flexible building of the scale of the Festival Plaza, Expo 70 at Osaka is rare and the average television studio requires almost continuous use to justify the capital cost of skilled operators and equipment available.

For the designer it is necessary to understand the techniques involved. Grids for lighting and sound equipment, control consoles; the electro-mechanics of moving panels and platforms to effect spatial change, acoustic qualities or as a means of transporting people or equipment; audio-visual effects of projected images and synchronised sound, either as a means of communication or as a means of providing a spatial ambience, etc. The vocabulary is extensive both as direct experience to the audience and the mechanics of presentation.

Structurally, the adaptable space is a reflection of the diversity of contemporary life. An architectural monument limited to a specific entertainment pattern ultimately suffers until the conservationists embrace it as part of the national heritage. The Roman amphitheatre at El Djem rests amongst the low-rise traditional North African housing like a marooned liner. In the UK the survival of piers is threatened and cinemas have been transformed. The life-span of popular entertainment forms varies; the theatre can enjoy continued support through creative and cultural momentum, whereas bowling alleys proved to be a short-lived interest.

The form adopted by the cinemas of the 1930s and 1940s and the Disney Park adventure buildings, represent an interesting compromise with an apparently permanent and 'styled' street front (which conveys the character of the entertainment provided), and a vast studio space behind, outwardly barn-like, but with an interior appropriately contrived and elaborate. This masks the anonymous flexible space by a façade structure that prepares the visitor for the entertainment or relates the total building to the street context. It is a measure of the skill of the design, the extent to which these aspects can be integrated in the overall concept.

Space frames, pneumatic structures and tensile structures have been used to provide space, protected from the weather, in which the environment can be controlled, and in which free floor area provides flexibility of use. Such structures are particularly appropriate to seasonal uses to provide a semi-enclosed performance with moderate protection.

Design: fantasy and illusion

The specific design of structure and surroundings can be an integral part of the entertainment, either by conveying the reality of the production, by creating an illusion of reality or by conveying a fantasy image.

The desire to create fantasy or an illusion is very evident in architectural history. Each generation has reconstructed images of a elysian past, conveyed the images patronised by one section of society to another, or anticipated the wonder images of the future. The 19th-century leisure buildings, such as the Blackpool Tower and Alhambra, conveyed an opulent environment (normally enjoyed by wealthy society) to ordinary day trippers. The Victorian follies that included enormous sham castles, reproductions of Greek temples, obelisks and things otherwise associated with Druid priests, provided an escape from wealth and reason. Today, the leisure centres sustain a tropical ambience through the bleak English winter; the Mediterranean marinas provide a fishing village innocence to wealthy yacht-owning escapists from city life, and the Las Vegas Caesar's Palace provides a setting of autocratic indulgence for a nation freed from European inequalities. The themed environment plays a significant part of design for entertainment.

The selection and quality of presentation is an important basic decision. To the entrepreneur, the theme or evocative character of a discotheque or casino interior is conveying both a unique identity for the particular enterprise, and an ambience conducive to enjoyment. For the designer, the theme can provide a structure for cohesion (as in the case of the 'Expo') or a means of enriching the entertainment experience. The magic of the baroque theatre interior as a background to the encompassed audience, the extravagant cinema foyer that provided a prelude to spectacular film entertainment, the 'Bavarian' discotheques and Russian themed restaurant in Hamburg, or the 20s style discotheques in London all aim to convey an ambience synonymous with the particular mood.

'Russian' themed restaurant in Hamburg

Design as media

The technology of electronics, electro-mechanics, laser projection, holography and cinematography can provide a realistic illusion. The capacity for stage realism, as the raging floodwater of the Lido Spectacular, projected three-dimensional images, and the stage manoeuvring of electro-mechanical devices, provide a new dimension to design. The mechanics integrated into the buildings are used to create a realistic image synonymous with the form of entertainment.

Stardust Showroom, Las Vegas. Great flood spectacular water effect

Architect, interior designer, stage designer, lighting and acoustic experts, all must work as a team to resolve audience-performance parameters. For example, the flexibility of the Cottisloe at the National Theatre in London, the acoustic monitoring of the Pompidou Centre Acoustic Laboratory, the change of ambience at the Paris Lido; each uses the building as an instrument to the entertainment experience.

Also, the audio-visual use of space can replace or enrich the physical enclosure by a projected image (for example the hemispherical cine-screen provides a total enclosing cinematic image for the audience), the interplay of synchronimous space form and projection techniques of Exposition buildings, the 'disco' dynamics of moving light patterns that are an analogue of the music; each extends the environment from enclosing walls or static decor, to animated space. The enclosure is dynamic, changing, defined by intangible light images, personalised by sound.

The word entertainment comes from the French words 'entretenir' to hold or 'keep among' and has many meanings including 'to engage agreeably the attention of'. Thus for the designer (without confusing the need for adaptability in buildings for leisure entertainment), environmental design is a media for entertainment. Not only in the evocative image, contrived decor or fantasy rides, but in the synthesis of entertainment technique and the fabric of the building. Furthermore, in the broader context of the urban environment, planning, conservation and urban renewal leisure entertainment can humanise the urban structure otherwise easily at the mercy of traffic and work priority.

There is a wide vocabulary of design experience and technology to enrich the growing demands for leisure entertainment.

13. Tendances et opinions—Résumé

La vie urbaine doit incorporer des activités de loisirs adaptés à tous les âges, sans qu'il y ait conflit. Les spectacles, avec ou sans participation d'audience, offrent une grande variété de solutions au niveau de la conception. Toutefois, on remarque une nette tendance vers une relation plus étroite entre l'artiste et le public, une importance plus accentuée de la participation et de l'expérience du jeu, une plus grande intégration de la fantaisie dans la réalité, mettant le fantastique au niveau du tangible. En même temps, la machinerie du spectacle, les animations électro-mécaniques, les systèmes de transport, les effets audio-visuels, le son et l'utilisation de la structure elle-même en tant que

moyen actif, ouvrent la porte aux projets d'imagination. L'expérience des expositions et parcs à thème est particulièrement importante pour la planification de l'environnement. On peut citer comme exemples: le restaurant 'Russe' à Hambourg, Allemagne, et la salle Stardust à Las Vegas, aux Etats-Unis.

13. Tendenzen und Stellungnahme—Zusammenfassung

Das Leben in der Stadt und im Urlaub muß Vergnügungsstätten für alle Altersgruppen enthalten, ohne Konflikte zu schaffen. Für Zuhörer- und teilnehmende Unterhaltung gibt es viele verschiedene Konstruktionslösungen, jedoch besteht eine Tendenz zu einer ängeren Verbindung zwischen Veranstalter und Zuhörern, zur erfahrungsmäßigen Bedeutung des kreativen Spiels, zu Teilnahme, größerem Realismus in bezug auf die Vorstellungskraft und dazu, da wirklich Phantastisches greifbarer zu gestalten. Gleichzeitig bietet die Vergnügungsmaschinerie elektromechanische Animatronik, das Beförderungswesen, audio-visuelle Effekte, Tonanlagen und den Einsatz der Konstruktion selbst als Mittel für die Unterhaltung Gelegenheiten zu einfallsreicher Konstruktion und Planung. Ausstellungen und Vergnügungsparks mit besonderen Themen sind auch für die Umweltplanung der Zukunft von Bedeutung. Beispiele sind das 'russische' Restaurant in Hamburg, der Stardust Showroom in Las Vegas, USA.

١٣ ـ الاتجاهات والتعليق ـ موجز

ان حياة المدينة وحياة العطلة يجب أن تشمل نشاطات الاستجمام وقت الفراغ لكل الأعمار بدون اثارة النزاع . ان كلا من وسائـل الترفيه التى نشاهدها أو نشترك فيها لها مجموعة واسعة من حلول التصميم ، غير أن الاتجاه هو نحو الترابط الوثيق بين المؤدى والجمهور والأهمية التجريبية للعب الخلاّق والمشاركة والواقعيـة الأكثر بالنسبة للخيال وجعل الشئ الخيالي حقاً أكثر مادية . وفي نفس الوقت فان اجهزة الترفيه والالكترونيات ووسائل المواصلات والمؤثرات السمعية المرئية وأجهزة الصوت واستخدام البناء نفسـه كوسيلة للترفيه ، كل ذلك يهيئ الفرصة للتصميم والتخطيط البارع . ان تجربة المعارض وحدائق الموضوع ترتبط أيضا بتخطيط البيئة في المستقبل . الأمثلة : فكرة المطعم «الروسي» في هامبورج بالمانيا ، ستاردست شوروم في لاس فيجاس بالولايات المتحدة الأمريكية .

Index

Index